献给我的父亲

感谢
国家留学基金委联合培养博士项目
江西财经大学博士科研启动经费
支持

SPEECH ACT AS INVESTMENT
—A STUDY ON
THE DISCOURSE PRACTICE
OF *TAOCI*

作为投资的言语行为
——"套磁"话语实践研究

肖琳 著

浙江工商大学出版社 杭州
ZHEJIANG GONGSHANG UNIVERSITY PRESS

图书在版编目（CIP）数据

作为投资的言语行为："套磁"话语实践研究 /
肖琳著 . — 杭州：浙江工商大学出版社，2021.12（2023.2 重印）
ISBN 978-7-5178-4762-5

Ⅰ.①作… Ⅱ.①肖… Ⅲ.①高等学校—留学教育—
研究 Ⅳ.① G648.9

中国版本图书馆 CIP 数据核字（2021）第 254339 号

作为投资的言语行为——"套磁"话语实践研究
ZUOWEI TOUZI DE YANYU XINGWEI——"TAOCI" HUAYU SHIJIAN YANJIU

肖琳 著

责任编辑	张莉娅　姚媛
封面设计	浙信文化
责任校对	鲁燕青
责任印制	包建辉
出版发行	浙江工商大学出版社
	（杭州市教工路 198 号　邮政编码 310012）
	（E-mail：zjgsupress@163.com）
	（网址：http://www.zjgsupress.com）
	电话：0571-88904980，88831806（传真）
排　　版	杭州市拱墅区冰橘平面设计工作室
印　　刷	广东虎彩云印刷有限公司绍兴分公司
开　　本	889mm × 1194mm　1/32
印　　张	14.875
字　　数	287 千
版印　次	2021 年 12 月第 1 版　2023 年 2 月第 2 次印刷
书　　号	ISBN 978-7-5178-4762-5
定　　价	56.00 元

序

传统上的跨文化交际语言研究，常会聚焦"语用失误"，用英语本族语者的语用规范，去衡量二语学习者的英语使用，找到模仿的差距。也就是说，英语学习者/使用者应是本族语者忠实的模仿者，遵守其语言文化规范。新近的研究，则多将二语学习者/使用者的英语使用纳入"英语通用语"（English as a Lingua Franca）的框架，强调语言通用的交际价值。在拒绝本族语者语言霸权的同时，也有可能忽略其深层的社会文化意义。由此，在全球化的视野下，关注具有本土特征的二语学习者/使用者言语行为及话语类型，揭示其社会文化功能，难能可贵。

《作为投资的言语行为——"套磁"话语实践研究》正是这方面的有益尝试。这项研究考察了中国学生写给国外导师争取留学机会的"套磁"电邮。这里的"套磁"言语行为来源于本土，然而用于国际情境，是用英语交流的。它并无"巧舌如簧地与陌生人拉近

1

关系"的贬义,而是一种中性的,既本土又全球,既古老而又新颖的语言构建或创造。作者带着强烈的好奇心,带领读者去探索了这样一个有趣的现象。个人认为本书有以下亮点:

首先,研究不局限于微观的语言现象描述,而是将扎实的微观话语分析与社会科学视角的中观解读密切结合起来。作者借鉴社会学家布迪厄的场域、资本和惯习理论以及社会语言学家诺顿的二语投资概念,来分析中国留学申请者的"套磁"话语,将其解读为全球文化资本的投资行为,并修订了达文和诺顿(2015)的投资模型。这就丰厚和深化了言语行为意义的揭示,既细致生动又视野开阔。

其次,研究指出了话语及文化"惯习"的可重塑性、动态性。以往对于布迪厄理论的理解、阐释和应用,多从社会结构主义的视角出发,强调结构关系和资本分配方式的再生产,突出其稳定的特性。而作者更多采用社会建构主义的站位,在提炼出"处理人际关系""展现学术自我""协商机构录取"三大中观言语行为的基础上,指出"展示学术自我"言语行为占言语行为综述的五成多,体现出受西方个人主义影响的"个人能力取向惯习"逐渐在年青一代留学群体中形成,并与"处理人际关系"言语行为所标志的"关系取向惯习"传统形成竞争。这样的理论阐释和应用具有新意,符合布迪厄的本意,也适合快速变迁中的社会现象解读。

最后,研究还有一个可圈可点之处,就是作者对不同身份、不同视角的整合。研究的主要材料来自研究对象即留学申请者，但其辅助材料还包括更广范围的英语培训机构套磁信写作培训，以及本人申请国外访学与教授交流过程的反思笔记。这就使得研究兼具"局外人"和"局内人"的视角，也得以将二语学习者/使用者个体与机构层面的社会话语联系起来。这样的多视角融合也给研究增加了魅力和深度。

    期待在阅读本书、经历套磁电邮的考察之旅的过程中，每个读者会迸发出自己的思维火花。

2021年于北京

自　序

本书基于我在北京大学所完成的博士论文修改而成。

"套磁"本是北京方言，指通过说话与不熟悉的人拉近关系。对于中国的出国留学群体，"套磁"是一个耳熟能详的术语，专指在申请过程中写给外国导师的私人电邮，通过电邮联系增加被录取和获得奖学金的机会。在全球化的高等教育竞争中，套磁可被看作申请人全球"猎学"（global offer hunting）的重要话语实践之一。本研究以二语投资理论和布迪厄的惯习、投资、场域等关键概念为理论视角，从言语行为角度分析中国留学申请者的"套磁"实践，试图探讨两个问题：（1）套磁在何种意义上是以言行事；（2）套磁话语在何种意义上是对留学想象认同的投资。

以布朗和莱文森（1987）的礼貌理论为语言分析框架，这项研究借助质性研究软件ATLAS.ti对所收集的套磁邮件文本进行标注、分析、统计和归类；相应的访谈内容则为文本分析结果提供支撑性证据；引入达文和诺顿（2015）投资模型讨论了各类言语行为的使用与申请人出国留学投资之间的关系。基于这些讨论，本研究把目的性和情境性的言语行为引入达文和诺顿（2015）投资模型的核心，用动态的惯习替换原投资模型中相对静态的意识形态，强调文化在个体乃至一个群体中的动态而微妙的变化。该模型动态呈现了资本、认同和惯习在投资中与话语实践的关系，丰富了投资理论的社会语用视角。

在完成博士论文和出版专著的过程中，我得到了多方襄助。首先要感谢我的导师高一虹教授。她在教学和学术工作上的魅力和毅力，为我树立了优秀学者的榜样；她的睿智和耐心照亮了我前进的方向，她富有洞察力的建议和发人深省的批评督促我进步。感谢她把我培养成一名独立且自律的教育科研工作者。

同时，这项研究离不开那些慷慨热心的参与者。每位参与者都非常支持我的工作，其中一些人成了我的朋友，并在我写作最艰难的时候施以援手。

感谢我的博士论文答辩委员会成员——姜望琪教授、杨鲁新教授、封宗信教授、冯捷蕴教授、董洁教授、刘璐教授，他们的建议中肯而锐利，帮助我不断完善和改进这项工作；感谢答辩秘书李桂东博士，整个答辩过程顺畅完成离不开他的帮助。

在北京大学求学期间，我得到了胡壮麟教授、高彦梅教授、姜望琪教授、钱军教授、申丹教授、段晴教授、张薇教授、胡旭辉博

2

士、郑萱博士、孟玲博士等的悉心教导。同窗好友和媛媛博士、李芳博士、王景云博士在我撰写论文时，常与我分享交换想法、碰撞思想火花。访学期间我还得到了纽约州立大学 Istvan Kecskes教授和 Robert Sanders教授的多次指导，他们对我的文本分析进行了细致评估，并为本研究的开展提供了慷慨的帮助。

感谢我的丈夫周宝健博士对我无私的包容和殷切的鼓励。感谢我的家人的支持和尊重。最后，特别感谢我的父亲，他勤奋的精神和可爱的倔强一直激励着我努力做最好的自己，谨以此书献给他。

肖琳

江西财经大学慧园小区

Contents

2

Chapter 4   Investment Through Speech Acts: A Panorama / 133

Chapter 5　Writing to Act: An Individual Investment Trajectory　/ 331

Chapter 6　The Dynamic Investment Model / 385

Chapter 1

Introduction

Going abroad for further education has become more and
more popular all around the world, concomitant with the increasing
cross-border higher education mobility propelled by the globalized
economy and politics, free market and international collaboration, and
unprecedented progress in science and technology in the twenty-first
century. In this global educational market, a predominant trend for the
cross-border flow is from less developed countries to developed nations,
usually the English-speaking ones, which are often considered to provide
first-class educational resources (e.g. faculty, equipment, funding), a
free academic environment, diplomas with more "gold content" and
well-paid jobs in the future. Borrowing Bourdieu's (1977) terms,
going-abroad to these countries for education can be analogized as an
investment practice to pursue more social, cultural and even economic
capital. The Chinese going-abroad heat is riding the tide as well.
Applicants seeking for education in America, Britain, and Australia
have taken the largest share of the whole study-abroad population.[1]
Chinese applicants are involved in an international competition for
education offers, i.e. global offer hunting, with rivalries from all over
the world. In their studious efforts to seize an offer, particularly for
PhD programs, *Taoci* email, a quasi-established electronic genre for

---

[1] https://baijiahao.baidu.com/s?id=1654754800023594688&wfr=spider&for=pc.

Chinese applicants to communicate with potential foreign supervisors, has become a must on their application "to do" list. Against this milieu, the issue of *Taoci* becomes a possibly significant site to examine the use of English in Chinese L2 learners' email discourse, to glimpse the cultural confluence trend of the traditional Chinese and the "Western" (running the risk of an oversimplified dichotomy) in globalization, and to overhear the dialogue between traditions and modernity within individuals.

1.1   The Motive

My interest in the topic of *Taoci* email (usually simplified as *Taoci*) originated from a piece of chapter writing that I collaborated with my supervisor Professor Gao Yihong in the year of 2013. She was invited to contribute to a book named *Email Discourse Among Chinese Using English as a Lingua Franca* edited by three scholars, Yuan-shan Chen, Der-Hwa Victoria Rau and Gerald Rau. Professor Gao asked me whether I would like to join her and I said "yes". When I was fumbling for a theme for that contribution, *Taoci* email popped up in my mind, as I had been one of those student applicants, albeit failed, for overseas PhD programs and ever wrote English *Taoci* email to foreign professors. After a brief discussion, Professor Gao and I decided to pool our efforts into this genre of English writing practiced by mainland Chinese English learners. We found interesting pragmatic strategies performed discursively by those applicants in their email communication with foreign scholars. Finally, our work turned out a chapter titled "Intercultural *Taoci* email: New wine in an old bottle" collected in that book published by Springer Publisher in winter, 2015. The experience of writing the article, for me, was not just a crucial part of my academic training, but also opened my eyes to an iceberg of the complexity of English writing among Chinese study-abroad applicants and their keen investment into further international education and imagined academic identity, which might be interesting topics worthy of further exploration.

One year after the commencement of that small research, I had a chance to apply for a visiting scholar program sponsored by China Scholarship Council (abbreviated as CSC) affiliated to the Education Ministry of China. To be honest, I had been very interested in going abroad to "gild" my academic credential partially for getting a position as research faculty at domestic universities after graduation, since the job market was more competitive and attached increasing importance to overseas education or training experience. The prerequisite of the application for CSC program was to receive a letter of acceptance

4

with free admission from a hosting university or professor. Thus, I needed to find a desirable foreign professor who would like to hand me that offer "pass". I emailed several professors of different cultural backgrounds in Britain, Australia and America, i.e. doing the so-called *Taoci* for the invitation letter. Both positive and negative responses came back, but most professors, after several rounds of back-and-forth email correspondences, were generous and willing to give me the letter of acceptance, perhaps because I made a good presentation of myself through using the writing tips that I gained from that *Taoci* investigation.

However, even as an English major student, having learned and used English for more than a decade, I still had to face the entanglement in writing English email to a completely strange professor and struggling to position myself appropriately in the email communication. It was not so much of difficulty of expressing myself in English, but of making myself presented in a proper way, or to quote Bardovi-Harlig and Hartford in their research on students' English email to teachers,

> On the one hand, students must play a subordinate role and be polite, modest, and unrebellious. On the other, they must show themselves to be worthy potential members of the intellectual community which demands that they demonstrate

"independence of opinion". (Bardovi-Harlig, Hartford, 1990: 473)

It is apparently not an easy task to strike a balance between being subordinate and expressing independent idea as Bardovi-Harlig and Hartford (1990) argued for, in particular when students need to use a language other than their mother tongue and when their counterparts are foreigners. Hence, my personal experience of doing *Taoci* awakened in me a stronger empathy with those research participants undergoing some kind of similar dilemma reported in Xiao & Gao (2015), intrigued my intense curiosity to take a closer and deeper look at Chinese applicants' *Taoci* email, and most importantly gave me an insider perspective to inspect the *Taoci* discourse practice among Chinese applicants.

1.2 *Taoci* in Beijing Dialect

Taoci, written in Chinese characters as "套磁", is originally a Beijing dialect term. *Tao* (套) is used as a verb and means "to obtain", like in *tao-guanxi* (to build up rapport). *Ci* can be written in two alternative Chinese characters. One is the ceramic *ci* (瓷) and in Beijing dialect means solid relationship between intimates. The other

6

is the magnet *ci* (磁)[①] and refers to the magnetic force drawing one party to another. Both characters are oriented toward the closeness of two communicating parties, and mean the same when respectively combined with the character *tao* (套). Chinese dialect dictionary explains *Taoci* as "trying to build up *guanxi* (interpersonal relation or rapport) with, chum up (*tao-jinhu*) with or cotton up (*la-guanxi*) to unfamiliar people, mainly through talking and chatting" (Gao, Fu, 2001). Doing *Taoci* is supposed to place oneself into an effective *guanxi* network for practical purposes through linguistic means, similar to the Yiddish word "schemooze", and hence can be regarded as speech act in a broad sense. In Beijing vernacular with heavier *r*-sounding, locals usually add the subsyllabic retroflex [ɹ] after *ci* and render it into *Taoci'er*. The final rhotic serves as "Beijing smooth operator" (Zhang, 2005) and gives an impression of an "oily" quality or character of people doing *Taoci*. Hence, the dialectal *Taoci* often assumes a negative sense.

The action of doing *Taoci* is closely related to the Chinese society built upon *guanxi* (Xiao, Gao, 2015). *Guanxi*, if simply put, refers to relation, but goes far beyond the literal meaning of relation. As a Chinese indigenous concept, it emphasizes the interpersonal connection

---

① The magnetic *ci* is used more frequently among study-abroad applicants.

and its maintenance as important and useful social asset (e.g. Chang, 2010; Chang & Holt, 1991; Fei, 1948; Hwang, 1988; Jacobs, 1979; Qi, 2013) in the area of business, political and social fabric. *Guanxi* is often portrayed in terms of Confucian role relations (Fei, 1992; King, 1985) exemplified in the hierarchical social structure and the concentrical familism/clannism (group formation based on patriarchal family networks) with the self located at the very center (Redding,Wong, 1986). Hierarchically "There is government when the prince is the prince, and the minister is the minister; when the father is the father, and the son is the son"[1]. On the other hand, horizontally "there is always a self at the center of each web" of relationships (Fei, 1992) while the related others are discerned by virtue of their closeness (such as blood ties) to the concentric center of family, and affinity and estrangement are clearly distinguished. Each individual occupies a spot in this *guanxi* coordinate. Maintaining these relations hierarchically or horizontally is a way to fulfill the principle of Chinese *li* (ritual or propriety) (Chen, 2010; Gu, 1990; Yum, 1988). The whole social networking web can be strengthened either hierarchically through linguistic practices such

---

[1] This episode is from *Confucian Analects* (by Yan Yuan). It is Confucius' response to the duke Ching of Chi who asked about government. The English version is translated by James Legge (2014).

as the use of position-linked addressing terms, or horizontally through linguistic practices such as the use of endearment expressions like pseudo-kinship addressing.

However, an individual's position in a *guanxi* network, though shaped by pre-existing social ties, is not at the total mercy of the ensuing interdependence (Fei, 1992). People in a *guanxi* network can take advantage of *guanxi* to obtain practical benefits. For people out of the *guanxi* circle, "it is possible for two parties to become closer by appealing to a third party who shares a relationship with each of them" (Chang, 2010). Therefore, relationships can be created or built upon established relations, and non-familial ties are possible to turn into insider relations. Each individual can be the architect of his/her own *guanxi* network. In Bourdieu's (1986) term, *guanxi* is a kind of social capital, the aggregate of existing or potential resources deriving from such membership as *guanxi* between friends, *guanxi* among coworkers, *guanxi* within a family. Different types of *guanxi* capital could be invested by *guanxi* owners in order to attain other material or immaterial wealth in relevant fields, i.e. pulling *guanxi*①. The

---

① "Pulling *guanxi* is a literal translation of *la-guanxi*, referring to actions of initiating and establishing a connection, and the translation is used in the field of management and organization." (e.g. Chen, Chen, 2004)

practice of pulling *guanxi* could probably lead to the flow of economic, cultural and (or) social capital between different *guanxi* circles (or fields), and breed a rupture in the existing structured connection. Once the flow and rupture become more fixed in and digested by the new network, it will be inserted into the previous structure as expansion and enrichment, and perhaps generating new dispositions of habitus.

The dialectal *Taoci* as a form of pulling *guanxi* is a way of social networking complementary and alternative to the traditional maintenance of Chinese *li*. Otherwise stated, *Taoci* is illegitimate since *Taoci* doers are not "native" in the *guanxi* network but needs to break into it, thus disturbing the existing social structure of appropriate li. Through talking or doing things with speech act, *Taoci* practioners create opportunities to develop their social resources outside the legitimized social structure. Some unconventional or unwelcomed methods may be used for networking between unfamiliar people. In an earlier dictionary, *Taoci* is even labeled as a word used by hooligans in modern Chinese society (Chen, 1985).[①]Nevertheless, *Taoci*, as a form of building up *guanxi* through discourse practice, became a norm of communication, reified in dictionary entries (Gao,

---

① *"Taoci* means pulling *guanxi* with targeted persons for practical purposes. It is a catchword used by hooligans in modern Chinese society." (Chen, 1985)

Fu, 2001). Through continued practice, the unconventional will turn into the conventional. The derogatory connotation may fade out and new meanings may fade in under a new context.

1.3   *Taoci* in the International Higher Education Market

1.3.1   *Taoci* Email

The original meaning of *Taoci* might not be widely known to the Chinese people since it is only a local term mainly used in the northern part of China. However, *Taoci* email (usually simplified as *Taoci*)[1] becomes a catchword among the young generation of overseas education applicants[2] growing up in the digital era. It refers specifically to writing personal email (in English under most circumstances) to foreign supervisors with the hope of achieving a kind of familiar relationship so as to increase the chances of admission and scholarship before the final offer is decided.

The earliest online record of *Taoci* in the study-abroad application

---

[1] Unless otherwise noticed, *Taoci* in the following discussion is short for *Taoci* email for the sake of convenience.

[2] The applicants can be college students, teachers or staff in any other vocation.

sense appeared in 1996[①], when Internet technology was introduced to China, and private service agencies for overseas application mushroomed. A model of *Taoci* email was then shared on a study-broad application website to give applicants some guidance of email writing to foreign professors. In 2007, *Taoci* was created as a separate vocabulary item on Baidu Baike.[②] In 2008, the entry was enriched with a supply of definition, explanation and examples. Although the meaning of *Taoci* in the overseas application area has not been entered in any authoritative dictionary, it becomes an accepted notion among foreign education applicants, used both online and offline, and even spreads among applicants for domestic graduate programs. This kind of folk usage of *Taoci* captures the vitality of language practice in the information age and one of the fascinations of the present study. Now, when people surf on the Internet for the word of *Taoci*, there are thousands of search results concerned about writing email to targeted foreign professors. Almost all overseas-program application websites,

---

① http://www.jxjxx.org/resource/application-letter-sample/547.php. A *Taoci* email written in English is provided on this website as a sample for applicants who intend to apply for computer science PhD program in America.

② The word of *Taoci* is defined and explained on the website in the following link: http://baike.baidu.com/view/1385927.html.

such as New Oriental, *Taisha*, Jituo,[1] have a special column/forum for *Taoci*, where people can obtain *Taoci* tips, share their *Taoci* experience, and find *Taoci* FAQs (frequently asked questions). *Taoci* has become a contemporary genre of English writing for Chinese students who have a specific foreign professor to reach for. Therefore, for most applicants, *Taoci* comes into their mind as an established signifier (de Saussure, 1960), to wit, denoting the email writing practice to foreign professors, and few of them know about its original dialectal sense. The regional concept of *Taoci* is revived and refreshed in the Chinese study-abroad application situated in the global higher education, undergoing what Bauman and Briggs (1990) called "recontextualization".

1.3.2   The Global Higher Education Market

About a century ago, international relations were largely marginal to the daily operation of higher education systems in most countries and districts. However, over the past half a century, high-level education ushered in a new stage thanks to the irresistible globalization trend and fast-developing technology in computerization and transportation. It is

---

[1] New Oriental is the first and most famous private English training institution in China, providing service mainly for oversea-education application. *Taisha* and *Jituo* are two well-known forums for study-abroad application information affiliated to private companies who provide paid service for study-abroad application.

reported that at present there are over 2 million international students around the world each year and the number will rocket to 8 million in 2025 (Altbach, 2013), not including those personnel involved in visiting, exchange and collaboration programs. It is a fact that "the first global university market has emerged" (Marginson,van der Wende, 2009) and "there is a general trend to increased international engagement of higher education" (Marginson, 2010).

On this market, resources are unequally distributed. The configuration of different sorts and volumes of resources, or capitals is influenced by pre-existing economic and political structure of different countries. For instance, developed nations such as the United States, the United Kingdom, Canada, represent the power of economy, politics, science and technology, so does their education. "In nearly all cases, superior national performance relative to economic capacity is correlated to relatively high public investment in research in higher education" (Marginson,van der Wende, 2009). The three countries of American, Britain and Germany[1] took a dominant proportion of almost 70 percent of top 100 research universities in the world. Advanced countries boast not only in "hardware" of funding, facility and infrastructure, but also

---

[1] China has gradually become a hot destination for foreign education.

14

"software" of intellectual minds and academic environment, functioning as a magnet for world-wide talent. By contrast, less developed countries are relatively weak on both aspects though they are pressing hard to catch up in recent years.

In accordance with the marketization law, strong nations especially English-speaking countries have a more gravitational attraction for overseas education seekers, while less developed countries become exporter nations. The dominant unidirectional influx from the less developed to the developed characterizes the objective structure of relations and power differences in the field of international higher education, which exerts an invisible yet possessed impact on individual choices. "One of the most important properties of fields is the way in which they allow one form of capital to be converted into another—in the way, for example, that certain educational qualifications can be cashed in for lucrative jobs." (Thompson, 1991) Thus, the cultural capital of prestigious degrees and diplomas received from foreign education systems has the potential to be transformed into economic capital (e.g. well-paid jobs after graduation), social capital (e.g. internationally disciplinary membership), or symbolic capital (e.g. honor, reputation, superiority, prestige). The large-scale cross-border flow of students in modern society is both driven by and drives at gaining more capitals through investment in overseas education, forming a site of struggle among participants involved in this field (Bourdieu, Wacquant, 1992).

1.3.3　Chinese Students in the Global Higher Education Market

China's study-abroad policy and situation has also undergone significant changes along with its remarkable progress in the social, political, and economic areas. In 1978, China officially inaugurated the policy of "reform and opening-up" and restated the goal of achieving "Four Modernizations" (industry, agriculture, national defense, and science and technology). Spurred by this national strategic goal, the government made the decision to resume the exchange of scholars and students with capitalist nations, which witnessed the unprecedented increase of study-abroad personnel from 1978 to the present[1]. In the early 1990s, the Ministry of Education developed a new policy of "supporting study abroad, encouraging returning home and giving the

---

[1] "Waves of Chinese studying abroad". http://www.china.org.cn/top10/2011-12/24/content_24220658.html.

16

freedom to come and go" [1]. In 1998, the government acknowledged the legitimacy of privately owned intermediary agencies providing services for people who wanted to apply for overseas education, such as the New Oriental Corporation. In 2003, study-abroad formalities were further simplified by the Chinese authorities, which further stimulated the overseas education market to a great extent. Going-abroad for education enjoys an unprecedented popularity, as Fig. 1.1 shows that the number of the going-abroad personnel increased manifold from less than 50, 000 in 1978 to more than 400,000 in 2012. At the national level, the policy of educational internalization has become a strategic investment to achieve the national prosperity as it is stipulated in the "National Long-term Education Reform and Development from 2010 to 2020" [2].

---

[1] In 1992, Deng Xiaoping made a series of speech during the Inspection Tour in the South. Following the spirit of his speeches, the Chinese government made the policy of "Supporting study abroad, encouraging returning home and giving the freedom to come and go" and it became an official guideline for the study-abroad on the Third Plenary Session of the 14th Central Committee of the Communist Party of China in 1993.

[2] http://www.moe.edu.cn/publicfiles/business/htmlfiles/moe/moe_838/20 1008/93704. html.

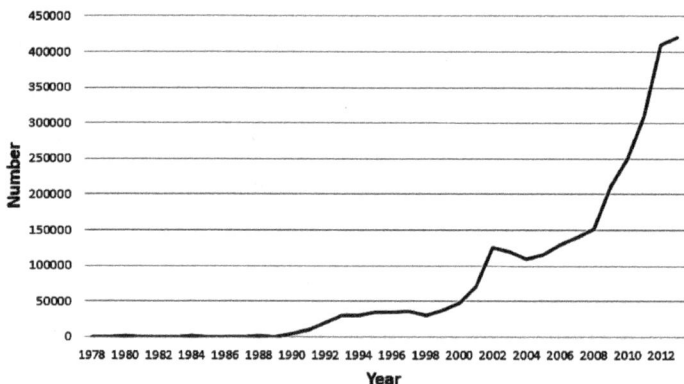

Fig. 1.1   Study-abroad personnel number from 1978 to 2012

At the individual level, receiving higher education in foreign nations indicates an opportunity for better self-development. Foreign education can expose students to an alluring array of educational resources that are perhaps not available domestically. Personal investment in overseas education is usually expected to bring back more capitals. Obtaining a foreign diploma or overseas educational experience often gives its owners more competitiveness on the domestic job market since many Chinese universities are now preferring to recruit returnees graduating from prestigious foreign universities and offer them more salary and stronger start-up funding compared to domestic

18

graduates. Moreover, people with foreign educational experiences are supposed to connect internationally in terms of friendship, membership and other networking ties, which means they are equipped with more and different social capitals.

For most Chinese students, top destinations for overseas higher education include America, Britain, Australia, Canada, New Zealand,[1] among which developed English-speaking countries take the dominant share, and matches the international cross-border mobility direction mentioned before. America has been the most favorite destination, which is related to its top status in the world. By contrast, China has become the top exporting country for sending students to study at American universities since the 2009–2010 school year and Chinese students constituted roughly one-third of all international graduate students in the US.[2] The total of Chinese studying for postgraduates surpassed that of undergraduate program[3] in America in the past decade as Fig. 1.2[4] shows.

---

[1] "Top foreign destinations for Chinese students study-abroad". http://www.eol.cn/html/lx/2014baogao/content.html.
[2] Source from Council of Graduate Schools "Findings from the 2013 CGS International Graduate Admissions Survey".
[3] *Taoci* is usually done among graduate program applicants.
[4] Data obtained from http://news.cntv.cn/2013/01/30/ARTI1359496238768767.shtml.

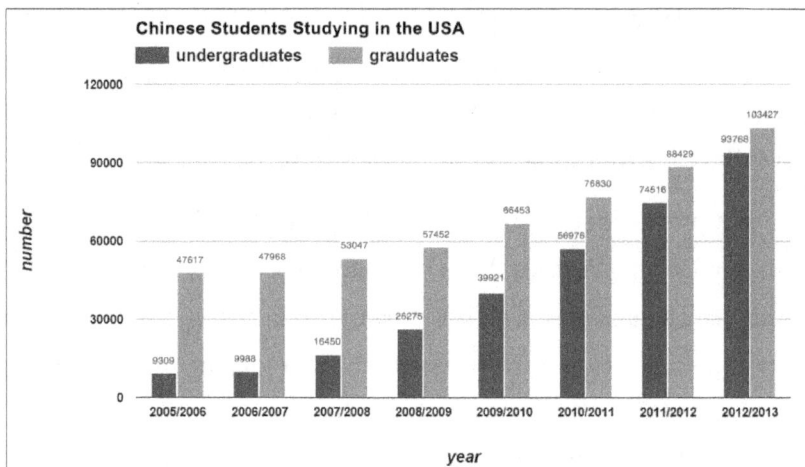

Fig. 1.2   Number of Chinese students in the USA for undergraduate and graduate
program

1.3.4   *Taoci* as a Means to Hunt Global Education Offer

The application package for foreign education usually includes applicants' language proficiency certificate like TOEFL (Test of English as a Foreign Language), GRE (Graduate Record Examination), or IELTS (The International English Language Testing System), school performance records, personal statement, recommendation letters, and/or sample writing. The package stands for an institutionalized report about applicants. Foreign supervisors may not know about their

20

applicants well enough through these documents. As it is widely known, the cooperation between student and advisor is a long-term project in PhD programs, so students will be careful to choose an advisor just as professors careful to take a candidate. Recruitment decision made only based on a review of official application file could lead to serious problems as what Zhao (1996) observed,

> "...North American graduate schools faced increasingly more financial difficulty in accepting Chinese students even though many Chinese students had impressive academic records. In fact, as the number of applicants increased, some applicants with excellent curriculum vitae and letters of recommendations turned out to be quite poor students when they entered graduate programs. Since few people knew the Chinese education system, to enroll Chinese students became a risky investment." (Zhao, 1996)

Before the massive use of the Internet and online application system, there was a communication gap between Chinese applicants and their potential supervisors as both sides didn't know each other personally before the former arrived. That is why Zhao (1996) emphasized the significance of early contacts with academic tutors. With the spread of the Internet in China in the late 1990s, applicants began to have a better pre-arrival understanding of targeted culture, education system and academic programs, and more crucially their future advisors. A professor at a North American university posted a message online to elaborate the reason to make early contacts for prospective candidates:

> You might be wondering, "Do I even need to write letters to potential supervisors? Can't I just fill out university application forms?" The fact is—hundreds of people apply for each spot and if you just fill out the application form without actually contacting any of the professors at the university in question, then you're not likely to get noticed. Furthermore, most graduate students (especially PhDs) and Post-Docs are admitted because a particular professor has expressed an interest in recruiting them, so if you've not been in contact with a professor, chances are, nobody there is going to push to get you admitted.[1]

The message in this post explains the necessity for PhD applicants and potential supervisors to know more about each other before the

---

[1] Source from https://thesistips.wordpress.com/2012/07/30/how-to-write-to-a-prospective-phd-supervisor/.

final enrollment decision, and illustrates partially why so many Chinese applicants choose to contact with potential foreign advisors through *Taoci* email in advance.

The birth of Chinese applicants' *Taoci* practice is inseparable to the modern information technology since *Taoci* email is done electronically. Internet was first introduced to China in 1994.[1] As it is mentioned, the first online *Taoci* email model was shared in the middle of 1990s, when in 1997 online technology was reported to spread to every corner of the Chinese society, including media, central and local governments, banks, electronic trade, higher education, etc.[2] Surfing on the Internet became easily accessible for ordinary people in China. Therefore, overseas graduate program applicants could know more about their targeted professors and graduate programs on foreign university homepages and could have a convenient yet cheap way to make themselves noticed by foreign professors through writing a

---

[1] On April 20th, 1994, China was officially acknowledged as a country with full-featured Internet in the world. http://www.cnnic.net.cn/hlwfzyj/hlwdsj/.

[2] In Novermber 1997, China Internet Network Information Center announced the first "China Network Development Situation Statistics ": till Oct., 31st, 1997, there were in all 299,000 computers in China, 620,000 netizens, 4,044 domain names, 1,500 websites and 25.408M international exit broadband. http://www.cnnic.net.cn/hlwfzyj/hlwdsj/.

personal email. The digital literacy of using the Internet and email becomes an embodied asset as a type of keyboard skill behind screens and empowers Chinese applicants to embrace cross-border mobility.

Different from the institutionalized application materials, *Taoci* is quite a personal way of self-presentation to foreign supervisors, which can accommodate more individuality and cultural uniqueness. Perhaps, at the beginning, *Taoci* practice was only individual, regional and temporary at the end of the last century. With repeated and frequent practice, *Taoci* has become almost a default step in application. *Taoci* genre circulates among graduate applicants and has probably formed a kind of small culture (Holliday, 1999) among *Taoci* doers. The dialectal *Taoci* gains rich meaning beyond its local sense. Using Blommaert's (2010) terms, local *Taoci* is upscaled to the national, trans-temporary and general level, influenced by the increasing mobility of codes, norms and expectations between different scales. Even the original connotation of "derogatoriness" gradually becomes fuzzily recognized among the younger generation of applicants. New meaning has been enregistered (Agha, 2003) in a bottom-up fashion, i.e. mediated by constant usage among applicants and the ongoing meta-discourse about *Taoci*.

1.4   Summary

In the international higher education field, universities in developed countries attract a growing number of foreign students who invest enormously in order to seek alluring educational resources and profitable degrees. Chinese students are involved in this cross-border influx as well, preferring to move to English-speaking countries to further their graduate programs. A *Taoci* email, an unauthorized way to strive for international offers, has become a conventional practice among Chinese applicants for high-stake self-presentation with regards to foreign supervisors, which represents a resistance or complement to the impersonal institutionalized overseas application system. Enlightened by the ethnographic masterpiece of "Global Body-shopping" authored by Xiang Biao (2007) in which he described and interpreted the Indian IT workers' migration to powerful English-speaking countries, we consider Chinese applicants' *Taoci* practice as a means of "global offer hunting" to capture the fact that they are competing with worldwide talents and invest intensively into their study-abroad programs and imagined future.

This study, by drawing in the two strands of theoretical rationales—speech act theory and investment model, aims to unveil Chinese study-abroad applicants' *Taoci* email practice, to uncover their personal communication with unfamiliar foreign professors, and to explain the found-out discursive features of *Taoci* by situating it in a broader social cultural background, such as applicants' investment into their imagined identity on the global higher education market.

The potential significance of this research is threefold. *Taoci* email is an emerging type of self-promotional genre of Chinese applicants' doing their international application with English email, which is a less-known topic. Therefore, the present research on *Taoci* fills in the niche of the underexplored area of Chinese English learners' writing practice. Second, as a locus intermingled between the scales of local (a dialect term), national (Chinese nationwide applicants) and global (a means to communicate with foreign professors), *Taoci* constitutes a significant site for the encounter between unfamiliar students and supervisors, applicants and gate-keepers, individuals and institutions, and even different cultures such as the traditional Chinese values and Western individualism. Hence a close examination of Chinese applicants' *Taoci* practice may illuminate the sleek and subtle cultural dialogue or confluence between different cultures in the ongoing globalized environment. Third, the application of investment theory to examine discourse practice extends the application of Bourdieu's

26

key concepts of field, capital and habitus to sociolinguistic analysis, and provides corroboration, reinforcement and enrichment for the existing investment theory with insights from social pragmatics.

Chapter 2

Theoretical Framework and Relevant Work

Speech act theory sheds great light on second language learning research. L2 investment theory was mainly inspired by and built upon Bourdieu's key concepts of habitus, field and capital. Norton's L2 investment and the new model proposed in Darvin and Norton (2015) are scrutinized with its inadequacies pointed out.

2.1 Second Language Investment Theory

2.1.1 Bourdieu's Theory of Practice: Habitus, Field and Capital

Pierre Bourdieu was a French sociologist. His theory of practice attempted to overcome or transcend such dualities as subjectivism and objectivism, internalization and externalization, structure and agency, and individual and society (Bourdieu, 1990, 1995; Bourdieu, Wacquant, 1992). He explained social practice by teasing out the complex interplay of field, habitus and capital, which is summarized via the following formula: [(habitus) (capital) + field]=practice (Bourdieu, 1984: 101). Language occupies an important position in Bourdieu's theory and is understood as a form of more general social practices of distinction. The following section elaborates the details of the triplets and their relations with language.

(a) Habitus and Linguistic Habitus

Habitus is not entirely Bourdieu's invention. The Aristotelian hexis (usually translated as "state") is the precursor. Bourdieu re-elaborated Marcel Mauss' definition of habitus by including *habits* and dispositions to Marcel Mauss' beliefs, behaviors, and characteristics that people take in and apply in daily practice. Habitus refers to "systems of durable, transposable dispositions, structured structures predisposed to function as structuring structures" (Bourdieu, 1995: 72). Structured structures are the regulated and regular principles of the generation and structuring of practices, that is the objective *opus operatum*, such as langue, the way Saussure viewing language as a structured system. Structuring structures, as *modus operandi*, are "instruments for knowing and constructing the world of objects, as 'symbolic forms'" (Bourdieu, 1991: 164). Therefore, it is a kind of schemata of thinking, feeling, speaking, such as the active aspect of cognition noted in Marx (Bourdieu, 1995). The structuring power is only exercised because it is structured, which justifies habitus as a way of being for doing, a habitual state (predisposition, tendency, propensity, or inclination) to steer actors' action and reaction.

Habitus is used to mediate the opposition between objectivism and subjectivism and to establish the science of the dialectic of "the

31

internationalization of externality and the externalization of internality"
(Bourdieu, 1995: 72). Habitus is sedimented situations lodged inside
the body that wait to be reactivated. It has a historical dimension
in that the structure of dispositions takes shape over time through
people's constant practices in fields. Dispositions are inculcated by
objective conditions, a kind of the internationalization of externality.
When habitus is triggered in a specific field, its dispositions operate
from within social subjects, and produce or reproduce programmed
improvisations, thus the externalization of the socialized subjectivities.

The historical inculcations are deposited in social subjects' mind
and body across time and space as they enter the society. Once the
tendency to act the same way in similar situations is formed, it becomes
inertial, perpetuated and long-lasting. Thus, habitus enables social
individuals to deal with unforeseen situations, and simultaneously
"integrat[ing] the past experiences, functions at every moment as a
matrix of perceptions, appreciations and actions and makes possible
the achievement of infinitely diversified tasks" (Bourdieu, 1995: 83).

Bourdieu used a lot of words like "determination" (*ibid*: 86),
"determine" (*ibid*: 81), "perpetuate" (*ibid*: 82), "regulated" (*ibid*: 72)
when illustrating the relation between habitus and the externalization
of its dispositions. Perhaps because of this style of rhetoric, his ideas

misled following scholars to conceptualize the construct of habitus as invariable structures under most circumstances. However, Bourdieu also emphasized that habitus is "durable, but not **eternal**" (Bourdieu, Wacquant, 1992: 133, bold added by the present author). Habitus evolves and continually adjusts to the current context and reinforced by further experience. In particular in the modern society where fields are transformed quickly and revolutionarily, the inculcation and appropriation of habitus may have a chance to encounter "a creation of unpredictable novelty" (Bourdieu, 1995: 95).

Habitus expresses itself through one of its dimensions of linguistic habitus. "The language habitus, [is] the generative, unifying principle at the basis of all linguistic practices...", or more specifically,

> "...a set of socially constituted dispositions that imply a propensity to speak in certain ways and to utter determinate things..., as well as a competence to speak defined inseparably as the linguistic ability to engender an infinite array of discourses that are grammatically conforming, and as the social ability to adequately utilize this competence in a given situation." (Bourdieu, 1977: 660)

People with acquired linguistic habitus are inclined to speak (or write) in a particular and roughly consistent manner. It seemingly resembles Chomsky's universal grammar but differs essentially from it in that habitus is engendered throughout a person's social history while universal grammar is regarded as an innate gift of human gene endowed from birth. Linguistic habitus could signal a dimension of class habitus, as it represents "an expression of (synchronically and diachronically defined) position in the social structure..." (Bourdieu, Wacquant, 1992: 145). To illustrate the linguistic habitus of the bourgeois class, Bourdieu (1977) gave an example of the petty bourgeois' tendency to give hyper-correction in speech.

(b) Field and Language Market

Both the production and the operation of habitus must happen in fields. "In analytic terms, a field may be defined as a network, or a configuration, of objective relations between positions." (Bourdieu, Wacquant, 1992: 97) Therefore, field is not a material or tangible space, but comprises a network of forces generated by positions and relation, that are objectively defined by social structure. In this sense, it resembles magnetic field in the science of physics. The relations between different positions define the structure of a field as well as capital distribution within it. Although field has boundary, it doesn't mean field is completely self-enclosed. One field interacts with other fields and has itself transformed and that is why new dispositions of habitus can be engendered. To carry out the study of a certain field, Bourdieu elucidated three facets to take into account: the position of the field, the objective structure of relations, the habitus of agents (*ibid*). The relation between habitus and field operates as follows, "the field structures the habitus… Habitus contributes to constituting the field as a meaningful world" (*ibid:* 127). Because of this dialectic relation, habitus is not a fixture forever, but changing concomitant with new contingencies of a specific field or the formation of a new social field.

Bourdieu (1977, 1991, 1995) used the words of "field" and "market" interchangeably. Therefore, a linguistic market is also called a linguistic field. Linguistic market is defined as "a system of relations of force which impose themselves as a system of specific sanctions and specific censorship, and thereby help fashion linguistic production by determining the 'price' of linguistic products" (Bourdieu, Wacquant, 1992: 145). "Utterances receive their value only in their relation to a market, characterized by a particular law of price formation." (Bourdieu, 1991: 67) For instance, on the language market constituted by all human languages, English, in particular American English and British English is top priced, which explains L2 learners' keen investment of money and energy in grasping an American or British accent with the hope to gain more economic return and higher social status, partaking of the competitive distribution or redistribution of resources internationally. At a micro level of language, linguistic features such as expressive style, choice of words or syntactic structure, and conversational turns are also congruent with power relations of a linguistic field. For instance, Thompson noted at the introduction part of Bourdieu (1991), "Tact is nothing other than the capacity of a speaker to assess market conditions accurately and to produce linguistic expressions which are appropriate to them." Therefore, people will be careful in "doing things with their words", though their inculcated habitus may not remind them of it.

(c) Capital and Linguistic Capital

Bourdieu (1977) expanded the Marxist material capital (means of production). He categorized capital into economic capital, cultural capital and social capital, all of which could be symbolic capital in certain fields. Economic capital is characterized by its immediate convertibility into money and institutionalized form of property rights, for example, stocks, deposit, and real estate.

Cultural capital, also called "information capital" (Bourdieu, Wacquant, 1992: 162), has three forms: embodied, objectified and institutionalized. The embodied state (*forme incorporée*) of cultural capital refers to long-lasting dispositions of the mind and body, such as athletic skills, talent, and gift. It is stable and represents a person's totality of intellectual cultivation and qualification as a result of time-consuming labor of inculcation and embodiment (Bourdieu, 1986; Bourdieu, Passeron, 1985). The objectivized state (*forme objective*) of cultural capital exists in the form of material objects, for example, books, paintings, monuments, instruments, etc., which are transposable in their physical state. Finally, the institutionalized state (*forme institutionnalisée*) of cultural capital is a form of institutional objectification, such as formalized academic qualification (e.g. diploma) that is socially sanctioned by an institution.

"Social capital is the aggregate of the actual or potential resources which are linked to possession of a durable network of more or less institutionalized relationships of mutual acquaintance and recognition— or in other words, to membership in a group." (Bourdieu, 1986: 51) A person's entirety of social relations indicates the actual or potential resources at his/her disposal. The amount of social capital owned by a person depends on the membership that s/he can effectively mobilize. Therefore, the Chinese concept of *guanxi* can be regarded a kind of social capital. Fei (1948) compared the Chinese patterns of *guanxi* to a concentric order of layers, with the innermost interpersonal connections typically being family members among whom members have the most solid and reliable *guanxi* capital to use, and as the order extends outwards to non-kin relations, friends, colleagues and acquaintances, the manageable capital varies accordingly. The relational ties define a person's position in a social network and the social capitals that s/he could make use of from context to context.

> "The instrumental value attached to a give relationship leads many Chinese to speak of having with someone, a factor which is extremely important in their language use ... It implies a sense of specialness and a greater range of mutual rights and obligations ... If one does not have *guanxi* with a target who one needs to get something done, one could either appeal to some commonalities with the target ("pull" or "climb" *guanxi*) or go through others who have already had *guanxi* with the target individual." (Chang, 2010: 51)

Different forms of capital are convertible into each other. Cultural capital like computer skills is convertible, mediated by the activity of selling and buying on a job market, into economic capital of salary. Social capital, made up of social connections, is convertible into economic capital. For instance, Chinese parents used to (perhaps still

38

prefer to) climb *guanxi*[①] in order to find profitable jobs for their kids (Chang, 2010). Because of the exchangeability of different capitals and marketization, people can trade one form of capital with another, and reap more capitals through investment practice.

Symbolic capital is a subordinate capital, related to honor and recognition (Bourdieu, 1995). It refers to "the form that one or another of these species [different capitals] takes when it is grasped through categories of perception that recognize its specific logic or … misrecognize the arbitrariness of its possession and accumulation" (Bourdieu, Wacquant, 1992: 119). The word of "symbolic" indicates no direct material effect, but in a certain social field, economic, social and cultural capital could be transformed into symbolic capital that is "worthy of being pursued and preserved" (Bourdieu, 1995: 82) and vice versa. Anything that is recognized as rare and worthy of being sought after such as fair words, compliments, honor, and power could have symbolic value. "…the exhibition of symbolic capital … is one of the mechanisms which (no doubt universally) make capital go capital." (Bourdieu, 1995: 183) That is to say, symbolic capital

---

① "Climb *guanxi*" in Chinese is *pan-guanxi* (攀关系). It is a synonymous expression of pulling *guanxi*. Only the Chinese character of "*pan*" implies reaching the *guanxi* network hierarchically higher than the person who is climbing *guanxi*.

becomes a currency in circulation to enable the inter-changeability of the three forms of capital. Fig. 2.1 gives a summary of Bourdieu's classification of different capitals.

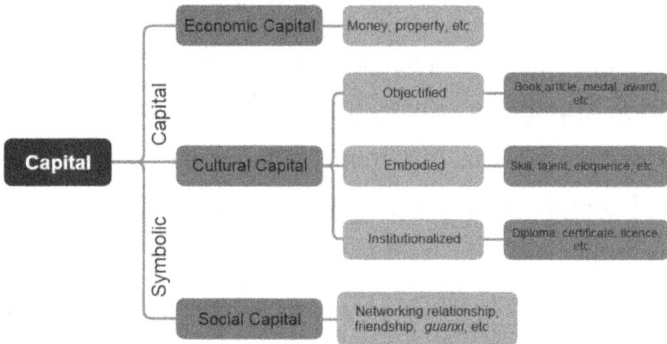

Fig. 2.1　A summary of different capitals in Bourdieu (1977) (The vertical display of "symbolic capital" indicates it as a subordinate to each type of capital.)

"Language forms a kind of wealth." (Bourdieu, 1991: 43) The wealth is taken as a kind of cultural capital and symbolic capital to constitute the world of symbolic exchanges. To view language as linguistic capital instead of linguistic competence is to align with communicative competence of language users emphasized by Hymes (1972a) and to part with the Chomskyan linguistic competence inherent in human genes. As a valuable asset procuring either material or symbolic profit, language itself becomes the goal of people's investment, for example, Chinese students' investment in English learning in the past decades. It can become a means of investment for more capitals, for instance, using the acquired English competence to look for a high-paid job. Having access to a language implies access to other resources that are produced and circulated in a regulated way, which allows for competition for resources of typically unequal distribution. Language investment as a means and as an end is thus in a dialectical relationship. Moreover, the investment and profit of linguistic capital is inseparable from the macro social structure of economy, politics, and education.

To summarize, the rules of games and individuals' position in a given field depend on the possession of capital in terms of quantity and quality. The relations of different positions lead to the distribution, flow and conversion of different forms of capital. Practice is the result of the interplay of field structure, habitus and capital, which contributes to the reconciliation between the macro and the micro, or structure and agency. In Bourdieu's theory of practice, language is a pervasive theme. Jones, cited in Grenfell and Kelly (1999: 41), recognized that Bourdieu's scope included "language at the international, the national and the regional level, language as a terrain on which the social classes do battle, language at the group level and the interpersonal level". Bourdieu's emphasis on language in and as social practice and his criticism of structuralist linguistics inspired researches in sociolinguistics and second language learning, among which Norton's investment stands out and comes next.

2.1.2 Second Language Learning Investment

L2 Investment owes its credit to the Canadian scholar, Bonny Norton, who emphasized the role of language in constituting learner identity and placed L2 language learning in a bigger social and historical background. The previous section on habitus, field and capital and language, has already paved a way for this part. A relook at Bourdieu's notion of investment is necessary to examine the current L2 investment construct.

(a) Bourdieu's Concept of Investment

A given field is occupied by bearers of capital of varying volume and types, which leads to power differentiation and channels capitals to flow and circulate with their bearers into a certain direction. Therefore, scarce capitals become the pursuit object for field occupants. Dominant class (or group) tries to maintain their *status quo* while the dominated tries to break it down and to fight for redistribution in their favor. Movement and adjustment of capital is done through the practice of investment.

> "By investment, I mean the propensity to act that is born
> of the relation between a field and a system of dispositions
> adjusted to the game it proposes, a sense of the game
> and of its stakes that implies at once an inclination and
> an ability to play the game, both of which are socially and
> historically constituted rather than universally given."
> (Bourdieu, Wacquant, 1992: 118)

Investment is closely related with habitus, "the propensity to act",
which then occurs at a subconscious level. Nevertheless, investment,
driven by a specific desire or goal, will also become conscious and
conscientious to investors, as Bourdieu used "game" to further illustrate
the notion of investment—"the moves that she makes, more or less
risky or cautious, subversive or conservative, depend both on the
total number of tokens and on the composition of the piles of tokens
she retains" (*ibid*: 99). Investment defined by Bourdieu is threefold:
sense, inclination and ability. Investors know about the game rules and
its consequence, i.e. sense of practice. Field rules and dispositions of
habitus steer investors' actions for their own benefit. Habitus endows
its actors "the art of estimating and taking chances, the ability to
anticipate through a kind of practical induction, the capacity to bet on

the possible against the probable for a measured risk, the propensity to invest, access to economic information, etc." (Bourdieu, Wacquant, 1992: 124).

All forms of capitals could be employed to invest on certain markets for benefits. Linguistic capital, such as English, becomes a popular investment object in the market of second or foreign language teaching and learning, as a lingua franca works as a profitable means of investment for other forms of capitals.

(b) Investment in Second Language Learning

Norton Peirce[①] (1995) introduced the economic metaphor of investment to L2 learning research in order to zoom in the social and historical aspect of female immigrants' English learning and their changing identity in Canada. In her own words, the concept of investment was drawn in to deal with "the complex relationship of language learners to the target language and their sometimes ambivalent desire to speak it" (Norton Peirce, 1995: 9). Diverting from the classical psychology perspective to investigate learners' motivation, which presupposes language learner as unitary, fixed and ahistorical, it

---

① Bonny Norton's paper published in 1995 was authored with the name of Norton Pierce.

emphasized that language learners' identity was multiple and dynamic. When they were moving to different situations, they carried with them their social roles and life history. Thus, "The concept of investment … signals the socially and historically constructed relationship of learners to the target language" (Norton, 2000: 10).

Learners invest in the target language across situations (or fields), because they believe they would gain benefits or interests in the future through investment, as "Learners expect or hope to have a good return from that investment—a return that will give them access to hitherto unattainable resources" (Norton, 2000: 10). For example, Gao et al.' s (2007) serial studies of Chinese English learners suggest that a substantial number of Chinese students regarded English as a valuable resource for self-empowerment. Gao, Cheng, Zhao and Zhou (2005) found that Chinese learners are "particularly motivated by self-esteem needs", which include positive attitudes towards life, pursuit of social positions, and fulfillment of individual potentials. Imagined identities and imagined communities are central in the struggle for legitimate language usage and to explain how and why people make sense of their relations with other people and the world. "There is a focus on the future when learners imagine who they might be, and who their communities might be, when they learn a language." (Norton,

Toohey, 2011: 422)

In the early development of the construct of investment in applied linguistics, access to the target language community was canonized as the primary imagined identity that learners desire to attain. For instance, Norton and Gao (2009: 114) argued "the people in whom learners have the greatest investment may be the very people who represent or provide access to the imagined community of a given learner". Pittaway (2004) claimed that acceptance into the L2 community was the desired return of students' investment in L2 learning because integration into the language community would offer learners opportunities to gain more capitals. However, as devices of language learning become diversified due to the progress of technology such as the Internet, being a part of target language community is not the only imagined identity that learners long for. "Advanced education, professional opportunities, study abroad, and other opportunities have become part of imagined futures and imagined identities." (Darvin, Norton, 2015: 40)

The concept of L2 investment is significant in the following two aspects. First, it takes a social historical perspective to examine learners' desire and commitment to learn as well as use a second/foreign language, which supplements the dominant psychological view of L2 learner motivation. Learners are identified as social human beings with complex and rich history yet constrained and empowered under different circumstances. Second, investment underlines the importance of language, which is "constitutive of and constituted by a speaker's identity" (Norton, 2000: 12). Language is regarded as a particular way of meaning-making practice and identity construction, as "discourses are the complexes of signs and practices that organize social existence and social reproduction" (*ibid*: 14).

As the effect of digital technologies (e.g. email, Skype, social medium, website) on identity and language becomes celebratory in the twenty-first century, "Networked electronic communications have given rise to new social spaces, linguistic and semiotic practices, and ways of fashioning the self" (Lam, 2006: 171). The spaces for people to traverse become further de-territorialized as they can participate in and retreat from different virtual communities as they like. People are endowed with more options thanks to digital literacy, which paradoxically creates new forms of power difference between those who have and those who don't have access to the Internet and its related technology. This situation renders the mechanism of power more invisible on the world-wide free market. To cater for the new challenges in the information age, Darvin and Norton (2015) proposed a model of investment navigating the three separate yet overlapping

47

constructs of identity, capital and ideology, locating investment at the very center of the interface as Fig. 2.2 presents.

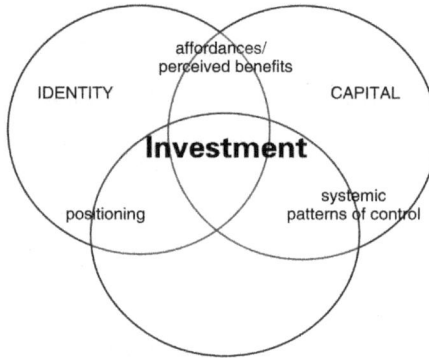

Fig. 2.2　The Darvin and Norton (2015) Investment Model

This model highlights the macro level of power represented by ideology, which is not just language ideology that indexes voices of social positions in communicative events, but a broader construct of ideology of a normative set of ideas embedding race, ethnicity, gender and social class. It enables us to "analyze the relation between communicative practices and systemic patterns of control at both micro and macro levels" (Darvin, Norton, 2015: 43). The flow and circulation of capital are subject to existing social structures. Through the integration of ideology, capital could be examined more closely and

48

critically. However, learners are equipped with capitals when they enter fields and these capitals help them to acquire other assets. Therefore, we should treat "the linguistic and cultural capital of learners as affordances rather than constraints" (*ibid*: 45). Capitals afford foreseeable and potential interests, so language learners are willing to invest, which at the same time shape and reshape their sense of self and relations with others. Carrying with them capital as affordances and driven by their desire of imagined identity, learners are empowered as choosing subjects to exercise their agency. Therefore, "...identity is a struggle of habitus and desire, of competing ideologies and imagined identities" (*ibid*: 45).

Darvin and Norton's investment model has several strong points to be chosen as the theoretical framework. First, by taking into consideration the macro construct of ideology, this model places the sociocultural approach of language learning into the systemic control of globalized power. Under the lens of systemic control pattern, the tension between imagined identity and investment could be examined more closely. Second, capitals are looked upon as affordances instead of constraints. Thus, learners are given more agency in particular in language and literary practices, illustrated by the investment praxis of Henrietta in Uganda and Ayrton in Canada (Darvin, Norton, 2015).

Third, the comprehensive model goes beyond the arena of second language learning and target language community. It is potential to be applied to a broad spectrum of investment practice driven by investors' desire, such as Chinese applicants' imagined future of studying abroad. Actually this has just responded to challenges from researches on investment in context of learning English as a foreign language, e.g. China, posed by such scholars as Rui and Gao (2008) and Gu (2008). Another merit lies in the fact that L2 investment places language or discourse at a crucial position in constituting identity. In addition, the freedom of movement and the decentralization of spaces emphasized by Darvin and Norton (2015) in constructing multiple identities and reconfiguring power is highly related to the subject matter of *Taoci* (a type of digital literacy) as a means of global offer hunting on the international higher education market.

However, there are some problems not adequately accommodated by this model. First, it runs roughshod over the concrete properties of language form and language use. Although Norton (2000) emphasized that the power at the micro daily encounters influenced investment, and Darvin and Norton (2015) drew in both the macro and micro structure, analysis at the micro level of L2 learners' language use, such as vocabulary, style, speech act, was not touched upon at all.

The majority of empirical investment researches concentrated on L2 learners' meta-discourse, that is, research participants' reflection on their language use or life experience (e.g. Pittaway, 2004; Arkoudis, Davison, 2008; Vasilopoulos, 2015). The learners' actual second language production is rarely under scrutiny. As the role of discourse is recognized as an essential part of the very social practice by many scholars (to list some, Bourdieu, Foucault, Gee, Fairclough), i.e. to speak is to act, the present investment model seems too metaphysical if we want to make linguistic analysis of people's discursive behavior in their investment practice.

Secondly, the model over-rationalizes investment as they claimed, "Learners invest in particular practices not only because they desire specific material or symbolic benefits, but also because they recognize that the capital they possess can serve as affordances to their learning" (Darvin, Norton, 2015: 46). L2 investment is depicted as conscious and purposeful activities, which precipitates investment into a dangerously mechanical subjectivism or rationalism driven by investors' sensibility of benefits, and ignores those seemingly epiphenomenal effects, which can be deeply rooted in the sub-consciousness of individuals of a certain group. Investment can be mindful and strategic, but if all practices are channeled only through a conscious mind, it fails to capture the essence

51

of Bourdieu's conception of investment, which refers to "the propensity to act" (Bourdieu, Wacquant, 1992: 118). Investment is wrought from the interaction between habitus and field. There is a fundamental link between people's action and their expected returns (or interests), but what is expected can be either knowingly or unknowingly pursued. Hence a subconscious aspect of investment is possible even though L2 learners are constantly monitoring their English production. In particular under the context of learning English as a foreign language, the L1 habitus may intervene from time to time, evidenced by, for example, pragmatic transfer of mother tongue.

Thirdly, the leverage of ideology in this model is rather static and could undermine the dynamism of investment. "…ideologies are dominant ways of thinking that organize and stabilize societies while simultaneously determining modes of inclusion and exclusion, and the privileging and marginalization of ideas, people, and relations." (Darvin, Norton, 2015: 44) They further claimed, "Ideology shapes these institutional patterns and practices, and it structures habitus." (*ibid*: 46–47) Therefore, an investors' field position and his/her quantity and quality of capital are decided once s/he carry out an investment project. This spotlights the tension between capitals of affordances and imagined identity under the systemic patterns of control. The focal valuing of ideology and power may fall short of revealing the dynamism of investment as a process and missing those significant cultural changes happening to individuals as well a collective.

These theoretical concerns challenge the existing investment model and need an immediate response in order to enhance its explanatory rigor and to be applied to different investment practices. Further development and modification can be built upon with more theoretical prudence and new empirical support from linguistic analysis. That is why the previous section reexamines its theoretical sources and the next part sails into the details of speech act.

2.2   Speech Act Theory

Speech act theory dates back to Austin's lecture book of *How to Do Things with Words*, in which he claimed that "we should say that in saying these words we are doing something" (Austin, 1962: 13), such as naming a ship, pronouncing man and wife, sentencing a criminal. Later scholastic development of speech act theory can be divided into two camps: the philosophy-cognitive line and the socio-cultural line.

53

2.2.1 Th Internalist Perspective: Intrinsic to Language Signs

The philosophy-cognitive line of speech act represents an internalist perspective, which highlights the autonomy of language and claims that the effect of utterances is intrinsic to linguistic signs. It covers two major research topics: taxonomy of speech act and illocutionary force, both of which originated from Austin's work.

Austin (1962) distinguished performatives from constatives. Constatives refer to utterances that describe activities or things. For example, the sentence of "I pour some liquid into the tube", if "I" failed to pour some liquid, can be verified as a false proposition. "The term 'performative' … is derived, of course, from 'perform', the usual verb with the noun 'action'…" (*ibid*: 6) It refers to the fact that the articulation of an utterance constitutes the accomplishment of an action. For instance, when "I apologize to you" is uttered, the action of "apologization" is made. The constatives are about statement being true or false, while performatives are about action being happy or unhappy (*ibid*).

For the performatives to be done, there are some linguistic rules to follow, as he argued "… any utterance which is in fact a performative should be reducible, or expandible, or analysable into a form which a verb in the first person singular present indicative active (grammatical)" (*ibid*: 61-62). Moreover, performatives have to meet some felicity conditions listed in Table 2.1. The first condition of (A. 1) is about the existing norm for the speech action performance. The second condition of (A. 2) is about the required situation for the speech action. The third and fourth condition of (B. 1) and (B. 2) are about the execution of the speech action, which could have included (Γ. 2). The last two are about the actor's mental qualification for the speech action.

Table 2.1   Felicity conditions

Name	Conditions
(A. 1)	There must exist an accepted conventional procedure having a certain conventional effect, which includes the uttering of certain words by certain persons in certain circumstances, and further.
(A. 2)	The particular persons and circumstances in a given case must be appropriate for the invocation of the particular procedure invoked.
(B. 1)	The procedure must be executed by all participants both correctly and completely
(B. 2)	
(Γ. 1)	Where, as often, the procedure is designed for use by persons having certain thoughts or feelings, or for the inauguration of certain consequential conduct on the part of any participant, then a person participating in and so invoking the procedure must in fact have those thoughts or feelings, and the participants must intend so to conduct themselves and further.
(Γ. 2)	Must be actual so as to conduct themselves subsequently.

However, in the later part of his lecture book, Austin gave up the contrast between constatives and performatives because it is impossible to identify common and precise linguistic features (such as person, mood, tense, predicates, voice) to distinguish them. One sentence can be used as either performative or constative as far as its context suffices. Even a slight change of tone or intonation could render a different category of it. Therefore, "The dichotomy between performative and constative was not discussed for its own sake, it serves another purpose, it paves the way for a new theory—the theory of illocutionary acts" (Jiang, 2000: 206). Austin (1962: 120) made a distinction of "the locutionary act (and within it the phonetic, the phatic, and the rhetic acts) which has a meaning; the illocutionary act which has a certain force in saying something; the perlocutionary act which is the achieving of certain effects by saying something". When an utterance is issued, the three acts are carried out simultaneously. The illocutionary force of utterance is the focus of pragmatics.

Previously Austin argued that "every performative could be in principle put into the form of an explicit performative, and then we could make a list of performative verbs" (*ibid*: 91), and classified five types of speech act: (a) verdictives, typified by giving a verdict; (b) exercitives, such as ordering, warning; (c) commissives, like promising, undertaking; (d) behabitives, such as apologizing, congratulating; and (e) expositives, like argument. This categorization is based on a semantic distinction of verbal meanings. However, in real life the performativity of these verbs could be countervailed by contextual factors. Given appropriate contextual and textual conditions, it is possible that any utterance could be used to achieve a certain illocutionary effect while a piece of utterance could deliver a variety of illocutionary force, a tension that pragmatic theorists like Horn (1984), and Sperber and Wilson (1986) tried to solve.

Austin's theory triggered a hot discussion in the 1960s and 1970s. The most notable inheritor of speech act theory might be Searle, who tried to tease out the systematic rules to pin down a certain speech act and propose another taxonomy of speech act. Searle (1975) proposed four essential felicity conditions to distinguish one type of speech act from another—the illocutionary point, the direction of fit between words and the world, the psychological state expressed and the propositional content. The illocutionary point means the purpose of a speech act. The direction of fit between words and the world means that some expressions are getting the words to match the world, for instance, making an assertion while others getting the world to match the words, for example, making promises. The psychological state expresses

57

speakers' attitude or feelings. The propositional content refers to the reference and sense of a locution. The four dimensions were developed into preparatory conditions, propositional content conditions, sincerity condition and essential condition, which are exemplified in the following citation of the speech act of "promise" in Table 2.2.

Table 2.2　Felicity conditions of "Promise"

(1)Propositional content conditions	(a) S expresses the proposition that p in the utterance of T.
	(b) In expressing that p, S predicates a future act A of S.
(2)Preparatory conditions	(a) H would prefer S's doing A to his not doing A, and S believes H would prefer his doing A to his not doing A.
	(b) It is not obvious to both S and H that S will do A in the normal course of events.
(3)Sincerity condition	S intends to do A.
(4)Essential condition	S intends that the utterance of T will place him under an obligation to do A.

Searle's felicity conditions are mainly concerned about the cognitive procedures needed to define a speech act: the content of the utterance in (1), the speaker's intention and the hearer's expected reaction in (2), the speaker's psychological state in (3) and designed action in (4) in Table 1.2. Comparatively, Austin's felicity conditions include more elements other than the cognitive processing, i.e. a prior ritualistic norm in (A. 1) and the situation in (A. 2) in Table 2.1 that contextualize the upcoming cognitive activity. Austin focused on how speakers realized their intentions through speaking, whereas Searle focused on how listeners responded to utterances, that is, "how one person tries to figure out how another is using a particular utterance" (Wardhaugh, 2000: 285). Searle's proposal of the felicity conditions is an idealized assumption of people's mental processing of a speech act. In reality illocutionary force derives not just from a sequence of preset inductive formula.

Based on the four conditions, Searle classified illocutionary acts into five categories: assertive, directive, commissive, expressive and declaration. The assertive is about expressing a proposition and almost conflates with Austin's constative. The directive is to get the hearer to do something. The commissive is to commit the speaker to some future action. The expressive is to convey the speaker's psychological state, like emotion, attitude. The declaration is to bring about some alternation in the status or condition of the referred object. However, this classification is too limited to cover all the possible actions done through speech acts. Jiang (2000) argued that there should at least be more subclasses under each of the five, and that is why we need more speech act categories.

Leech (1983) criticized both Austin's and Searle's analysis of illocutionary verbs by claiming that their discussion led to futile efforts of grammaticalizing pragmatic force devoid of context. Illocutionary force "is more subtle than can be easily accommodated by our everyday vocabulary of speech-act verbs" (Leech, 1983: 175). Only the metalinguistic performative, a small number of it, can be syntactically defined. He proposed the extended performative hypothesis that "the illocutionary force not only of a direct speech act, but also of an indirect speech act, can be appropriately formalized in a performative deep structure" (1983: 194). For example, the deep structure of "Can you close the window?" is "I request that you close the window.". Therefore, Leech hammered out a semantic analysis of the relevance of verb meanings of performatives. Considering the absence of sub-categorization of speech acts under the glossary of five speech acts in both Austin (1962) and Searle (1975), Leech made some progress on this aspect. For example, he divided the "directive" into further specific speech act verbs of tell, command, order, demand, ask, request, beg, advise, recommend, suggest and invite, which could be applicable to discourse analysis.

The afore-discussed speech acts are all utterance-based or sentence-based, more exactly, verb-based. Levinson (1987) appraised that any theory about speech act was trying to match utterances with speech act categories to predict the functions of sentences in context. However, if contextual sources of speaker, hearer, and their social relations are acknowledged for the generation of illocutionary force, the complexity goes far beyond linguistic signs per se. "Together, these acts produce a total speech act that must be studied in the total speech situation." (Schiffrin, 1994: 54)

Van Dijk proposed a discourse-based approach to speech act in the study of global structures in discourse, interaction and cognition. "Macrostructures are higher-level semantic or conceptual structures that organize the 'local' microstructures of discourse, interaction and their cognitive processing." (van Dijk, 1980: V) Macro speech act is a kind of macrostructures. "…certain sequences of various speech acts may be intended and understood, and hence function socially, as one speech act. Such a speech act performed by a sequence of speech acts will be called a global speech-act or MACRO-SPEECH ACT." (van Dijk, 1977: 238) Through such rules as deletion, generalization and construction, a macro speech act could be mapped out from discrete speech act sequence of a text.

Van Dijk's idea about macro speech act is an expansion of speech act from sentence-based performance to textual analysis. It provides a discursive perspective to put speech act into its unfolding discourse.

61

In other words, it provides a bird-view on information processing. Macro speech act plays the role of giving coherence to a piece of discourse. However, it is also related to those social and cultural factors that van Dijk didn't take much into consideration in his analysis of macro speech act. Unlike Austin and Searle, van Dijk didn't provide a list of specific speech acts used in his model. Types of speech act in a sequence could possibly vary across texts, which will jeopardize analytical consistency. On top of all, his macrostructure theory is primarily based on semantic meaning of text.

Speech act theory does offer a "kind of mini-scenario for what is happening in language interaction and ... a simple way of explaining the more or less predictable sequences of conversation" (Mey, 1993: 207). It gives us lens to scrutinize the explanation of linguistic construction of the sentences. Nevertheless, classical speech act theory only gives analysts a detached toolkit, without taking into account those social and cultural parameters adequately. "Despite the emphasis on language function, speech act theory deals less with actual utterances than with utterance-types." (Schiffrin, 1994: 60) Thus when it is applied to discourse, the issue of identification of speech acts will raise eyebrows. Furthermore, it seems a mission impossible to categorize all speech acts, and the zeal of speech act taxonomy has gradually dwindled away. However, researches on a specific speech act, such as request and apology, have flourished. In particular the speech act of request has received much research attention, to list some Ervin-tripp (1976) on English request, Blum-Kulka and House (1989) on the direct, the conventionally indirect and the nonconventional indirect request[1], Blum-Kulka and Olshtain (1984) on the cross-cultural difference of request, and Huang (1993), Zhang (1995), and Wong (2000) on request in Chinese, Kirkpatrick (1991) on English request produced by Chinese learners.

Speech act in the internalist approach is restricted to the study of linguistic signs, which leads to an irreconcilable contradiction: the illocutionary force of signs derives from the outside world, which is historically illuminated, but linguists are determinedly bent on the mere

---

[1] Direct request includes (a) mood-derivable, the grammatical mood of the verb; (b) explicit performatives in Austin's sense; (c) hedged performatives; (d) locution derivable, deriving the illocutionary force directly from the semantic meaning of the locution; (e) scoping stating, expressing the speaker's intention, desire or feeling. The conventionally indirect request contains the suggestory formula and the query-preparatory formula. The non-conventionally indirect request seems the most irrelevant to the request and there are two types of realization: the robust hint containing partial reference to object or elements needed for the implementation of the act and mild hint making no reference to the request but interpretable through the context (Blum-Kulka, House, 1989; Blum-Kulka, Olshtain, 1984).

symbols. The large social, cultural and historical elements should be invited to solve this problem, which is the externalist perspective in the coming section.

2.2.2 The Externalist Perspective: Beyond Linguistic Signs

The externalist perspective on speech act matches the socio-cultural line of pragmatics, which stresses the dynamic emergence of meaning in communication influenced by socio-cultural factors (Kecskes, 2014). Tapping into speech acts from a sociocultural perspective has produced insightful findings (Blum, 1997; Kasper, Rose, 2001; Gee, 1999), which has later developed into conversation analysis, politeness theory, discourse pragmatics, and discourse analysis in the broad sense. For instance, the SPEAKING grid proposed by the ethnographer Dell Hymes who emphasized that a communicative event was formed by the interrelationship of its components. "Discourse may be viewed in terms of acts both syntagmatically and paradigmatically: i.e. both as a sequence of speech acts and in terms of classes of speech acts among which choice has been made at given points." (Hymes, 1972b: 57) The smallest unit in communication is act (message of both form and content), including speech acts such as commanding and greeting. Separate speech acts are embedded in a larger unit called speech event, "activities, or aspects of activities, that are directly governed by rules or norms of the use of speech" (Hymes, 1972b: 56). The largest communicative unit is the speech situation, like different social occasions. The hierarchy of speech act, speech event and speech situation resembles the Russian doll, with the lower level nesting in the higher. Therefore, the analysis of speech act is the most fundamental, local, turn-by-turn level of discourse embedded in the larger context or "frame" in Goffman's (1974) term. The ethnography of communication sheds light on the fact that the force of each speech act lodges in its sociocultural milieu, not merely confined to its linguistic forms. Although Hymes also noted the need for more contextualized speech acts, he concentrated more on the large context, without turning into the micro analysis of speech act at the linguistic level.

Brown and Levinson's (1987) politeness theory has more concern about the microstructure of utterances and is adopted the main framework for linguistic analysis in the present research. The study of politeness of language focuses on the appropriateness of linguistic behaviors by bringing social norms and cultural models into consideration. Blommaert (2010: 4) commented "In pragmatics, such phenomena of selection [of linguistic forms] for preference have been described for decades in terms of ranging from 'felicity conditions' to 'appropriateness criteria' (Levinson, 1983), and let us not forget 'politeness' research as culmination point in such studies...".

Politeness was regarded a universal constraint on language usage (Brown & Levinson, 1987). They borrowed (or followed) Goffman's concept of face, which is defined as "the positive social value a person effectively claims for himself by the line others assume he has taken during a particular contact" (Goffman, 1967: 5). The term of face developed from Goffman's (1959) earlier work of "The Presentation of Self". Face is the image that speaker projected into a specific situation together with his or her hearer and audience if there is any. Brown and Levinson distinguished negative face and positive face, which are respectively defined as "the want of every 'competent adult member' that his actions be unimpeded by others" and "the want of every member that his wants be desirable to at least some others" respectively (Brown, Levinson, 1987: 62). Therefore, positive face and negative face are both about face needs, which should be taken care of in communication through words.

Given the universality of face and rationality in communication, certain kinds of acts "intrinsically threaten face, namely those acts that by their nature run contrary to the face wants of the addressee and/or of the speaker" (*ibid*: 65). Face-threatening acts (abbreviated as FTAs) should have been called face-threatening speech acts as "By 'act' we have in mind what is intended to be done by a verbal or non-verbal communication, just as one or more 'speech acts' can be assigned to an utterance" (*ibid*: 65). One speech act can be expressed in very different forms. Some forms are preferable while others tend to be shunned by rational minds. The choice of a specific form reflects the impact of people's sociocultural background of doing things with words, or in Bourdieu's terms "the body hexis" (Bourdieu, 1977: 660). Brown and Levinson (1987) postulated three social determinants that influence linguistic choices especially those face-threatening expressions: social distance (D), social power (P) and imposition (R).

To calculate the weight of threat of a speech act, they composed a formula of "$Wx = D(S,H) + P(H,S) + Rx$". D (S, H) is the social distance between speaker and hearer, similar to like-mindedness and social similarity in Brown and Gilman (1968), familiarity in Holms (1990), and solidarity in Scollon and Scollon (1991). P (S, H) means hearer's power over speaker and Rx refers to the imposition degree of the threat. Generally, the more distance between interlocutors, the more power hearer over speaker and the more imposition of the speech act, the more prudence and carefulness will be invested in wording. The effects of the three variables are orchestrated to determine the weight of threat and politeness strategies. Brown and Levinson (1987) also pointed out that these factors were culture-specific and had emic correlates.

There are three super strategies raised in Brown and Levinson (1987): positive politeness strategy, negative politeness strategy and off record strategy. Each super-strategy is further dissected into sub-strategies, which are realized through specific speech acts and linguistic forms. "Positive politeness is redress directed to the addressee's positive face, his perennial desire that his wants (or the actions/acquisitions/ values resulting from them) should be thought of a desirable." (Brown, Levinson, 1987: 101) Thus, positive politeness expressions resort to common ground, and share wants with the hearer, e.g. using in-group identity markers like jargons, to minimize the distance between speakers. Negative politeness is oriented towards hearer's claims of territory and autonomy so as to preserve the other's face. Sub-strategies include being direct, not presuming or assuming, not coercing hearer, apologizing, showing deference, etc. "A communicative act is done off record is it is done in such a way that it is not possible to attribute only one communicative intention to the act" (*ibid*: 211), for instance, using metaphor, irony, understatement or rhetorical questions. The politeness theory proposed by Brown and Levinson indicates that the encoding and deciphering of speech acts are not just about message of forms, but related to various social and cultural factors.

A large number of empirical studies have supported the relationship between the three social variables and the speakers' choice of communicative strategies of various linguistic forms. However, Brown and Levinson's politeness theory also received constant criticism. For instance, Matsumoto (1988) and Watts, Ide and Ehlich (2005) criticized that the model overemphasized negative politeness, i.e. individual freedom/autonomy, which is basically an Anglo-Saxon norm, not necessarily suitable for, say, the analysis of Asian communication. Spencer-Oatey (2002, 2007a, 2007b) claimed that Brown and Levinson's face was pre-defined, static, and centered on the individual and proposed a relational view of rapport management. Leech (1983) proposed more specific maxims politeness: generosity, modesty, approbation, agreement and sympathy to deal with politeness-concerned communication. Mao (1994) argued that negative and positive face were not empirically adequate for all cultures. For example, the Chinese has both *mianzi*[1] and *lian*[2] translated into "face" in English and a relative face orientation construct was needed to explain the

---

[1] In Chinese it is written as "面子".

[2] In Chinese it is written as "脸".

cultural variation. Chinese scholars raised different super-strategies of politeness. He and Chen (2004) argued for three facets of Chinese politeness: be respectful, be considerate (always thinking for the others, not bothering the others), and be warm (Don't be cold, and show concerns.). Bi (1996) pointed out that the Chinese politeness lied in self-modesty, respecting the others, showing concerns for each other, attaching importance to feeling and *renqing* [1]. Gu (1990, 1992) proposed four maxims in the politeness system of modern Chinese culture: the self-denigration maxim, the address maxim, the attitudinal warms and refinement, the balance principle of *huanli*[2] and *renqing*. These principles or maxims guide Chinese people's choices of linguistic forms in interpersonal communication.

In spite of all the criticism, Brown and Levinson's (1987) demonstration of analyzing politeness strategies, with rich and concrete examples of speech acts (often sentence-based) and their concrete linguistic forms, are still enlightening for further researches to expand the explanatory spectrum of speech act. However, they failed to unravel the deep social and cultural structure underlying language use. The

---

[1] In Chinese it is written as "人情", referring to feelings and emotional ties between people.

[2] In Chinese it is written as "还礼", and means the return of *li*, the reciprocity of ritual.

root of politeness

> "go[es] deep into the history and moral constitution of a society and as such require more than just attention to verbal and non-verbal manifestations. Its origins and workings are woven into the social fabric of interpersonal behaviour and only multidisciplinary research can hope to shed further light on them." (Bargiela-Chiappini, 2003: 1467)

In other words, "Tact is nothing other than the capacity of a speaker to assess market conditions accurately and to produce linguistic expressions which are appropriate to them…" (Thompson, 1991: 20). Thus politeness is not an independent linguistic phenomenon but the manifestation of the negotiation between a certain context (or linguistic market) and speakers' linguistic habitus. Speaking politely is a kind of habitus, a body hexis that is inculcated throughout the history of social and cultural practice, which is in line with the postmodern arguments on the performativity of discourse.

2.2.3   Performativity in Postmodern Sociology

Austin's "performative" is revitalized in the postmodern sociology of language. Performativity is reviewed briefly because it underscores the constructivist role of language in shaping and reshaping people's identity. Therefore, it appears to fall into the socio-cultural camp of speech act, but differs greatly from the previous two approaches in that it pays less attention to linguistic forms.

Bourdieu criticized Austin's illusion of ascribing the efficacy to the symbolic expressions themselves in that "Austin's account of performative utterances cannot be restricted to the sphere of linguistics. The magical efficacy of these acts of institution is inseparable from the existence of an institution defining the conditions..." (Bourdieu, 1991: 73). The power of words stems from social conditions, which "does not reside in the symbolic systems in the form of an 'illocutionary force' but that it is defined in and through a given relation between those who exercise power and those who submit it..." (*ibid*: 170). It is necessary to examine the institution from which illocutionary power comes and the conditions that are needed to exercise such power. "Most conditions that have to be fulfilled in order for a performative utterance to succeed come down to the question of the appropriateness of the speaker—or, better still, his social function—and of the discourse he utters." (*ibid*: 111) These conditions, like the felicity conditions Austin and Searle tried to tease out, are actually social conditions, which constitutes the power of a speaker's acting upon the world through words.

While Bourdieu argued that the performative effect of utterances boiled down to social institutional power, Butler concentrated more on the performative power of language use in identity construction. The performative is "not merely an act used by a pregiven subject, but is one of the powerful and insidious ways in which subjects are called into social being, inaugurated into sociality by a variety of diffuses and powerful interpellations" (Butler, 1999: 125). Performativity deconstructed the concept of identity, which "is performatively constituted by the very expressions that are said to be its results" (Butler, 1990: 25). Pennycook appraised Butler's development of performativity as "open[ing] up a way of thinking about language use and identity that avoids foundationalist categories" (Pennycook, 2007: 70). What we perform constitutes who we are. On the other hand, each new performance will lead to new entailments to sedimentation cumulative from previous practices. In this way, it "is able to accommodate concepts of both structure and agency" (Benwell, Stokoe, 2006: 33). As the performative calls into the subjects into social subjectivity, and once the subjectivity is reinforced through constant and frequent repetition, new stable identities or new attributes of identity will be formed. Thus, "the notion of the performative ... depends on a history of repetition, of sedimented effects" (Pennycook, 2007: 77). The performative breaks both linguistic and social shackles, and "to the extent that speakers are agentive, we can indeed say that they are always performing language" (Bell & Gibson, 2011: 556). In this sense, all utterances in communication are performative, echoing Austin's argument in the later part of his lecture book, and shape and reshape language users' identity.

Performativity draws our attention the ways in which discursive components utter or write language users into an identity. For example, academic discourse "socialize[s] students into academic practices as they write themselves in their disciplines" (Hyland, 2009: 5). Identities are consequently hailed in through linguistic performances. The concept of performativity underscores the fact that identity is passed on or brought to life through discourse. This view of identity construction enables us to perceive how subjectivity can be presented, invented and negotiated at speakers' disposal. However, performativity doesn't happen in vacuum to construct identity at speaker's discretion. The performativity of linguistic signs is not produced out of thin air. New meaning nests upon the old, just as Sapir asserted "The birth of a new concept is invariably overshadowed by a more or less trained or extended use of old linguistic material..." (Sapir, 2002: 14).

To summarize, the philosophy-cognition line has mainly studied speech act in terms of taxonomy and the illocutionary force in order to figure out the abstract linguistic ways of how speech act is used,

74

"divorced from broader theoretical and explanatory concerns" (Thompson, 1991: 2). It is the socio-cultural pragmatics that explores communicative strategies by taking into consideration of social norms and cultural models. Although the postmodern performativity cannot be simply reduced to specific linguistic forms of speech act, it sheds light upon the constructive role of language and reminds us the underlying mechanism behind linguistic forms.

Bourdieu and Wacquant (1992: 193) noted, "Any speech act or any discourse is a conjuncture, the product of the encounter between, on the one side, a linguistic habitus…; and, on the other hand, a linguistic market." Habitus stores the cultural and historical connotation of speech act while linguistic market highlights the relations of interlocutors and power difference within social groups. Upon entering a linguistic market, speakers carry with them their linguistic habitus and doing things with words could happen in a misrecognized-as-arbitrary way (Bourdieu, 1991), to produce the structure of a given field. When the boundary of and tension within that field undergoes change, old habitus will supervene and new dispositions are underway. Speech acts partake of this process of transformation and their characteristics may reflect as well as contribute to the negotiation between habitus and market. Hence, "It becomes clear how artificial it is to oppose external

75

linguistics to internal linguistics, analysis of the form of discourse to analysis of the social function it performs" (Bourdieu, 1977: 658). Therefore, the present research pays great attention to the social and cultural nuances inscribed into even the minute speech act.

2.3 L2 Learners' English Email Writing and Self-promotional Discourse

Previous empirical researches on English email and self-promotional discourse are reviewed to pin down the research niche in L2 email writing.

With the fast development of the Internet technology, email has gained widespread popularity in daily life. Being able to use email for communication, both knowing the email technique and phrasing email appropriately, has become a component of digital literacy, or in Bourdieu's word, a cultural capital (perhaps the embodied form of capital as a skill of keyboarding). Email communication is characterized by a blending of both written and spoken language features: It is actually preplanned and composed owing to its asynchronous without reference to those face-to-face paralinguistic characteristics, while it is also more interactive than the traditional letter-writing owing to its instant messaging nature (Herring, 2002; Baron, 1998). The

76

hybrid medium still depends on such a variety of contextual factors as sender/recipient relation, power distribution, topic concerned, and personal preferences. In this sense, the analysis of email discourse is not different from that of discourse in other mediums. Established linguistic analytical framework such as speech act can be applied to email texts as well.

This part reviews empirical researches on English email from students to faculty, in particular from second language learners, since the subject matter here is Chinese applicants' *Taoci* email. Researches on self-promotional discourse in genre analysis including job application letter and personal statement in graduate application are reviewed because they are highly relevant in that *Taoci* email is a form of self-promotion for Chinese applicants to fight for an offer from foreign universities.

2.3.1　English Email from Student to Faculty

Email is an important means to facilitate teacher/student interaction (Crystal, 2001). This part zooms in those studies of email between student and faculty, with a focus on that of Chinese college students in academia. "Broadly defined, student-faculty interaction involves contact between a faculty member and graduate student and includes conversations and discussions related to course work and assignments, thesis writing progress, job search and professional development issues, as well as informal and social exchanges of information." (Danielewicz-Betz, 2013: 25). For any kind of student-faculty interaction, such email exchange could be very personal.

Many previous researches on student-faculty English email made cross-cultural comparison between native speakers and non-native speakers, and problematized English learners' pragmatic strategies by referencing to native speakers' politeness yardstick. It is impossible to exhaust all literatures in this area, so representative researches about L2 learners' English email in the world are exemplified and discussed, ensued with a focused review on the Chinese learners' email practice.

(a) Researches on L2 Learners' English Emails in the World

By contrasting the native and non-native speakers' English emails to faculty, Bloch (2002) generalized four types of communicative topics: phatic communion, asking for help, making excuses and making formal requests. The English learners were reported to be able to use various strategies and to accommodate their email under different contexts. Block (2013) also argued for the good demonstration of pragmalinguistic competence of those non-natives who had an advanced level of English proficiency. Biesenbach-Lucas (2005) examined both American and international college students' email to faculty and generalized three functions of these emails: facilitative function, substantive function and relational function. It was reported that the non-natives might lack the ability to use email in appropriate ways that might have contributed to their academic success. Non-native speakers' lack of enough email literacy implied that they should be more acculturated into the native style of email writing.

Motallebzadeh, Mohsenzadeh and Sobhani (2014) investigated the pragmatic features in English email sent by Iranian university students to their professors. They followed the three email functions generalized in Biesenbach-Lucas (2005) and found that the most frequent communicative topic in both male and female corpora was the facilitative (scheduling appointment, submission of work, class attendance, self-identification and message confirmation). What is interesting in their research was that gender was found influential in the choice of communicative topics and strategies. For instance, in the female email data, relational strategies were more frequently used and in the male corpus, substantive strategies took a higher percentage.

Hardford and Bardovi-Harlig (1996) compared the request emails written by international students and those by U.S. students both to professors at an American university. They discovered that international students used fewer mitigating forms, less institutional explanation and less linguistic expressions of acknowledging imposition on the faculty, but mentioned their personal needs more often. Impoliteness was thus impressed on professors due to L2 students' inappropriate linguistic behavior. Similar to Biesenbach-Lucas's (2005) findings, it alluded to non-native speakers' imperfect email literacy, an inadequacy of cultural capital.

Biesenbach-Lucas and Weasenforth (2001) applied the framework of cross-cultural study of speech act realization patters (abbreviated as CCSARP) (Blum-kulka et al., 1989) to non-native speakers' and native speakers' request email to faculty. They found that there was only a minor difference in the degree of directness of the e-requests (i.e. request in email) between the two groups. To explore further, Biesenbach-Lucas (2007) again applied the CCSARP framework to examine the degree of directness and the politeness features of students' request email (including both native and non-native speakers of English) to university faculty. Not surprisingly, combination of syntactic modifiers was used by native speakers in high-imposition requests while non-native speakers failed to make use of a combination of mitigating devices. Economidou-Kogetsidis (2011) looked into

200 pieces of email produced by English learners at Greek Cypriot University. It was found that non-native speakers used direct request, little downgraders, improper forms of addressing and omitted necessary greetings and closings in email writing, which instigated pragmatic failure. This research collected perception questionnaires to testify that these pragmatically inappropriate request emails would inflict negative impression upon native English speakers.

Findings in these researches were often correlated with L2 learners' language competence. Other social variables have influence on L2 learners' linguistic performance in email. For instance, Akkaya (2007) studied the relation between the use of pragmatic markers (e.g. hedges, intensifiers) and English learners' gender, nationality and status. Based on a corpus of 160 emails sent by American and international students to professors, it was found that the international, female and undergraduate groups were significantly associated with the use of formal pragmatic markers whereas the American, male and graduate groups employed informal pragmatic markers. Seemingly, the international students were more respectful and formal compared to their American counterparts.

(b) Researches on English Email of Chinese Learners

The majority of researches on Chinese L2 learners' email are in a comparative manner as well. Chang and Hsu (1998) narrowed down the comparison between Chinese English learners' email and American native speakers'. They collected 44 pieces of request email initiated by 25 Chinese graduate students and 19 American students at an American university. Chinese students were reported to consider email communication as formal letters or telephone conversations. By contrast the American students regarded it as written memos. The requests use by Chinese learners was in indirect sequences, bearing out Kirkpartrick's (1991) schemata of Chinese request—salutation, preambles (facework), reasons and the request, but the linguistic forms were reported more direct in want-statement with less downtoners. Hence some of the Chinese students' emails were thought impolite from native speakers' perspective. The researchers suggested that Chinese English learners should be taught to follow American way of making request, i.e. "short, to the point, direct, clear and which give the recipient options" (Chang, Hsu, 1998: 145), but they neglected the underlying cultural connotation embedded in those unorthodox requests used by Chinese learners.

Cross-cultural comparisons in email usually took a deficit view of second language learners, but there were also scholars who took a "difference" perspective and focused on the linguistic features in relation with sociocultural parameters including learner identity. Chen (2001) compared the request strategies in emails to professors between Chinese students and American students and interpreted them from culture-specific notions of politeness and socio-cultural identities. The Chinese students tended to use formal address terms and salutation to show deference, but they used self-introduction emphasizing their nonnative identity. The Chinese students were reported more of pragmatic infelicities due to being too direct, but they tended to use external modification (i.e. a series of other speech acts served as supportive moves) for the politeness concern. The author emphasized that she followed Faerch and Kasper's (1989) position of "difference" hypothesis instead of "deficit" hypothesis in interlanguage research so as to get more insight about the nature of communication in a multi-cultural world.

Lee (2004) analyzed 56 pieces of request email written by Chinese students in a Hong Kong university in China, 33 of which were addressed to Chinese-speaking English teachers, 23 to native English-speaking teachers. Three functions of request were found: asking for assistance, asking for an appointment, consulting information about assignments. Using the CCSARP coding system, the researcher found

83

that over 90% of the requests to Chinese-speaking English teachers contained an alerter and a request move after making salutation, while to English native teachers there was only 50% to follow the pattern. Students tended to use various softeners and requestive hints to show respect and to lessen the imposition of the request. Nonetheless, students used more hedged and explicit performatives to the Chinese-speaking teachers than to native English teachers. The author claimed that the students' linguistic behavior pattern conformed to the traditional value of teacher-student hierarchy. Regretfully, there was no further explanation of it.

Chen (2006) carried out a longitudinal case study and explored how a Chinese English learner developed her email literacy as a graduate student with professors in America. Adopting Fairclough's critical discourse analysis approach, she narrowed down on language features in relation to identity performance, power relations, and culture-specific ideologies of student-teacher interaction and politeness. It revealed that the research participant made changes in institutional email writing with regards to discourse style, message length, message structure, and request strategies. The changes were inseparable from the participants' evolving understanding of the nature of email as a medium, the student's identity, and her knowledge of appropriate

84

student-professor relationship in America. The strong attraction of this study lies in its emic view of email writing by taking interviews with the participant.

Chen (2015) investigated the efficacy of email-pragmatics instruction to develop L2 students' literacy in English email requests to faculty. Two rounds of email were collected in a pre-test and post-test discourse completion task by using four student-teacher request topics. After the pre-test, a genre-based approach of email-writing instruction was treated on the subjects. After analyzing the 224 solicited emails from 30 students, she claimed that the students had significant gains after the instruction in terms of the greater use of concrete subjects, appropriate greetings, proper self-identifications, and closing moves, which meant the instruction was effective on the post-test than on the pre-test. This is a pioneering study to cultivate students' digital literacy in intercultural communication. In this sense, English email writing is a kind of investment into students' cultural capital, which pitifully has never been explored in the light of L2 investment.

Taking the perspective of English as lingua franca, Chen, Rau and Rau (2015) edited a book titled *Email Discourse Among Chinese Using English as a Lingua Franca*, which filled in the gap of the few-researched area of written ELF in Chinese academia. Huang

85

(2015) examined 76 emails addressed to professors written by Chinese students. Eight different email functions were identified including request, inquiry, thanking, providing information, apologizing, asking for leave of absence, confirmation of appointment/information, and wishing, which have been discovered by Block (2002) and Chen (2003). Another Huang (2015) investigated the openings and closings of Chinese students intercultural emails' corresponded with Japanese or Italian key pals. The opening used by the Japanese and Chinese students is more formal than that of the Italian students. These differences could be attributed to the cultural incongruence, as Asians were often claimed to tend to deference more carefully, whereas Italians tended to show solidarity.

The Chinese subjects in the afore-mentioned studies were from Chinese students in English-speaking countries. There are also increasing researches about English learners' email practice in mainland China in recent years. Luo (2010) analyzed the politeness strategies used in students' request email addressed to an English-speaking teacher at a Chinese university. 46 pieces of email were collected from 30 college students. It is found that conventional indirect strategy characterized Chinese students. More specifically, query preparatory, pre-request supportive moves and typical inductive discourse organization were the most prominent features. The factors that might lead to such characteristics were situational factors, the medium, cultural influence, pragmatic transfer, and language proficiency. However, none of these factors were explored in depth.

Pan and Cai (2004) compared English email written by Chinese college students and American college students. They analyzed 36 pieces of email texts and found linguistic differences between the two groups at lexicon, syntax and textual level. It was found that American students composed longer emails with more personal characteristics while the Chinese students' emails were shorter and the lexicon was limited. Perhaps due to the transfer of Chinese writing style, the sentences written by Chinese students were not as layered (e.g. complex and compound sentences) as the American ones. They explained these differences only in terms of English proficiency difference, which is too simplified.

Likewise, Zhu (2012) compared the strategies used by English learners in English request emails between English major (EM) and non-English major (NEM) students in mainland China. The researcher elicited data by giving students a task of writing request email of different topics to instructors. The CCSARP coding framework of head acts was mainly adopted and social distance, power and rank of imposition (Brown & Levinson, 1987) were identified as situational variables. It was found that the EM group employed much more indirect requestive strategies than the NEM group. The EM used much more syntactic mitigators in the head request to decrease the imposition than the NEM, and by and large the EM could use the politeness devices more flexibly than the NEM. The research implied that both groups seemed to exhibit inadequate sociopragmatic competence and pragmalinguistic knowledge in writing English email, which was closely related with their English language proficiency.

Chen et al., (2015) also investigated how identities were constructed in Chinese graduate students' emails to international researchers. A sample of 12 request emails respectively written by 12 Chinese graduate students to hypothetical international researchers were collected as the data, together with informal interviews with three of them. The emails exhibited a high degree of formality and use more formal words and long complex sentences. The students were reported to construct a deferential relational identity.

The three researches demonstrate mainland Chinese students' linguistic strategies in email writing practice. However, their data were elicited instead of natural and spontaneous ones, and Chinese students' English usage was also problematized in Pan (2011) and Zhu (2012).

Ren (2015) used authentic email data to explore how Chinese university students used remedial and preemptive pragmatic strategies to solve misunderstanding and non-understanding problems in intercultural email communication. 215 emails were collected from 30 Chinese university students. It was found that when the students encountered misunderstanding in email communication, they employed metalinguistic comments to articulate the problem. When they could not understand the email content, they tended to point them out straightforwardly through focused questions and metalinguistic comments. They often employed preemptive strategies like building common ground to ensure the success of the ELF email communication. This study sheds light on the pragmatic strategies used by Chinese students in intercultural communication.

In the same collection, as a first try to study English *Taoci* discourse, Xiao and Gao (2015) discussed the pragmatic strategies used in Chinese applicants' *Taoci* emails. They analyzed 26 initial *Taoci* emails plus 11 packages of *Taoci* emails written by 19 applicants. Two broad categories of *Taoci* strategies were summarized—*guanxi Taoci* and academic *Taoci*. *Guanxi Taoci* strategy is about using interpersonal relations and is associated with the original sense of *Taoci* in the Confucianism tradition. It subsumes the linguistic practices of honor statement, using formal titles, making compliments, showing magnetic attraction, keeping frequent contact, resorting to previous association, referring to ingroup members and creating chances for further interaction. Academic *Taoci* refers to demonstrating personal academic competence and research ability to convince the targeted supervisor. It resorts to claiming mutual academic interest, and self-promotion (self-evaluation of academic competence, listing publication and research work, discussing academic questions, talking research plan and referring to possible contribution). The data showed that academic *Taoci* was favored more by the Chinese students to exemplify their academic strength and boost their quality face, which renders a positive connotation of acknowledging personal endeavors. This new added feature the individualism-based self-promotion was named "new wine in old bottle" based on a Chinese idiom. This preliminary study in Xiao and Gao (2015) serves as a starting point for the present research.

Emails written by English learners were examined from the deficit perspective in most of the studies reviewed above. English native speakers' norms are prioritized that learners should follow. What deviates from the norms of native speakers is viewed as imperfect or inadequate, in particular in terms of the politeness standard which originates from the Anglo-European tradition. Non-native speakers are thus struggling and stigmatized in the linguistic market of English under the influence of Kachru's world Englishes (1982). This is understandable that most of these researches had a pedagogical concern to improve English learners' email performance. However, those seemingly impolite and unconventional expressions or strategies may reflect Chinese mainland students' sense of practice (Bourdieu, 1995) to communicate with higher-status and unfamiliar foreign faculty. These features might boil down to their cultural and linguistic habitus at lurk.

To give a brief summary, Chinese students' email writing still remains largely unknown to the academic world, which Chen (2015) also argued for. The majority of researches on Chinese students' emails were Chinese students in foreign countries, whereas the email practice of English learners in mainland China has received inadequate attention. Moreover, it is high time to move out of the deficit trap and look closely into Chinese English learners' ways of doing things with their emails to better understand their linguistic behaviors and enhance intercultural communication. In case of the subject matter of *Taoci* emails in the present study, it is not only Chinese applicants' efforts to communicate with foreign academia, but also a generative effort to strive for their imagined identity to study abroad and build up their professional career. To write is to act. In order to achieve

91

that, Chinese applicants have to make tremendous writing-efforts to promote themselves in front of higher-status foreign supervisors.

2.3.2 Self-promotional Genre in Application

Self-promotional discourse is mainly to promote self for a certain candidature of a job, a prize, or a program, etc. It is usually in a persuasive style by resorting to such strategies as establishing credentials, offering positive evaluation of candidates, or highlight the most important aspect of candidature. Many researches on promotion discourse in application have been done for such genres as job application letters (Bhatia, 1989, 1993), grant proposals (Connor, Mauranen, 1999) and personal statement in application for graduate programs (Swales, 1996; Henry, Roseberry, 2001). *Taoci* bears a lot of similarities to these persuasive texts in that it aims at a convincing self-presentation to targeted professors so as to enhance the chance of successful application. Therefore, this part is going to review representative researches on some subgenres of self-promotional discourse in application.

Genre analysis of job application letter has revolved around the structure of moves and steps to identify textual regularities. A move was defined by Swales (1990) as a functional unit used for some identifiable purpose and a step the strategy of rhetorical options to

92

realize that move. Bhatia (1993) analyzed the move structure of a typical example of westerners' letter of application, which included the moves of establishing credentials, introducing candidature, offering incentives, enclosing documents, soliciting response, using pressure tactics, ending politely. Under each of these moves, there were more specific and optional steps. Bhatia (1993) argued that application letter from western writers was more oriented to self-appraisal, i.e. adequately relevant, positive and credible description of the candidate and a good indication of its potential value to employers. By contrast, in Bhatia (1989) of job and scholarship application letters from South Asia (Pakistan, India, Sri Lanka and Bangladesh), most applicants just gave up the opportunity of application letter to offer self-appraisal, and only used cover letter attached to their CV. Among the scholarship application letters, Bhatia (1989) identified three types of moves: self-glorification, self-degradation, and adversary glorification, which were rarely used by westerners. Bhatia assumed these features found in applicants from South Asia might be related to their cultural values, or in Bourdieu's term, cultural habitus. In particular, self-degradation was said to be relevant to the inequality of economic strength between applicants from developing area and employer in affluent countries. This could be a very interesting topic, but it is a pity that Bhatia didn't go deep into it.

Connor, Davis and Rycker (1995) juxtaposed job application letters between Americans and Flemish. The typical American applicants were reported better at promoting themselves by giving more supporting evidence for application, and discussing incentives for both the applicant and the employer, which confirmed Bhatia's claim of self-appraisal characterizing western applicants. Flemish lacked self-promotion and had less supporting argument for their credentials.

Henry and Roseberry (2001) analyzed native English speakers' letter of application for jobs in Britain. Different moves were distinguished in their data and more detailed information about the Promotion move was provided. They argued that their Promotion move encompassed Bhatia's (1993) moves of Establishing Credentials and Offering Incentives. It was subdivided into the following steps of listing relevant skills, abilities; stating how skills, abilities were obtained; listing qualifications; naming present job; and predicting success. Henry and Roseberry's research was original in that it had a focus on more linguistic analysis at the lexicon and syntactic level. By using the software of Wordsmith for corpus analysis, they found high frequency words, prominent syntactic structure and other significant linguistic features between different generic steps.

In the tide of globalization and marketization and under the influence of increasing intercultural communication, the style of lack of self-appraisal featuring those Asians may change as well, as what Khan and Tin (2012) found. They analyzed a total of 26 letters of job application obtained from two organizations in Pakistan. It revealed that the Pakistan applicants no longer used the self-degradation moves discovered in Bhatia (1989). Establishing credentials also emerged as the most central and elaborate move. However, the applicants still resorted to glorifying the employer and used old-fashioned courtly expressions to appeal to the sentiments of compassion of the employer. The change of generic moves was significant in that it could allude to the change of Pakistan's traditional cultural habitus under the challenges from the competitive job market.

With regards to academic discourse, Hyland (2012) proposed a genre of prize application based on his research of application essays written by graduates in a Hong Kong university in China for educational scholarship. The prize application was persuasive, designed to convince judges of the significance of a thesis and the credentials of its author. Therefore, it was a conflating genre of promotional and academic discourse, a kind of discourse hybridity. The applicants resorted to the display of a skillful adoption of a disciplinary value system, evaluation, research expertise and (or) self-aggrandisement in order to construct an academic competent self, to wit, their cultural capital of academic competence and achievement. Hyland's research indicated the applicants' strategic manipulation of rhetoric moves for more capitals (scholarship) competing with rivalries on the international education market.

As a self-promotional genre, personal statement in application for graduate school admission serves to demonstrate one's academic background, professional qualifications, and personal strengths to gain admission into target programs. Swales (1996) ascribed personal statement (also called submission letter) to a type of those occluded genres, various text types integral to knowledge production and decision-making in the academy but rarely circulating in the public sphere. In the last century, these genres remained largely hidden. Therefore, it attracted scholarly attention especially for pedagogical purposes. For instance, Brown's (2004) study of personal statement of psychology applicants highlighted the need to provide evidence of disciplinary appropriation and socialization as well as to present oneself as an apprentice scientist rather than an outsider. He also argued for a possible disciplinary variation of personal statement. For example, the psychology expected a fair degree of critical and disciplinary sophistication through the articulation of research areas or research questions while medical students may name-drop their research experiences.

Ding (2007) applied genre analysis to move structures, underlying patterns, text-audience relations, and communicative purposes in 30 personal statement samples collected from commercial websites. Five procedural moves were identified in the corpus, namely, explaining the reason to pursue the proposed study, establishing credentials related to medicine/dentistry, discussing relevant life experiences, stating career goals, and describing personality. It showed that successful personal statements devoted more efforts to and better developed the first four moves but paid less attention to the fifth move.

Taking a more constructivist approach, Li, Gao and Li (2007) discussed identity construction in nine Chinese students' application letters for American graduate programs. Using J. Martin's appraisal theory for discourse analysis, they found how Chinese students evaluated themselves and presented their imagined research identity. It also revealed a potential conflict between the English individualism self-appraisal (Bhatia, 1993) and the Chinese traditional value of self-efficacy and being modest (Bi, 1996), an implication of potential habitus change among the Chinese young applicants.

97

Due to the spread of the Internet technology, it is now highly doubtful that there are any occluded genres left (Swales, Feak, Barton et al., 2004). Websites offer us many samples of, like, personal statement samples used as data in Ding (2007). What is more, the South Asian region, in particular China, has undergone enormous changes in the social, political, and economic spheres. The trend of globalization and information technology has ushered in an era of more freedom and liberalization, and "the socially aware educated middle class" (Khan, 2012: 396) is expanding, whose habitus may bear out the transformation in these fields, and the reconfigured structure and positions within each of them.

To summarize briefly, the analysis of self-promotions genres, as Bhatia (1993) also noted, serves to identify moves and strategies of a certain genre and their linguistic features, and to explain how these findings will enlighten L2 pedagogical practice, more specifically how to write these texts to meet their communicative purposes through words. In this sense, self-promotional genre is a perfect example to represent the performativity of speech acts' doing things with words. However, most of the previous researches have prioritized English native speakers' generic norms in writing application letters, and treated those local cultural values embedded in such moves like self-denigration too loosely. It is necessary for following researches to explain those unconventional and localized features with more theoretical insight. The Internet technology has demystified many once-occluded text types and even bred new self-promotional genre such as *Taoci* in China. The popularity of *Taoci* among Chinese applicants shows that they have developed a sense of genre expertise in this kind of writing, which, like job applications, gives an "open-ended creative opportunity for favourable self-presentation" (James, Scholfield, Ypsiladis, 1994: 325) and aims at capturing readers' attention, establishing the writer's competence, appealing to readers' expectations, and/or claiming for the fit between the recruiter and the recruited.

As the details of the literature review shows, there are both theoretical and empirical gaps in the present scholarship. With regards to the empirical aspect, Chinese students' English email is still underexplored (Chen, 2015), particularly that of mainland Chinese students. Even less has been known to the academia about the emerging genre of Chinese applicants' *Taoci* emails, which could still be considered an occluded genre, hard to get access to and understudied due to its strong flavor of privacy. In addition, no researcher has taken L2 investment perspective to investigate learners' English emails. As for the theoretical concern, a threefold inadequacy of the present investment model (Darvin, Norton, 2015) has been articulated as follows: (1) This model runs roughshod over the concrete properties of language form and language use. Actual linguistic product has been rarely under scrutiny; (2) The model over-rationalizes investment as conscious and purposeful activities, which precipitates investment into a dangerously mechanical rationalism; (3) The leverage of ideology in this model is rather static and could undermine the dynamism of investment. A focal valuing of ideology and power may fall short of revealing the viability of investment as a process and missing the delicate change occurring to individuals as well a group. There is still a large space for the empirical application and theoretical enrichment of L2 investment, in particular under the Chinese context.

2.4   Research Questions Based on the Present Work

To fill in the scholarly gaps mentioned in the last section, the present study took *Taoci* as its research object to examine the investment of Chinese applicants in study-abroad education. Two broad questions were asked.

First, what is *Taoci* as "doing things with words" in study-abroad application in China?

This question is further broken down into two sub-questions.

(1) What speech acts were used in *Taoci* email texts?

(2) How were the speech acts employed across situations in the application process?

Second, in what sense was speech act, as cultural and historical encounter between linguistic habitus and linguistic market, investment into applicants' imagined identity and imagined future?

The second big question is likewise decomposed into the following ones.

(1) What and how capitals were served as affordances for applicants' application for overseas education in their *Taoci* process?

(2) Through the investment of different speech acts, in what way did the Chinese young people's habitus undergo changes perceived through the massive and repeated *Taoci* practice?

The first big question is supposed to understand Chinese applicants' *Taoci* email discourse at the level of microstructure of language and to pave the way for building speech act into the existing investment model. The second big question attempts to tap into the cultural and historical factors to explain in the sociolinguistic phenomenon of *Taoci* and to build upon the current investment theory.

These questions must be approached in a both sensitive-to-empirical-detail and theoretically informed way. To address the first big question, Brown and Levinson's politeness theory is adopted as the analytical framework for speech act analysis. However, the concept of speech act is not just used as a rigid analytical unit, but its soul of performativity is kept to further explain the concrete analysis. A hierarchical classification of speech acts is followed to establish different levels of communicative function, which will be introduced in detail in the findings. Request is of special importance here since *Taoci* is essentially a request for offer. Previous researches on promotional and academic genre are also referred to for analysis. The investment model by Darvin and Norton (2015) serves as the primary theoretical framework to tackle with the second big question and to provide in-depth discussion on the features of found-out speech acts in the first big question. Reexamination of Bourdieu's concept of capital, habitus and field are assumed to infuse fresh insight into the existing model. Speech act, as the product of the relation between a linguistic habitus

102

and a linguistic market, is supposed to bridge the macrostructure and microstructure of language analysis exemplified through the *Taoci* investment practice.

Chapter 3

Research
Methodology

The present study adopted a mixed design, with qualitative as the primary and quantitative as the complementary method, to explore Chinese applicants' *Taoci* discourse. Two major types of data, successful applicants' *Taoci* emails and interviews, were collected. The email data was scrutinized in a qualitative way with reference to Brown and Levinson's (1987) politeness theory to categorize and gain deep understanding of the speech acts of *Taoci* through detailed and intensive description. Analysis of the interview transcripts and other types of supplementary data was used to offer an insiders' view and to provide more in-depth insights into speech act as investment. We drew on the L2 investment model to interpret applicants' speech act investment tied to their global education offer hunting. The following sections are going to present the research procedures in more details.

3.1 Data Collection

There were two kinds of data collected: primary data and secondary data. The primary data referred to Chinese applicants' *Taoci* emails with foreign supervisors and individual interviews with me. The secondary data included my field memo of the interviews, field notes with American professors, postgraduates and PhD students, and observations of existing online *Taoci* discourse. Research participants were regarded not as objective data providers, but collaborators who actively shared with me their email and experience to help attain the goals in the present research.

3.1.1   Participants

The participants recruited in this study were Chinese students applying for higher education, either PhD program or visiting scholar position, in such developed countries as America, Britain, Australia. For the purpose of collecting naturally occurring email data, I tried to reach potential informants after they finished their *Taoci* with foreign professors, or more precisely, after they received an offer from foreign universities. In other words, only successful applicants were recruited. There were two types of applicant involved: applicants for foreign PhD programs and those for foreign visiting positions, the second of which was not originally targeted, but turned out crucial to enrich the email data.

To Chinese applicants for fall admission PhD programs, offers begin to be released in spring and the deadline is usually in the middle of April each year. Around that time, successful applicants share their offer (s) on their own university's online bulletin board system (abbreviated as BBS) and try to find companions to fly together or

107

rent an apartment abroad. Therefore, only successful applicants were accessible in this research partially for the reason of consistency, and partially for the fact that unsuccessful applicants would not post on BBS or would not be willing to join this study. I chose to start getting access to prospective research participants in spring in the first two rounds of data collection. For the last round, I found an easy access, which will be detailed later. All participants were accessed through personal online contact. Three rounds of data collection in the year of 2013, 2014, and 2015 were carried out respectively.

The first round took place in 2013 and 7 participants were recruited who had received official offer from American universities. I registered on the BBS of a prestigious Chinese university (hereafter called A University) and sent a brief online message to those offer sharers (usually with a cyber name) and asked whether they did *Taoci* with foreign professors and whether they were interested in participating in the *Taoci* project.[①] Once a positive reply was received from them, I made further contact with them through personal email or cellphone, introduced the research briefly, and invited them to provide their *Taoci* email. All the research participants chose to forward their *Taoci*

---

① The online recruit email was written in Chinese and is added at the Appendixes section.

email to me through email, either in the email body or as a PDF or Word attachment.[①] When I knew about their *Taoci* content, and got familiar with them, I asked whether they would like to provide their professors' feedback email as reference and participated in the interview part. Some participants took face-to-face interview while some took email interview, and some others were not available for either form of interview. The face-to-face interviews were audio-recorded after getting the participant's oral consent at the beginning and were transcribed and rechecked twice by myself.

The second round of data collection occurred in 2014 and recruited 10 participants who were admitted to American PhD programs. It followed almost the same procedures as that of 2013. I learned from the experience of the previous round and got registered on another three key universities in Beijing (hereafter called B University, C University and D University) and had access to more participants from more institutions.

The third round took place in the spring of 2015 and 46 informants were reached. A little different from the previous two rounds, data in

---

① Few of them forwarded me the complete *Taoci* email including email subject, which could have been highly relevant for the analysis of communicative function. However, the absence of email subject turned out not a big problem for the textual analysis.

the third round were collected from applicants for visiting positions in foreign institutions. In 2014, when I discussed with fellow students about the application for a visiting position, I happened to know that applicants for visiting position also wrote *Taoci* emails to their desired hosting professors. As I was one of the applicants for the CSC sponsored program, I got access to a full list of contacts of all the program applicants in the school year from 2014 to 2015 in my own university. There were in all 282 students and I began to send separate email to each of them in February 2015, to introduce myself, my project and to ask whether they were willing to provide their *Taoci* emails. Luckily, 59 responses were received, but some respondents didn't keep their *Taoci* emails, or were not willing to join with me. At last, 46 respondents' emails were included in the text data pool. There was a richer spectrum of study-abroad destinations, including America, Britain, Germany, Japan, and France, which were all developed countries and academically powerful nations. All of the emails were written in English. No interview was made with this group of applicants because this round of data was mainly intended to enlarge the data pool and support the focused themes discovered from the previous two rounds of data, but new features were integrated into the existing discoveries.

3.1.2   Data Collected

This part describes the data into the following categories: emails, interview data and supplementary data after giving an overview of the participant distribution across the three years. In this study, the researched *Taoci* emails were all written in English. All emails written by applicants to foreign professors from their first contact to the final official offer release during their application, which were shared by the research participants, were included as *Taoci* email.

During the first round, 7 participants were enrolled. All of them provided their first *Taoci* emails. Two of them shared with me their full *Taoci* email package, to be explained later, and two of them partial email package. Two of them joined a one-time email interview and three of them took face-to-face interview. All of them were from A University. In the second round, 10 participants were recruited. Likewise, all of them provided their first *Taoci* emails. Two of them shared with me their full *Taoci* email package and three of them shared partial email package, among which one participant gave two partial packages. Four participants joined the face-to-face interview and two took the email interview. Five of them were from A University, while the remaining three were from B University, C University and D University respectively. In the third round, 46 pieces of initial *Taoci*

111

emails were collected from 46 participants respectively. All of them were from A University.

Additional background information is briefed here, but with no in-depth details (except the case analysis in Chapter 4)[①] since the present research didn't aim at correlational investigation. All of the participants were of very high-level English proficiency. Those in the first two rounds passed TOEFL with scores of more than 90 out of 120 and had a GRE score that met the requirement of American universities. The English proficiency test taken by students in the third round varied, such as IELTS, TEM 8 (Test for English Major Band 8), GRE, TOEFL, etc., but all of them must acquire a quite high English proficiency required by the CSC program. In all there were 29 females and 34 males, and 21 of them majored in art and 42 in science. Table 3.1 is an overview of the participants with their contribution of data types in the three rounds. The successive calendar year in the following table doesn't mean it was a longitudinal research but gives more information about the data collection.

---

① The data for the case analysis will be specified in Chapter 4 for the sake of more coherence and clarity of discussion.

Table 3.1   Participants distribution in the three rounds (F=female, M=male, A=art, S=science)

Data collection time	Email providers			Interview participants		Gender	Major
	Initial email	Partial package	Full package	Email	Face-to-face		
2013	9	3	2	2	3	3F 4M	1A 6S
2014	11	4	2	2	3	4F 6M	2A 8S
2015	46	/	/	/	/	22F 24M	18A 28S
Total	66	7	4	4	6	29F 34M	21A 42S

Some participants did *Taoci* simultaneously with more than one professor and received several offers. Since the present research focused on Chinese applicants' *Taoci*, students' email was the concern of interest while professors' response email was used as a reference. The following section will detail the collected data.

3.1.2.1   Email Data

Taoci email, as is introduced in the first chapter, refers to applicants' personal email contact with foreign professors during their application process. In addition, whatever my research participants regarded as *Taoci* email and then shared with me was involved as

113

the *Taoci* email data. The collected emails were classified into three types: initial email, partial package and full package.

a. Initial Email

Initial email refers to the first *Taoci* email written by applicants, who usually follow those online *Taoci* model texts, but with exceptions. Since all research participants provided their initial *Taoci* email, there were in all 66 pieces of first email texts.[1] The shortest one contained 34 English words while the longest was up to 600 words. The total word amount of the collected initial email was about 18,440. I labeled each email text in the following manner: the year plus the order of access and a pseudonym (given name + family name) of the sender. For example, the initial email from the second research participant was labeled as "2013-02 Si Chen".

b. Full Package

A full package of *Taoci* emails refers to all the email correspondences between an applicant and his or her foreign supervisor from the beginning to the final decision of admission and (or) scholarship. Some of the packages had one or two emails amiss either because the

---

[1] Three participants sent me more than one version of *Taoci* email.

participants couldn't find them or thought them not proper to share with me. There were in all four sets of full packages respectively from four participants. Foreign supervisors' emails were included only as reference for contextual analysis.[①] The labeling method was similar to that of initial email: the year plus the order of access and a fake name given by me. Only a number indicating the order of occurrence was added to students' email and the number plus an apostrophe to professors' email. For example, the label of "2013-05-01 Qingwan Li" means that this is the first email of my fifth respondent of Qingwan Li collected in 2013 and "2013-05-01' Qingwan Li" means that it is the professor's first correspondence in Qingwan Li's package.

c. Partial Package

Partial package refers to both applicants' and professors' emails, but only includes several rounds of exchanges either in the beginning, in the middle, or at the end of the application. It is partial in the sense that I could not figure out the whole picture of the *Taoci* communication

---

[①] It was impossible to get foreign professors' consent then, so I asked my informants to delete all of the professors' personal information before they shared with me. The emails from professors were only used as reference for the analysis of applicants' emails when it was necessary. Some professors' response content that appeared in the findings was retrieved from the research participants' interview transcripts.

as there was only a partial picture of their *Taoci*. There were seven sets of partial packages, one of which were supplied by a full package of providers, and one participant provided two partial packages. A number was added to the end of the name to make a distinction between the two packages contributed by the same applicant. For example, "2013-04-01 Chu Gao1" means that it was the first email in the fourth participant's, renamed Chu Gao, first partial package collected in 2013. An overview of all the email data is sketched in Table 3.2.

Table 3.2   Email data overview

Email data type	Pieces of email		Words	
Initial email	66 from students		18,440	
Full package (7 sets)	81	46 from students	4,632	
		35 from professors		
Partial package (4 sets)	47	25 from students	2,100	
		22 from professors		
Total	194	137 from students	29,147	25,172 from students
		57 from professors		3,975 from professors

3.1.2.2   Interview Data

After I got a little familiar with participants, I began to schedule interviews with participants, because familiarity could create a relaxing atmosphere for them to share their stories and a secured sense of understanding and trust between us. The interview was supposed to be face-to-face, but some participants were not available physically then, so email interview with them was adopted. There were in all ten participants taking the interviews, six in face-to-face interview while four answered interview questions through email. Nevertheless, only four participants had been interviewed to a great depth. For the interviews, all respondents preferred to speak or write in Chinese with occasional code switch to English.

The face-to-face interview was designed semi-structured, which consisted of several key questions that helped to define issues to be explored, but also gave both the interviewees and me freedom to navigate back and forth in order to tap into an idea or response in more details. Interview questions were prepared in advance, which covered topics about the applicants' English learning experience, their application and *Taoci* experience, and their thoughts, attitudes and perceptions about the *Taoci* phenomenon, but were at the same time open to participants' free-style narration. The interview topics were structured into their English learning experience, why going abroad for PhD programs, opinion about *Taoci* (their knowledge, attitude and opinion towards it), reflection on their own *Taoci* experience (email

117

writing process; self-positioning with the supervisor; self-evaluation in the process).

Face-to-face interviews were carried out at coffee shops around the campus. All interviews were audio-recorded after the participants gave me the oral consent at the beginning. I used two recorders in case any accident might occur. Two participants didn't finish all the topics due to their personal reasons. Two participants were interviewed twice when the first interview didn't cover all the themes. Nonetheless, the in-depth interviews with the four participants mentioned above covered all the prepared topics. At the end, the collected interviews lasted from 30 to 70 minutes. I tried to transcribe the audios as soon as possible and rechecked the transcripts by myself. Moreover, follow-up contacts with the interviewees were made when there was any significant information amiss and needed to check with them.

The email interview, one of the means of E-interview (electronic interview) was also adopted. The mentioned interview topics were forwarded through email in questioning forms to research participants. However, some of them chose to answer certain questions and ignore the others. I tried to follow up the unattended questions but couldn't force them to exhaust all. Although the email interview was not as consistent as the face-to-face one, the information shared by the participants was still valuable to scaffold textual findings and was included as a part of the data.

Each piece of interview data was labeled in this way: the calendar year and month plus the participants' pseudonym following the lead of "Interview transcripts" or "Email interview". For example, "Interview transcripts, 2013-May Huyang Long" means that it was a face-to-face interview with the research participant renamed Huyang Long and the interview was carried out in May 2013. The interview data was summarized in Table 3.3.

Table 3.3　Overview of the interview data

Interview type	Participants	Chinese characters
Face-to-face interview	6	63,430
Email interview	4	4,301
Total	10	67,731

3.1.1.3　Supplementary Data

Supplementary data included online meta-discourse of *Taoci* and our field notes.

(a) Online meta-discourse of *Taoci*

Almost all overseas-program websites, such as New Oriental, *Taisha*, *Jituo*, reserve a special column for *Taoci* email writing, where

119

people can find *Taoci* tips, *Taoci* experience sharing, and *Taoci* FAQs. These constitute the online *Taoci* "meta-discourse", i.e. discourse about *Taoci* discourse, which tells applicants how to deal with *Taoci* email. *Taoci* meta-discourse also covers the communication between applicants and their peers, senior schoolmates and (or) teachers about the ways to write to foreign professors, some of which were retrieved from the interview content.

(b) Field Notes

The majority of the field notes were taken from my personal experience about student-professor relation at a foreign university in America during my visiting program. I observed the student-professor relationship in class and out of class and jogged down notes; I wrote down key points during casual talk with graduate students, including Americans, Indians, Koreans, Turkish, and Chinese; I also consulted American professors' opinions about some of the *Taoci* email samples that I collected.[1] In addition, when I took face-to-face interviews with the *Taoci* informants, I sketched observations about them. After the interviews, I wrote down carefully the memos in Chinese about the interview content, process, and my reflections. All field notes were

---

[1] Before I showed the collected email data to other people, I had already finished the anonymity work.

120

kept in separate files.

Before moving to the next section, I want to describe the multiple roles—insider, learner and butterfly collector—that I took along with my researcher role during the process of data collection and analysis. First, my role of insider was twofold: (1) my participants and I were both Chinese and we shared similar social and cultural membership; (2) I did *Taoci* email with foreign professors as I mentioned in the first chapter. This insider role enabled me to facilitate my understanding about my fellow students' *Taoci* email writing, such as the underlying subtlety of a seemingly weird expression. Second, I assumed the role of learner. I tried to learn from my informants (Glesne, 1999), in particular from their interviews. I was inspired by their unique experiences and insightful knowledge of student-teacher relationship and intercultural communication with foreign professors. Third, I was a butterfly collector. I went into the fields, i.e. website, BBS and online communication, and chased my data as much as possible. More importantly, I cherished each piece of my data and tried to turn its value into academic worth. However, overarching all the roles, my researcher or expert role was paramount. It is inevitable that the findings presented in the ensuing chapters bore out my own academic background and institutional training, which indicated a certain degree

121

of subjectivity.

3.2 Data Analysis

This part describes how email, interview and supplementary data were analyzed, with a focus on the analytical procedure of email texts.

3.2.1 Discourse Analysis Method of *Taoci* Email

Brown and Levinson's (1987) politeness strategies were taken as the major reference for email text analysis. In addition, the two themes, *guanxi Taoci* and academic *Taoci* found in Xiao and Gao (2015), which piloted the present study to some extent, shed light on the establishment of speech act as pulling *guanxi* and speech act as presenting academic competence in the present findings. However, care was taken to attend to categories coming from the data in a bottom-up manner. Therefore, I didn't design a completely strict analytical scheme for the analysis but preferred to let those prominent themes of speech act category emerge from the data under the guidance of existing categories. The linguistic analysis of email texts was thus both bottom-up and top-down.

Borrowing the concept of "coding" from qualitative studies, giving a speech act name to a piece of discourse segment was regarded as coding and the speech act name was considered a code. The discourse segment was at lexical, syntactic and textual level. Therefore, speech act was not just a sentence unit. Those metapragmatic units were not analyzed, for instance, "I am going to introduce myself below", because instead of capturing the sense of action of speech acts, they worked more for textual coherence, to wit, the textual function of language in Halliday (1994). The coding included two steps: the initial coding and the focused categorization.

The initial coding was mainly made at the clausal level, but when prominent meaning appeared at the lexical and textual level, it was also coded so as not to exclude interesting features. When a segment had alternative functions and could be coded into different speech acts, the most prominent one was decided after discussion with my inter-coder and supervisor.[If the other functions were also significant and impossible to exclude without undermining the explanation, they were kept. For the purpose of calculation, only the agreed prominent features came into statistics.] I tried to use coding names as concrete and descriptive as possible to describe the segment in the initial coding. In particular, gerund phrases, as recommended by Charmaz (2014), were used in order to capture the action performed by the word. Moreover, I tried to keep the coding names simple, short and precise to seize what Chinese applicants did with their discursive output. The initial coding was done in an iterative and ongoing process, which started right after I gathered a round of email data and continued side by side with the incoming texts. When the second and third round of data was collected and processed, I made back-and-forth comparison with the previous coding, and kept open to newly emergent features.

The initial coding of speech act was first conducted independently. I first coded the email data on printed-out papers since I could go back and forth more easily to compare the coding. In order to secure the coding reliability, another researcher, a PhD candidate in my institute who was interested in the similar academic field, was invited to do the initial coding independently. We subsequently collated our interpretative findings. It resulted in an inter-coding reliability of about 0.81 out of 1, which meant the two coders made the same decision on over eighty percent of all the data codes. The remaining discrepant coding differences were discussed after the coding comparison until agreement was reached. Still there were some coding differences unsolved between me and the other coder, where a third party, my supervisor was invited into discussion till all the disagreements were dismissed.

When the initial coding was finalized after inter-coding was made,

I input all the coding document and the analysis into a qualitative research software named ATLAS.ti. A sample of the final version of initial coding of a *Taoci* email (2013-01 Qiang Miao) stored in the software is screened in Fig. 3.1 below. The software was used to export the overall distribution, where the focused categorization was generated. Focused categorization referred to classifying the found speech acts at the micro-linguistic level into different types in terms of communication strategy by modeling Brown and Levinson's (1987) positive politeness strategy and negative politeness strategy, but with modification of terms to cater for the needs of the uniqueness of *Taoci* email. I assessed and compared the initial coding and conceptualized focused terms to subsume those miscellaneous initial codes. At last, three abstract themes of speech act were constructed upon the initial coding: speech act as pulling *guanxi*, speech act as presenting academic competence, and speech act as negotiating institutional entry.

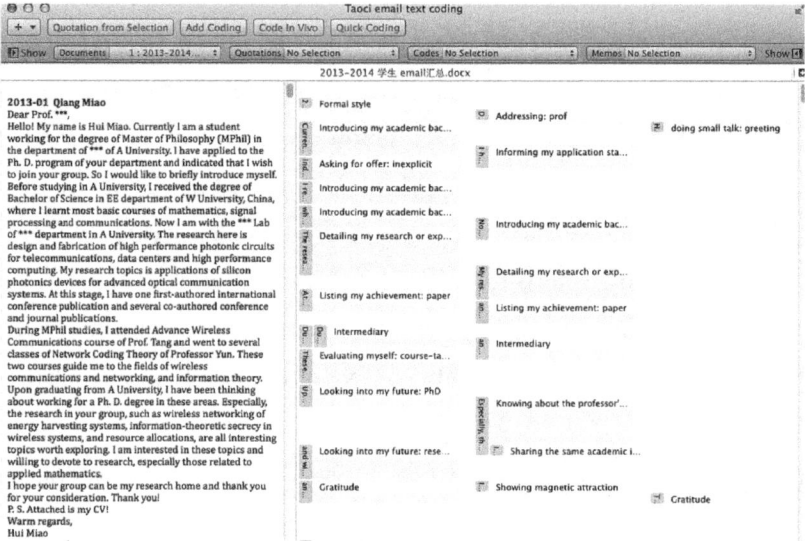

Fig. 3.1 Sample analysis of the initial coding of email text

Based upon the initial coding and focused categorization, I drew the hierarchy of speech act in *Taoci* emails. Following the broad sense of performativity, the genre of *Taoci* emails was regarded a macro speech act at a generic level, the highest rank of speech act. The medium level was meso speech act. Micro speech act was the lowest level of speech act mediated linguistic forms and action. Between the micro and macro was meso speech act. However, meso speech act was not a waste basket to hold all those unattended actions between the top and bottom level of speech act. The details of each speech act will be elaborated in the next chapter.

The hierarchy of speech act (micro, meso, macro) proposed in this research was intended as an analytical instrument, rather than a definite conceptualization of all speech act categories. At each level, there could be correspondent strategy types, which vary from one genre to another. Only at the lowest level will we observe concrete linguistic characteristics. Thus, the focus of analysis dwelled upon the meso and micro speech act. With regards to the statistics used in the present findings, the calculation of speech act occurrence was based at a clause-unit level for the sake of consistency, even though there were also textual features illustrated later.

3.2.2　Analysis Method of Interview Transcripts and Supplementary Data

Compared to email text analysis, the left data were used in a less complex way. The interviews and supplementary data were treated as scaffolding data for the textual findings. Important quotes were pulled out from the interview transcripts and field notes to explain or validate the discovered linguistic features. Meta-discourse materials about *Taoci*

127

from websites were also cited to support relevant arguments. My choice of data was concentrated on the participants' own understanding about their discursive practice, their perceptions, beliefs and values in doing *Taoci* with foreign professors. In particular, the social, cultural as well as the economic capitals represented through the *Taoci* emails and mentioned in interviews were examined, and applicants' commitment to and effort for their study-abroad application were conceptualized.

The hierarchy of speech act is intended to answer the sub-question of the first big question "What speech acts were used in *Taoci* email texts?" to give an overall picture of *Taoci* as investment, which will constitute the horizontal dimension of *Taoci*. Among all the data, Yunyang's email package was selected for the case analysis. The specific information of his data will be presented in Chapter 5 for the sake of a consistent discussion, but the analysis of his email texts was a part of the speech act analysis scheme in Chapter 4. Yunyang was selected as the subject of case analysis for the following two reasons. First, his package included all email contacts between him and his targeted professor with no email missing in between, so I could observe a complete picture of an individual's *Taoci* journey through email texts. Second, his email was a perfect example to exhibit the mixture of pulling *guanxi*, presenting academic competence and negotiating institutional entry, which varied across the situations he was confronted with. The case analysis will deal with the second sub-question, "How were the speech acts employed across situations in the application process?", which will constitute the vertical dimension of *Taoci*. The horizontal and vertical dimensions together will solve the first big question: "What is *Taoci* as 'doing things with words' in study-abroad application in China?".

Taking the theoretical perspective of Darvin and Norton (2015) investment model, along with the analysis of speech act, different types of capital, social capital, cultural capital or even economic capital retrieved from email content and interview transcripts will be teased out for discussion to answer the sub-question of the second big question, "What and how capitals were served as affordances for applicants' application for overseas education?". Simultaneously its sibling sub-question of "How did the investment of different speech acts in *Taoci* contribute to applicants' discourse identity and imagined identity?" will be solved. In all the reexamination of speech act as the product of the interaction between linguistic habitus and linguistic market in Bourdieu (1991) will be used to bridge the macrostructure and microstructure of language analysis to address the second big question of "In what sense was speech act, as cultural and historical encounter between linguistic habitus and linguistic market, investment into applicants' imagined identity and imagined future?". All the details will come soon in the next chapters.

3.3 Privacy Protection

A *Taoci* email is very personal, so the email content itself may well reveal sensitive information. Rich and informative data were shared by the collaborative participants, which reminded me more that their rights should not be neglected. I adopted the following measures to safeguard confidentiality.

First, the research followed the "volunteering" principle, i.e. recruiting participants on a voluntary basis. Participants were first consulted whether they would like to contribute to the project. If negative answer was received, I respected the choice and dropped out of further contact immediately. This applied to both email collection and interviews. Once participants showed willingness to join the research, I let the participants choose whatever email texts that they felt comfortable to share with me. In the audio-recorded interviews, I obtained participants' oral consent before turning on the recorders. For the informants who participated in face-to-face interview[1], informed-consent forms were shown to them and signed by them during the data collection process[2]. The consent form is attached at the Appendixes part for reference.

Second, anonymity was conducted twofold. On the one hand, potential participants were reminded to do the anonymity work (excluding any private information of people names, institution and place) before they sent their *Taoci* emails to me. On the other hand, I alone transcribed all the recorded data and anonymized the participants through the following means: using pseudonyms in email texts and interview transcripts; and uniformizing all data with the label of year and access order. Therefore, only I knew the participants' real identity.

Third, data storage was safely guaranteed. All the data were stored in my personal computer and in my cloud account as a backup, which only I had the password to get access to. I only shared the printed-out email texts and interview transcripts with my intercoder

---

[1] For those participants who only provided their emails, I got their consent to use their data only for academic purposes through their email response.

[2] My access to participants shows that the data collection started from my online contact with them when they responded my data solicitation email, so the consent form was actually obtained during the data collection.

and supervisor for discussion from time to time and locked them in safe drawers after each use.

To summarize briefly, this chapter has presented the research methods adopted in the study, including the process of data collection, different types of collected data, the detailed data analysis process in relation to the research aims and questions. Ethical consideration was discussed to show how I respected and protected the research participants' privacy. Although the speech act hierarchy was built upon bottom-up analysis, the following chapters will elaborate the findings in a top-down manner.

Chapter 4

Investment Through Speech Acts: A Panorama

This chapter gives a horizontal depiction of speech act as investment in *Taoci* email discourse. It maps out the speech act hierarchy and categories generated from the textual data analysis and to discuss investment of different capitals through speech act combined with the scaffolding data of interview transcripts, field notes and *Taoci* meta-discourse. Various capitals that applicants used to invest into their study-abroad programs are discussed in relation with Chinese applicants' identity precedes a succinct discussion in combination with Darvin and Norton's (2015) investment model.

4.1 An Overview of *Taoci* as Macro Speech Act

Following the sense of performativity of "doing things with words", the emerging genre of *Taoci* emails among Chinese applicants can be considered as a macro speech act at a generic level. Here the macro speech act differs from van Dijk's notion. Van Dijk's macro speech act is based on the semantic macrostructure of a given text and generalized through some predefined cognitive procedures of deletion, generalization, and construction. Therefore, his macro speech act is a semantic and cognitive term, applied to a single text. In this research macro speech act is more a sociocultural pragmatic concept, defined as the general function of a genre of discourse, directed at a goal of

134

bringing about changes into a situation and comprising an ensemble of communicative actions. Macro speech act is on the highest rank of the hierarchy of speech act, followed by lower layers of meso and micro speech act, which will be explained later. *Taoci* emails as a macro speech act, if composed in the boldest way, might have been reduced to the single line of:

Give me the offer.

This sentence represents the ultimate purpose of *Taoci* emails, requesting an offer. In Brown and Levinson's (1987) term, it can be categorized as a bold-on-record strategy of request without any redressive devices. However, never had such kind of request appeared in the present research data, and neither does it seem possible for any Chinese applicant to behave in this way. On the contrary, Chinese applicants spared no efforts in spilling ink (or typing) so as to produce less straightforward expressions to express that request.

Chinese applicants and their potential foreign professors were remote from each other both physically and psychologically. Social distance preexisted between them since most of them didn't know each other until their first email contact. Another factor adding to the social distance might be the fact that Chinese students used English as a foreign or second language while professors were either native speakers or near-native English users. Besides, there was a distinct power difference for the following reasons that (1) professors were regarded as gatekeepers by Chinese applicants. Otherwise, there would be no need to make the email contact; (2) even though the two parties were not in a factual student-supervisor relationship, this kind of power hierarchy was still cherished by Chinese applicants perhaps due to the traditional Chinese value of the insurmountable disparity between student and teacher. Moreover, *Taoci* emails contained the highly imposed request for admission or scholarship from the recipient. In short, there was a great social distance, an obvious power distinction and a heavy imposition upon the hearer, so the weight of doing *Taoci* can be rated on the top scale of weight represented by the upward arrows shown as follows:

$$W(x)\uparrow = D(H\ S)\uparrow + P(H,\ S)\uparrow + R\uparrow$$

Brown and Levinson appraised the speech act of request as follows:

"When formulating a small request one will tend to use language that stressed in-group membership and social similarity... When making a request that is somewhat bigger, one uses the language of formal politeness ... And finally, when making the sort of request that it is doubtful one should make at all, one tends to use indirect expressions." (Brown, Levinson, 1987: 57)

Since the weight of request in *Taoci* is especially heavy, applicants had to take great care in phrasing their words in order to decrease that weight of imposition on foreign professors through such strategies as being indirect, carefully polite and inoffensive. On the other hand, applicants needed to thrust the competent applicant "face" (Goffman, 1967) confidently, most importantly their façade of academic competence in order to convince targeted professors of their competitive candidature. This tension makes the less-explored *Taoci* email even more intriguing.

A *Taoci* email is not an officially required but a *de facto* step in overseas application. The very act of writing personal email to foreign professors can be regarded as a resistance towards the impersonal institution of international education application just as the dialectal *Taoci* used as an unconventional means to create *guanxi* between unfamiliar people. *Taoci* emails represent Chinese applicants' claim for the legitimacy to better display themselves besides the rigid application portfolio. Following Pierre Bourdieu's terms, *Taoci* emails are a site of struggle and competition where applicants' capitals (e.g. academic

137

capital, human resources and linguistic capital) which might not have been satisfactorily revealed in the application package, are brought into discursive performance for the global offer hunting purpose. To the applicants, the tension of being forceful and firm in self-presentation and the concern of doing a face-threatening act leads to the delicacy of *Taoci* communication. Therefore, applicants pay earnest attention to the form of language use in *Taoci* emails, echoing the emphasis of rational investment in Darvin and Norton (2015).

Three prominent themes of discursive action were abstracted from the initial coding: pulling *guanxi*, presenting academic competence and negotiating institutional entry, which constitutes the medium level of meso speech act in this study. Meso speech act is defined as the function of communicative strategy types to realize a certain communicative intention. It roughly equals what Brown and Levinson's termed as super strategies (e.g. positive politeness, negative politeness), but keeps open to accommodate further layer (s) of speech act for the sake of social and cultural sensitivities. That is to say, any level between the macro speech act and micro speech act can be taken as meso speech act, which makes the middle level more flexible for analysis.

Under the three focused abstractions, a repertoire of a lower level of speech act was teased out to mediate linguistic forms and actions.

138

Micro speech act is defined as the pragmatic function of concrete discursive occurrences, which includes various forms of message construction. It usually corresponds to the speech acts taxonomized by classical speech act theorists such as J. L. Austin and G. Leech, yet open to analysts' own nomenclature. It is the basic analytical unit, corresponding to the initial coding names. These specific linguistic devices were maneuvered by the relationally inferior applicants towards the superior professors and may result in: what on the surface seems to be equal could be made hierarchical, what seems hierarchical more balanced or flattened, what seems to be imposed less imposed, what seems to be distant closer. However, some subtle nuances of linguistic features in each speech act may still bear the vestige of an underlying habitus that renders the subconscious dimension of investment practice.

The hierarchy of speech act in terms of micro, meso, and macro is intended as an analytical instrument for the analysis *Taoci*, rather than cast a rigid conceptualization of all speech act categories. Under each level, there were correspondent strategy types, which vary from one genre towards another. Only at the lower level can we observe the concrete linguistic forms more clearly, so the analysis focuses on the meso and micro speech acts.

To give a preview, the meso speech act of pulling *guanxi* consists of deference-oriented and solidarity-oriented strategies, each containing seven subcategories and realized through a rich range of linguistic features under its micro speech acts. The meso speech act of presenting competent applicant is categorized into Me-oriented and Us-oriented strategies, with the first centering on self-promotion while the later on academic bonding with professors. There are five sub-strategies under the Me-oriented and four under the Us-oriented. The meso speech act of negotiating institutional entry consists of inquiring, briefing, following up and soliciting help, which are not meant to be exhaustive but to capture the most salient features in the *Taoci* email data.

4.2 Speech Act as Pulling *Guanxi*

Speech act as pulling *guanxi* refers to socializing or networking through words to work for the rapport with interlocutors and build up interpersonal connections that will become exploitative for practical purposes. *Guanxi* involves personal relation, in particular long-term relationships between individuals formed, maintained and accumulated over a long time. It is deep-rooted in the Confucianism of relational self, familism and hierarchy. *Guanxi* is often associated with malpractice, corruption, or bribery and so pulling *guanxi* is criticized as an unfair play by breaking rules and even laws (Qi, 2013), as it can be taken

140

advantage of as social resources for practical purposes (Hwang, 1988; Chang, Bolt, 1991). Other concepts like networking (King, 1991) or rapport management (Spencer-Oatey, 2002) also capture the sense of building up interpersonal relationship and have no derogatory connotation, but I chose to keep "pulling *guanxi*" in this study for the following reason. The word "pull" indicates strength, matching the magnetic force expressed by the Chinese character of *ci*, and reflects how Chinese applicants are engaged in their *Taoci* practice to invest into their study-abroad future. It is still well acknowledged as an important social resource (Chang, Holt, 1991; Chow, Ng, 2004; Chang, 2010; Fei, 1992; King, 1985).

Pulling *guanxi* is to negotiate personal relationship between applicant and professors, to alleviate the offer-request imposition, to bring them closer if possible, and/or to create a harmonious relationship. *Taoci* emails reflect the practice of tending *guanxi* among Chinese young applicants and become a locus of encounter between old habitus and new dispositions. Furthermore, the speech act of pulling *guanxi* is to nurture interpersonal relation, turning the unfamiliar to the familiar, the outsider into insider, and attain the social capital of *guanxi* so as to pave the way for the future student-advisor identity. Relevant social capital, such as intermediary, previous association, is also introduced to establish more trust and harmony between applicants and professors.

The meso speech act of pulling *guanxi* will be discussed in terms of two categories, deference-oriented strategy and solidarity-oriented strategy, which were differentiated based on Brown and Levinson's (1987) positive politeness strategy and negative politeness strategy but with slight modification to accommodate the present data. The two subcategories are further differentiated respectively into micro speech acts of various linguistic realizations, or "output" in Brown and Levinson's (1987) term.

4.2.1 Deference-oriented Strategy: Distancing

Deference-oriented strategy is used to celebrate the existing power difference between two communicating parties, and to show one's respect for the counterpart's higher social status. Here, we adopt the Goffmanian deference, defined as "that component of activity which functions as a symbolic means by which appreciation is regularly conveyed to a recipient of this recipient, or of something of which the recipient is taken as a symbol, extension, or agent" (Goffman, 1967: 56). Goffman's term of deference describes the appreciation delivered in both hierarchical and horizontal interaction, though it still keeps the difference or distance between interlocutors, whereas the term of power in Brown and Levinson (1987) often creates an impression of hierarchical patterns. Deferential behavior tends to be honorific and politely toned. It arises from either asymmetrical relation, for instance, that of superordinate and subordinate, or symmetrical relation such as that of coworkers. The asymmetrical deference could be done either by raising the hearer or abasing the speaker to convey the perception that the hearer is of higher social status than the speaker (Scollon, Scollon, 2001). Younger people, subordinates and students are expected to show respect and politeness when interacting with older ones, superordinates and teachers (see also Bond, 1991: 28–31; Gu, 1990; Lee, 2004).

In the case of *Taoci*, asymmetrical deference mainly derives from the hierarchy of student and teacher in traditional Chinese culture, while symmetrical deference might be related to the fact that applicants and foreign professors were equal academics interested in the same topic (though hardly accepted by Chinese students). In the Confucian doctrine, one's teacher is on a par with one's father. Chinese students are expected to show loyalty and deference to their teachers, which could be regarded as an inculcated cultural habitus. However, it is not impossible that students' deference to professors who holds their academic future in his hands could also be horizontal as academic peers. Thus, the term of deference could shun the struggle between vertical ranking and horizontal positioning but highlights the distance and difference to convey applicants' appreciation towards their targeted professors' academic capital, such as well-known publication, and symbolic capital such as their academic prestige. The deference-oriented strategy includes seven types of micro speech acts with different realizations of linguistic expression. To be consistent, all email examples start with capitalized "E" plus order of occurrence. For instance, E1 means the first example excerpted from email texts. Likewise, all interview episodes begin with capitalized "I" and field notes with "F". At the end of each example is a label of that piece of data's source.

4.2.1.1 Addressing Formally

To address one's hearer with titles is at the same time to recognize the hearer's social role. In the collected *Taoci* emails, most of the applicants (over 90%) used formal addressing terms, the V form (Brown, Gilman, 1960/1968), such as "Dear Professor ***", "Dear Prof. ***", "Dear Dr. ***", to show their respect for professors' higher position. In particular in the first email, no applicant used first name (FN) addressing and in *Taoci* packages, they kept using such formal address terms even though professors signed their first names at the end of their reply. This prominent feature confirms what Gu (1990) claimed that the lower-status tended to choose those formal address terms to deliver respect and politeness. On the other hand, in the *Taoci* email package, foreign professor all used applicants' FN in reply, which testified to what Brown and Gilman observed, "There is an interesting residual of the power relation in the contemporary notion that the right to initiate the reciprocal T belongs to the member of the dyad having the better power-based claim to say T without reciprocation" (Brown, Gilman, 1960: 260).

There were occasional deviations from the norm of V form used by the less powerful applicants. For example, In Huyang Long's *Taoci* package, the first email started with "Dear Prof. Kiong" (a Korean professor in America), but in the following contacts he shifted to first name addressing like "Dear Feon", "Hi Feon", or even zero addressing. Nevertheless, he reused the deferential term of "Dear Professor Kiong" from the eleventh email and the asymmetrical T/V resumed. Huyang reflected in his interview:

(I1) "I worked part time in a Western electronic company ... All of my habits [of addressing others] are formed there. Whenever I write to Chinese or English speakers, I'm used to an equal relationship in addressing others. No matter whether he is my boss or the big boss, we are equal, rather equal. So after chatting a little or four or five emails, I addressed him by his given name. But later, I felt that, Korean, Chinese, Japanese, or some Indians, probably do not like such kind of equality. They might expect you to respect your teacher much more. So suddenly one day, I felt that I should go back to use 'Dear Professor' in the email." (Interview transcripts 2013-May Huyang Long)

Huyang's feeling of being equal to the professor was only momentary and didn't last to the end of his *Taoci* email communication. The addressing relapsed into the power difference pattern, because the asymmetrical addressing is deeply rooted as linguistic habitus in Chinese students' mind, or even in Asian people's mind, which both conveys applicants' respect for professors and demonstrates a polite demeanor. Another research participant, Qingwan Li, recalled,

(I2) "At that moment I made some consideration about it [how to address professors], I searched it on Baidu and so on, either way, then I read some, some foreign students were discussing the addressing issue too. Because I am inclined to see how foreigners deal with it, because they are native speakers and their answer could be more reliable. They said, usually you addressed them by family name, like Professor *** or Doctor ***. Usually professor may well reply with their given names instead of family names ... Anyway, you will not offend them by using family name. But I'm not used to addressing a professor by their given names even if they allow me to do that. I don't know why, there is a line in my mind that cannot be crossed as we are teacher-and-student relationship."

146

(Interview transcripts 2014-Dec. Qingwan Li)[①]

Qingwan Li turned to the Internet to look for information about terms addressed to foreign professors, and she tried to follow what native speakers did. Although native speakers said that first names were acceptable if professors signed their first names, Qingwan still picked up the titled addressing all through her email package. She mentioned that there was a "line" between student and teacher that students could not crossed, which was engraved in her mind as a kind of cultural habitus. Confronting with the western egalitarian norm, the hierarchical value was kept all the same and even strengthened through such addressing terms. The default V form among applicants might also account for the fact that formal addressing was phrased unconsciously, representing the subconscious level of speech act investment, which was absent in Darvin and Norton (2015).

However, the V form may contradict what professors expect as Brown and Gilman (1968: 196) argued "The American professor often feels foolish being given his title, he almost certainly will not claim it as a prerogative; he may take pride in being on a first-name basis

---

① I got in touch with Qingwan in 2013, but she was not in Beijing then. I interviewed her through email during that year. In 2014 when I went abroad, I had the chance to interview her in person.

with his students". It might be due to the egalitarianism promoted in American universities. An English native speaker at an American university mentioned,

(F1) "Students address professors by their first names, which is not uncommon here. I was in the business field before and we cut through to the point, so we used first names a lot and [though] there is a hierarchy of employer and employee. But when I came to the educational [field], it is not that the boss-employee relation here. I usually use first names to my professors and all the faculty except one.

But if we are in a kind of formal occasion I will use more formal addressing terms, such as titles. But usually first name is enough. For example, in Kristen's course, we just call her by first name. And also for my own students, some of them call me professor, some of them call me Grace. I'm okay with either of these." (Field notes 2015-Mar. Grace)

Grace was an American, a native English speaker and was working for her PhD degree in the informatics department while she also took in charge of course instruction in that department. She mentioned that first name addressing was prevalent in her own community. However, she also observed,

(F2) "But I know that Chinese people's way is quite different as I have a friend and I really had a hard time to figure out dealing with her. I felt I'm a bull in a china shop, afraid of offending her. I know the hierarchical is more important than here. But we finally got along with each other well. Compared with the

Chinese, maybe the relationship between advisor and student here is equal, but it also depends on situations." (Field notes 2015-Mar. Grace)

As intercultural communication becomes more frequent and common than before, different norms of addressing are also mingled, struggling, conflicting and compromising with each other. Grace had her preference of first name addressing, but also showed toleration and understanding to the Chinese asymmetrical addressing.

Through something as simple as the micro speech act of addressing, interpersonal boundaries are defined, and rights and obligations can be negotiated as "naming practices reveal distinctions among what may be said, what may not be said, and what must be said, in monitoring the delicate balance of self and world" (Blum, 1997: 372). Meanwhile, the naming practice is undergoing modifications as different addressing norms are brought into contact. New dispositions of linguistic habitus might appear, as in Huyang's case, while durable habitus like Qingwan's sense of "line" could still maintain its propensity to guide her writing acts, as an facet of subconscious level of speech act investment.

4.2.1.2   Making Apologies

The micro speech act of making apology is used to convey speakers' regret about impinging on hearer's freedom. In writing *Taoci* emails, Chinese applicants were approaching unknown professors who had no institutional obligation to answer their question or consider their offer. Receiving a *Taoci* email and reading it interfered with foreign professors' autonomy. This sense of impingement was primarily due to the distance between the two parties and face-threatening act of the requestive nature of *Taoci* emails. To show their awareness of such infringement, applicants would apologize at the very beginning or the end of their email, as the following examples show.

(E1) Again, I apologize for interrupting. Looking forward to hearing from you.

Best,

Pianhong Yin   (2014-09-04 Pianhong Yin)

In E1, after she raised a series of questions concerning about her application, Pianhong Yin used the utterance of "I apologize for interrupting" at the end of her email. The word of "apologize" is a self-naming verb of apologizing, in which the uttering of the sentence refers to the act itself, i.e. the explicit performative in Austin (1962) and the expressive performative in Leech (1983). The word of "interrupting" indicated the reason for making such an apology and demonstrated Pianhong's awareness of infringing the professor's daily routine.

Another way to admit the transgression was led by the emotional expression in the "hope" form like Example (E2) below shows. The applicant, Dong Wang, indicated that her email might bring a lot of trouble to the professor, but she still had to go on with the face-threatening action as she longed for the offer from the professor. By reminding the professor that she recognized the risk of causing inconvenience, Dong Wang showed her consideration for the professor's autonomy so as to lessen the requestive imposition.

(E2) I hope this mail will not cause you too much trouble and many thanks!

Best wishes!

Dong Wang   (2015-40 Dong Wang)

Some apologies took place at the beginning of email. A less performative output of apology was in the form of "sorry" as follows.

(E3) Dear Sir ***:

I am sorry to bother you. I'm Professor Xu's student, and want to stay as a foreign visiting researcher in your lab for one year. (2015-29 Yue Xu)

The applicant in Example (E3) used "I am sorry to bother you." to ask for forgiveness from the targeted professor because he raised the request: to stay as a foreign visiting researcher in the professor's lab for one year. He recognized that his "want" might trespass on the professor's territory of autonomy. The usage of apology, phrased before his request, was intended as a way to alleviate the threat on the receiver's negative face.

Another way to deliver apology was the expression of asking for forgiveness in a request form of "Please excuse me for taking some of your time" in Example (E4) below.

(E4) Dear Professor ***,

Please excuse me for taking some of your time. I am *** (Chinese characters), a 2nd year Ph.D. candidate from *** University Law School. (2015-14)

Brown and Levinson (1987: 187) argued, "By apologizing for doing an FTA, the speaker can indicate his reluctance to impinge on H's negative face and thereby partially redress that impingement." In addition to the function of redressing a potential threat, which would be hardly redressed if the reader started to consider the request, the usage of apology was also regarded as a routine opening for a request in Chinese as a research participant reflected,

(I3) "The distance between student and teacher is large and that is one factor, more crucially, [I'm sorry to bother you] is a literal translation. Actually, in the Chinese contact 'Hi, I'm sorry to bother you' is an idiomatic expression. It is rather an opening of small talk, which I feel it's similar to how is your day today in America". (Interview transcripts 2014-Dec. Qingwan Li)

An English native speaker' commented on such kind of apology in email writing as follows.

(F3) "In the first email, I might not use this. For a written apology, it must be

152

something that you really feel sorry for or you did something wrong. There should be some specific reasons for the apology. But in the first email, you are just telling the professor you are going to apply for the program. You have nothing to apologize for. Although this sounds strange to the professor, this will not hinder the communication." (Field notes 2015-Apr. Nicolas)

Nicolas was a TESOL student at an American university. From his native speaker's point of view, using apology in the application email was inappropriate especially when there was nothing to apologize for at all. However, Nicolas also mentioned that the apology expression would not block the communication even though it sounded strange to the recipient. Taking into consideration of What Qingwan Li mentioned, the speech act of apology used by Chinese applicants could be regarded as a type of "situation-bound utterance" (Kecskes, 2014). The situation that the speaker was going to phrase his intention for request for his own benefit while the hearer's benefit (in any form) would be at risk is triggered through the usage of apology. It reflected applicants' cautiousness in dealing with higher-status hearers. Moreover, Goffman observed "A meek, apologetic manner may give the impression that the performer expects to follow the lead of others, or at least that he can be led to do so" (Goffman, 1959: 24), which testifies to the Chinese applicants' positioning themselves as a lower status with regards to their foreign professors. To some extent, the speech act of apologizing in *Taoci* emails indicates an old linguistic habitus coated in the new language of English to affirm the distance between applicants and professors. It might also be used by Chinese applicants without a conscious consideration but come into the textual lines as a subconscious propensity to act in front of authorities.

4.2.1.3 Magnetizing the Supervisor

The character of "磁" (*ci*) in Chinese means magnetic force. Foreign professors are compared to magnets because they owned the social, cultural, economic and even symbolic capital that applicants competed for, for example, their funding resources, academic prestige, publications, research achievements, etc., which drew Chinese applicants to apply for their programs and supervision. Applicants would state clearly that they were attracted by supervisors' achievements or charisma or conceived some personal affection towards supervisors. Most of these revealed feelings were not only positive but also accompanied with intensification vocabulary to emphasize professors' magnetic force and how greatly applicants were attracted to them. There were different kinds of linguistic realizations of foreign professors' magnetic attraction, through process structure, modality lexicon or attitudinal vocabulary (Martin, White, 2008).

(E5) Your research on this field **deeply attracts me**, so I write to you... (2015-

17 Rong Chen)

(E6) **I am fascinated** by the issue of explorations of complex networks [in your paper]. (2015-26 Yuan Zhao)

(E7)…and I **love** your taste as well as style. (2015-26 Yuan Zhao)

(E8) I **deeply admire** you for the scope and depth of your academic research, as well as the attitude and notions that behind your researches. (2015-34 Feng Huang)

In Example (E5), the word "attract", was up-scaled by the graduation term "deeply" in order to stress how attractive the professor's research work appeared to Rong Chen. In Example (E6), the passive structure "I am fascinated" together with the word the "fascinate" showed that the professor's research topic radiated a great charm to Yuan Zhao and thus he was beguiled. Another term was the emotive mental verb of "love", which indicated the applicant's strong inclination towards the professor. In Example (E7), Yuan Zhao used this intensified affection-laden word "love" to show his appreciation of the professor's "taste and style" of the research group. Likewise, in Example (E8), Feng Huang used the intensifier "deeply" to upscale his admiration not only for the professor's academic achievement but also the attitude and notions behind his researches, which could be interpreted as the professor's academic vision. Example (E5) and (E6) pointed out professors' academic capital while Example (E7) and (E8) alluded to

155

作为投资的言语行为
—— "套磁"话语实践研究

professors' symbolic capital of taste, style, attitude, and vision.

Because of the rich capitals that foreign professors possessed which applicants pursued, the latter would keenly show their willingness to be recruited by foreign professors' research team. The modal verbs and phrases in the following examples of (E9), (E10), (E11)—*wish, be more than willing, would like*—each combined with the subject of "I" (*wish to join your group, more than willing to apply for, would like to explore the possibility of doing research with you*), demonstrated applicants' strong desideration for the professors' capitals.

(E9) I have applied for the Ph.D program of your depart and indicate that **I wish to** join your group. (2013-01 Qiang Miao)

(E10) ...so I am **more than willing** to apply for the doctoral program in your department this year. (2013-06 Qin Huang)

(E11) ...and I **would like** to explore the possibility of doing research with you. (2014-03 Lin Jiang)

Some applicants also revealed their emotions in the form of "affect as quality" (Martin, White, 2008). For instance, in Example (E12) the excitement of becoming a member in the professor's team was attributed to the participant of "I", realized through the attribute of "excited" below.

(E12) ...and I would be **very excited** and grateful to become one of your team

156

members. (2015-13 Lan Luo)

The last way to show "being attracted" was to evaluate how foreign professors' research or their team looked like to applicants, which was typically realized through appreciation terms. For example, Si Chen in Example (E13) claimed that her targeted professor's group was the dream place that she longed for. Qiang Miao in Example (E14) described the professor's group as his research home. Such expressions conveyed a sense of belonging that applicants desired for and it emitted from the great attraction from the professors. The terms of "dream place" and "research home" also alluded to the professors' symbolic capital recognized by the applicants.

(E13) Therefore I found your group at U University **a dream place** for me to start my graduate education and research. (2013-02 Si Chen)

(E14) I hope your group can be my **research home**. (2013-01 Qiang Miao)

In a word, in the speech act of showing professors' magnetic attraction, the magnetic attraction force works from professor to student, that is, applicants let themselves be attracted by professors. This unilateral attraction indicates that foreign professors were positioned as capital owners and distributors, which led to the power difference between them. Moreover, the attitudinal enthusiasm embedded in the above-list examples also indicated professors' symbolic value to applicants, which mainly originated from professors' cultural capital of research achievement.

A note about the micro speech act of showing magnetic attraction is that it may be on the surface a solidarity strategy, but professors' magnetic attraction was stressed and the difference between them was enlarged. Thus, it is ascribed to the deference category.

4.2.1.4　Making Bribery Compliment

Compliment is an explicit expression of affection. Compliment refers to a speech act "which explicitly or implicitly attributes credit to someone other than the speaker, usually the person addressed, for some 'good' (possessions, characteristic, skill, etc.) which is positively valued by the speaker and hearer" (Holmes, 1986: 485). Compliment is, therefore, a clearly evaluative act to help the speaker accentuate the positive attributes of the addressee (Holmes, 1988).

Compliment is also regarded as a common form of "presentational deference" (Goffman, 1967: 72). It greases the interpersonal relationship because it elevates others (Gu, 1990, 1992), maximizes praise of others (Leech, 1983), and in most cases maintains a harmonious relationship with others (Chang, Holt, 1991). Complimenting as a kind of "gift-giving" is a frequently used strategy as a pre-request supportive move (Nash, 1983). The compliment made in *Taoci* emails falls into the category of "bribery" in Chen and Rau (2013). It "often happens in the situation where the complimentee has a higher status than the complimenter. Usually, the complimenter wants to bribe the complimentee in order to benefit from him of her in some way" (Chen, Rau, 2013: 21). Chinese applicants held a lower status compared with foreign professors and they did have a practical goal in mind. Bribery compliment is similar to the move of adversary-glorification found in South Asian job application letters in Bhatia (1989), which boiled down to "the best traditions of Asian hospitality" (Bhatia, 1993: 70).

As compliment and flattery is often a matter of degree and compliment-makers' personal preference, I used the umbrella term of "making bribery compliment" to subsume all positive evaluations of foreign professors. According to what was complimented, the categories of compliments towards the professors, research work/team and the institution they represent, were distinguished with specific examples given below.

(E15) As I know, you are the **leading scholar** of Center for Chinese Legal Studies of ** Law School. (2015-17 Rong Chen)

The expression of "leading scholar" in Example (E15) was an overall evaluation towards the professor's academic standing and influence in the discipline of Chinese legal studies. The attributive term of "leading" was highly value-laden and was a compliment on the person per se, which might be considered as flattery if the professor was factually not that influential. A piece of online meta-discourse is worth mentioning as presented in Example (M1). It was a *Taoci* email shared on *Renren* (Chinese version of Facebook), which incurred much critique and was considered "bizarre"[①].

(M1) You are in my view one of the most knowledgeable and authoritative scholars in the area of self-assembling materials … Therefore I am eager to be your intern student and learn from you the most helpful research skills. (Online *Taoci* discourse, 2014-Mar.)

The expression of "the most knowledgeable and authoritative scholars" was criticized harshly because of its lickspittle tone, since the targeted professor was just a novice lecturer, according to the sharer, and the compliment went far beyond the truth. This was posted as a bad example of writing over-stretched compliment. However, in the Chinese students' *Taoci* emails to Chinese supervisors (Xiao, 2014), lauding supervisors' character, morality and reputation was pervasive, which nevertheless was rare in the present English data. One research

---

① This *Taoci* email was posted on *Renren* and forwarded for many times. It was cited as a bad example of *Taoci* email writing with regards to its content, format, font, etc.

participant mentioned that:

(I4) I would like to say "you did great research work". Certainly I won't say you have a great personality. Instead I will say your research is terrific and I like what you did very much, and I feel that I can do an excellent job under your guidance and my academic research will be much better. That's it. I will not bow and scrape, 'cause you don't know the teacher that well actually, and you won't know anything more than his research from his website. (Interview transcripts 2013-May Huyang Long)

Just as what Huyang emphasized, compliments in the present data were more concerned about professors' academic work, i.e. their academic capital, like Example (E16) and (E17) below.

(E16) You have published quite **a lot of high level** scientific papers. (2015-30 Ningfu He)

(E17) Your group's researches are so **outstanding** that I believe if ... the experience in your team can **improve** my research capacity, **broaden** my academic horizon, and **enlarge** my knowledge in this field... (2015-28 Ting Hu)

In Example (E16), Ningfu He pointed out the fact that the targeted professor produced excellent publications, the objectified social capital that attracted him. The term "high level" was not only an evaluative term but also an infused up-scaling quantification, while the isolated term of "a lot of" further quantified the amount of the capital at

161

the up-grading end to stress the professor's academic authority and prolificacy. In Example (E17), Ting Hu used the upgrading term of "outstanding" to describe the excellent work done by the professor's research group. In the rest part, Ting Hu described how the experience in the professor's team would benefit him, by using "improve my research capacity", "broaden my academic horizon", and "enlarge my knowledge", a kind of imagined identity of the applicants which drove the applicant to bond up with the professor. The three verbs of "improve", "broaden" and "enlarge" showed the expected return of his *Taoci* investment, also a further demonstration of the value of the professor's research.

The last form to deliver a compliment was about the institution that applicants applied for. In Example (E18) below, the applicant used "world-famous" to evaluate the prestige of her targeted professor's affiliated university.

(E18) *** is one of the **world-famous** universities, where many students dream to go. (2015-36 Zhen Fan)

Making compliment is a way to boost interlocutor's quality face (Spencer-Oatey, 2002, 2007). "To establish relations with a total stranger, one has to manage the situation in order to create a pleasant appearance through tactics such as enhancing the face of the other."

162

(Chang, 2010: 55) The enhancement of the other's face could be beneficial for nurturing a harmonious atmosphere and turn the temporary relation into a long-term *guanxi* along with the production of social membership.

Khan and Tin in investigating job interview observed that glorifying the employer was a move "with the sole communicative purpose of gaining positive response through its appeal to the reader's sentiments" (Khan, Tin, 2012: 407). By resorting to bribery compliment, applicants also wanted to appeal to professors' positive sentiment since few professors would like to take students who didn't even recognize their research value. The speech act of bribery compliment conveyed applicants' deep appreciation towards professors. It originates from either horizontal deference (like academic peers in the same discipline) or hierarchical deference (like green hand and veteran in the academic hierarchy), or both, but it boils down to the inequilibrium of cultural capital (research achievement) or even symbolic capital (academic prestige) between applicants and supervisors, which casts the magnetic force of supervisors.

4.2.1.5   Stating Honor

Stating that to work with a targeted professor is a great honor could be a courtesy expression, but it still conveys applicants' deference

163

to foreign professors.

(E19) It would be an honor if I had the chance to work with you. (2013-04 Feifei Hu)

(E20) It will be an extreme honor for me to be under your supervision. (2015-15 Yi Wang)

In Example (E19), Feifei Hu claimed the honor in a subjunctive mood (*It would … if … had*). In terms of English grammar, the subjective mood structure could generate less imposition on the professor to deal with the request of "working with you" because it was not actualized. The intensification word of "extreme" in Example (E20) in claiming "an extreme honor for me", together with the adjunct of "under your supervision" illustrated well the hierarchy between applicant and professor. For English native speakers, here "honor" might be better replaced by "pleasure". However, as is mentioned, teacher-student relationship in the Chinese context is normally characterized as a hierarchical one under the influence of Confucianism, for example, "treat my teacher just as I treat my father" [1]; "He who teaches me for one day is my father for life"[2]; with teacher amounting to the role of father, one of the Five Codes of Ethics (*Wulun*, 五伦). As Scollon

---

[1] From "Encouraging leaning" in Lv's *Commentaries of History*.
[2] Folk adage.

164

and Scollon observed, "the teacher and student relationship is felt by Asians to be as permanent and all-pervasive as that between parents and children or that between elder and younger brothers" (Scollon & Scollon, 1991: 121). Consequently, to work with or for teachers is considered a great honor. The honor statement displays applicants' deep appreciation and respect towards targeted professors. Moreover, the honor that applicants longed for would only become true by professors' decision to recruit them, which highlights the symbolic value of the global offer in their imagined future.

4.2.1.6　Humbling Self

Denigrating self is a way to show deference (Brown, Levinson, 1987). "Humbling self" means the speaker places him/herself at a lower status, which simultaneously profiles the hearer's higher status.

(E21) I have known **a little information** of your researching project. (2015-11 Tao Feng)

(E22) Some other Ph.D. students in our department are using VASP to investigate nuclear materials, so I know **a little bit** about it (2014-10-03 Shunying Qin)

In the above-listed examples, both applicants used the down-scaling quantification term of "a little" and "a little bit" to claim minimal knowledge about the professors' research work, showing their limited amount of embodied form of cultural capital, knowledge. Compared to the applicants, the professors were usually experts in their fields, so even if the Chinese applicants knew more than "a little", they would not upgrade that volume of their cultural capital of knowledge. Example (E23) is an illustration of this feature.

(E23) I have done **some elementary** works about the HHT. In one study, the HHT is applied to the study of low-level jets in the atmospheric boundary layer which was published in the ***. The other accepted by the *** (in Chinese) is the basic discussion about the application of HHT in the boundary layer turbulence. (2015-12 Xu Liu)

Xu Liu said that he only did some beginning work about the HHT, which was a research topic in the professor's group. However, the following content actually invalidated his self-abasement as he had one related article published on an international journal and another one accepted by a Chinese journal, which indicated his possession of convincing academic competence forged through his research work.

Apart from such kind of self-devaluation of knowledge command, applicants would position themselves as "learners" instead of academic peers, another reflection of the traditional Chinese style of student-teacher dyad. The expressions of "learn from you" and "get your coach", separately in Example (E24) and (E25) below, indicated that they had less expertise, so they needed to learn from foreign professors and get trained.

(E24) I hope to learn from you... (2015-09 Xianxian Liu)

(E25) I do hope to have the chance to study in your school and get your coach. (2015-24 Lan Yang)

A field reporter, who was a TESOL student from an American university commented on the expressions in the foregoing examples as follows:

(F4) I will not use this kind of expression. Learning from you sounds like that you are not competent enough for the PhD project. If you just want to learn something from the professor, nobody would like to recruit you since professors need someone who will work with them, not learn from them. (Field notes 2014-Nov. Amy)

In the native speaker's understanding, "learning from you" was an expression of weakness and should have been avoided in competitive application for graduate programs. However, in the Chinese's mind, it was still cherished as a virtue of modesty. Gu (1990) proposed "modesty" as one of the Chinese politeness maxims to explain the self-degradation phenomenon in language usage. In the book of *The*

Book of Rites[①], *li* (politeness) is about humbling yourself and showing respect to others, an inculcated cultural capital still exerting its influence on the polite behaviors of Chinese people. Speaking with a higher-status hearer, the lower-status party is inclined, or has the propensity, to display humbleness in order to follow the requirement of li in the hierarchy of institutional power. Being modest and being humble is preferable particularly in this kind of "upward communication" from students to supervisors (Ho, 2010). With the cultural habitus of valuing self-efficacy, some applicants' speech act investment was oriented to the modesty end, instead of the popular western self-appraisal (Bhatia, 1993; Brown, 2004). An interviewee commented,

(I5) "If given a, suppose I was given a scale, a scale, one end is humble and the other arrogant, I will not hesitate to choose humble. I thought ritual would cost nothing … I kept, talking with my friends, that if I exaggerated just a little bit, I would feel a strong sense of guilt." (Interview transcripts 2014-Dec. Qingwan Li)

4.2.1.7 Formalizing the Writing

Formality is an important feature of ritual and exhibits the ritual performers' faith in doing the rites. In student–faculty communication,

---

① *The Book of Rites* (《礼记》) is a book complied by Dai Sheng during the West Han Dynasty. It is mainly about the social institution, rituals and values before the Han Dynasty.

168

polite emails are expected to reflect greater formality (Danielewicz-Betz, 2013). Professors thought that following a standard letter format in the order of subject, greeting, message, and closing is essential for a polite email (Chen, 2015). To show their deference, applicants made their *Taoci* emails appear quite formal, characterized by using an epistolary style and using formal formulaic expressions. Exhibiting an overall formal style is a feature at the textual level, but still a micro speech act with different linguistic outputs. A formal style also creates an impression of detachment, thus difference between applicants and professors.

Applicants' *Taoci* email texts were mostly composed in a formal epistolary style, including the ritual moves of addressing, opening, body, closing and signing, even in the shortest email. To give an example,

(E26)

Dear Prof. ***:

Nice to meet you! Thank you for reading my letter during your busy time.

My name is ***, a Ph.D. student of a five-year educational system major in *** from *** University, China, supervised by Prof. Fangxue Li. I will receive my doctor degree in ***.

… **(content left out by the researcher)**

Enclosed is my CV. I'm looking forward to your reply of whether I can refer to you as a prospective supervisor. Should you have any questions, please let me know. Thank you very much for your attention!

Thanks!

Yours sincerely,

*** (signature)   (2015-22 Rui Wang)

This email presents a typical example of epistolary style. Rui Wang in Example (E26) began her email with the titled addressing of "Dear Prof. ***". She used a warming-up opening of "Nice to meet you", which resembled the opening in face-to-face communication. The body part of the letter introduced herself and expressed the request. The email then ended with a gratitude expression and signed respectively. The epistolary format results in a formal impression and demonstrates applicants' decorum in writing the email. One probable reason for the epistolary style is that most Chinese students are taught how to write a letter before but not how to write an email, so they transferred their letter-writing knowledge to their email writing.

The formal tone is also colored through some formulaic rhetorical structures. Request email more often than not contains such formulaic expressions as thanking and wishing to be responded, the unmarked form of which is respectively the use of performative "thank" and the phrase of "look (ing) forward to...". It is understandable since "job letters are a genre and, as such, have not only a predictable structure but in many cases predictable formulaic expressions" (Upton, Connor, 2001: 322).

(E27) I would appreciate it if you took a look at my CV in the attachment. (2013-06 Qingwan Li)

(E28) Your comments and considerations will be highly appreciated. (2015-28 Ting Hu)

(E29) If any other information were needed, please let me know. (2015-27 Panpan Wei)

In Example (E27), Qingwan Li used the formulaic expression of "would appreciate" combined with the subjunctive mood in the if-clause, while in Example (E28) Ting Hu used the passive structure of "be appreciated". The two cases gave an impression of being sincerely serious. Instead of using "I'm looking forward to your reply", Panpan Wei in Example (E29) used the if-led subjunctive mood to convey this concern. Besides, the passive structure of "any other information were [was] needed" hid the grammatical subject of the foreign professor, and also left less impingement on the imposition. An applicant reflected,

(I6) "Because when I directly spoke with foreigners on Skype, I felt myself quite casual, I myself found that I'm especially formal when writing an email, which appears a little odd. I don't know why I become so courteous when I write in English. For example, several days ago, I wrote to the admission secretary that I planned to order the flight ticket and applied for the visa, so when you can send me that I-20 form, just that issue. And the correspondent replied, saying 'we are currently working on your form and your patience will be appreciated'. Just that, they write this kind of [formal words] and then you will follow them in writing." (Interview transcripts 2013-Apr. Si Chen)

The occurrence of each speech act under the deference-oriented strategy in all *Taoci* email texts is given in Fig. 4.1. Since the last category of exhibiting a formal style also includes textual level features, it is not calculated here. It is clear that formal addressing takes the largest proportion. Complimenting and showing professors' magnetic attraction are also frequently used to augment the value of professors' capital. Apologizing, humbling self and stating honor are comparatively less used.

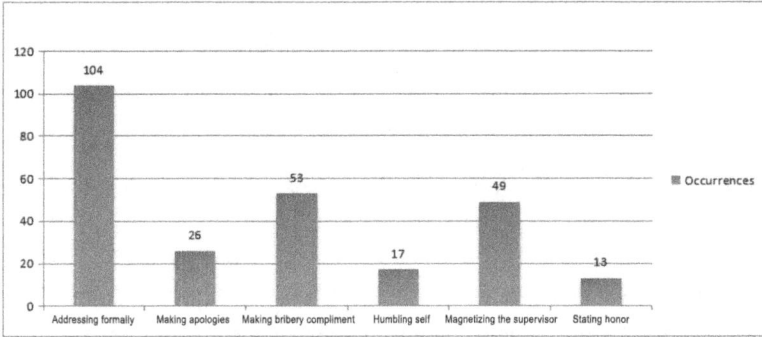

Fig. 4.1   Deference-oriented strategy distribution

The deference-oriented strategy of pulling *guanxi*, in both others-raising and self-debasing manner, is used to pay applicants' appreciation, respect and/or consideration to foreign professors' power or social status correlated with their alluring social, cultural, economic, and symbolic capital. In the traditional Chinese *guanxi*-oriented culture, self-efficacy and respect for higher-status people are two inseparable elements of politeness, which constitute a continuum of Chinese people's being polite (Bi, 1996). The Confucianism tradition of li has been engrained in Chinese people's hexis, which can be regarded as a cultural habitus. People should, therefore, behave status-congruently or at least status-appropriately in communication, which further produces and strengthens the existing social structure. Foreign professors, even if they were not

173

in the Chinese context, were assigned symbolic capital of authority and superiority recognized by Chinese applicants, who thus turned to such expressions as formal addressing terms, honor statement in their *Taoci* email to exacerbate the difference between them. This cultural propensity is also reflected through a research participant' reflection:

(I7) We have to be respectful and show deference to them, because after all you are students. The rank, student to teacher, is lower to higher, because they are at different ranks. At least, the lower posture is after. It's possible that the teacher prefers to an egalitarian relationship. But under the situation that you're not familiar with him, it's safer to place yourself at a lower position. Otherwise, it will make him uncomfortable too. I thought it might be related to the Chinese tradition, you know, the dignity and authority of teacher. Yes, that's it. (Interview transcripts 2014-Dec. Qingwan Li)

4.2.2 Solidarity-oriented Strategy: Bonding

The solidarity-oriented strategy, by resorting to similarity, i.e. the T-form expressions, is intended to build up common ground between interlocutors. "Solidarity is the name we give to the general relationship and solidarity is symmetrical." (Brown, Gilman, 1968: 189) It refers to a state of unity, trust and togetherness resulting from shared interest, value or belief. It does not necessarily mean that people hold equal status, but they are involved in the same cohort of any kind. The solidarity-oriented strategy in *Taoci* emails is to nurture closeness with foreign professors. Sharing similarities and having frequent contact could generate like-mindedness.

During the *Taoci* process, applicants and foreign professors were at first strangers to each other, and the distance between them was predictably large. The low-status applicants tried various strategies to create more common ground so as to pull their relation closer, which was thought to be beneficial for their application. Common ground is a cognitive term about shared knowledge between interlocutors (Clark, 2009; Kecskes, 2014), serving as the basis for understanding. However, in this research, common ground is used in a broader way, lumping all shared values, beliefs, context, relation and knowledge about each other. The common ground in *Taoci* emails was created from applicants' perspective, though not necessarily acknowledged by foreign professors.

4.2.2.1 Introducing the Intermediary

Guanxi is a significant social capital in that its expansion can create new relational ties and bring new capitals. Therefore, outsiders might try to enter the network through ingroup members, for example, "I am your father's friend's best friend." This is what Chang and Bolt (1991: 260) called "intermediaries" and "going through another" in

Chang (2010: 79). Chang further explained it as follows,

"Another verbal manifestation of intermediary activity occurs when someone requests something of the target directly, but mentions the name of a mutual acquaintance in order the make the exchange easier, or more profitable. In such cases the intermediary's presence is not direct, but symbolic, since it is constructed through words." (Chang, 2010: 85)

Through the introduction of a middleman, the potential social capital of networking resource and membership is activated when it is put into investment on a relevant market, which is taken advantage of by Chinese applicants in their *Taoci* emails.

There were different kinds of middleman introduced by applicants to mediate the relationship of "who I am to you through the third person", including "my Chinese professor", "professors I know other than my own", "my classmate", and "people in your group".

For the majority of applicants, who were still on their threshold to knit their academic networking web, "my Chinese supervisor" was the most available resource to invest into their academic future. Supervisors' names appeared in different parts of their emails.

(E30) <u>Prof. Fanyang Sun</u> is my current supervisor. (2013-04 Chu Gao1)

(E31) My supervisor is Huang Shen. (2014-06 Liguo Zhao)

The Chinese supervisors' names appeared in the "being" relational process, as subject or predicate, which was the most explicit form as Example (E30) and (E31) shown above.

(E32) My name is ... at ** University... and supervised by Prof. Tian Liu. (2015-17 Rong Chen)

(E33) At the present time, I am under the instruction of Prof. ***, focusing upon unconventional geology, sequence stratigraphy, and basin analysis. (2015-13 Lan Luo)

The supervisors' names appeared in the adjunct part. Supervisor-student relationship was represented through the action of "supervised" in Example (E32) and "instruction" in Example (E33) above.

When supervisors' name was not available for the mediation, "another professor that I know" was also introduced in Example (E34) and (E35).

(E34) During the last summer vacation, I was doing some work related to computational simulation under the guidance of Professor Qi in *** Academy of Science. (2013-05-01 Ran Xia)

(E35) I took the cognitive process seminar with **Prof. Mary Kung**... (2014-09-01 Pianhong Yin)

Ran Xia mentioned the name of "Professor Qi", who was a big

figure in Chinese science academy, and further claimed that his research work was guided by that professor. Ran Xia reflected in his interview,

(I8) "If the current supervisor and your targeted professor know each other, not necessarily that they are familiar with each other, anyway, they knew each other, at least they are in the same academic circle, you can mention it … In one letter, I mentioned Professor Qi's name on purpose because he and the other supervisor had previous cooperation and met each other before (Interview transcripts 2013-May Ran Xia)

In Example (E35), Pianhong Yin mentioned that she participated in a seminar with Prof. Mary Kung. Her targeted professor replied, "I know her—she's terrific!" acknowledging the common ground that Pianhong assumed—both of them knew a famous scholar and the applicant even worked with her, which indicated a kind of closeness between them. All of the middlemen mentioned were configured into the discursive interaction arena.

In the foregoing examples, applicants assumed that their Chinese professors and foreign professors could know each other since they were in the same research field. This connection on the one hand specified the applicants' academic background, and on the other hand brought the applicant closer to the potential supervisor. The intermediary mode works like this: *The person I am acquainted with is a famous scholar in the professional field, whose reputation you must know very well. As you know him, and I also know him, you and I belong to the same professional group, for which you might give more consideration of my application.* "Because someone is assumed to be close to you, there is a sense that 'we are in this together', and therefore that an individual's rights and privileges must be shared with others." (Chang, 2010: 57)

In addition, names of "my classmate" and "people in your group" also serve as intermediary. Although it couldn't draw the applicants and foreign professors in an actual or imagined academic networking, it still put the two into an existing interpersonal relationship mediated by the third person. In the following Example (E36), Wang Lin was mentioned as the applicant Zhi Gao's classmate, who was a student in the targeted professor's research group. In Example (E37), Dr. Douglas was a researcher of the professor's lab. The third person bridged the networking gap, creating a kind of common ground.

(E36) Wang Lin may have mentioned me to you. (2015-01 Zhi Gao)

(E37) I discussed with Doctor Douglas about my research interest, and he also agree that my research interest fits well the work of your lab. (2013-04-01 Gao Chu1)

As academic green-hands, most applicants had little available *guanxi* capital to make use of. The relational closeness, a kind of renqing symbolized through the mentioned names, was the only social capital that they could manipulate to invest into their study-abroad programs and future academic career. "…where there are no relational ties, it is possible for two parties to become closer by appealing to a third party who shares a relationship with each of them. Thus relationships can be built upon other relationships, integrating both familial and non-familial ties as parts of the relational web." (Chang, 2010: 45) This investment of social capital was anticipated to create an impression of closeness with foreign professors and added to their chances of successful offer hunting.

4.2.2.2　Doing Small Talk

Not all utterances are intended to carry substantial message but rather for the sake of lubricating interpersonal ties. The term of phatic communion, dating back to Malinowski (1947), means that the referential content of some utterances is disregarded by their users, but only their interactional functions are recognized (Brown, Yule, 1983), which is also called small talk. McCarthy (2000: 84) defined small talk as "non-obligatory talk in terms of task requirements". Small talk refers to unimportant subjects of conversation and functions as a warming-up or transitional move to the serious weighty business.

In this sense, small talk is similar to the Chinese "*xianhua*"[1] (idle talk). It is somehow viewed as ritual, habitual, and conventional. Gossip, phatic communication, and chit-chatting can all be included in the category of doing small talk. Although written language usually could not accommodate as much phatic communion as oral discourse does (Crystal, 2001), Bloch (2002) maintained perhaps because of its apparent immediacy, email was effective to express such opening of social interactions.

In our *Taoci* email data, small talk occurred at the beginning, in the middle or at the end of texts. Phatic communion at the beginning as an opening resemble that of face-to-face communication. For instance, "Nice to meet you" is a situation-bound utterance to greet a stranger used in Example (E38). "Hope all of you are well" expresses the student's kind greeting in Example (E39).

(E38) Nice to meet you! (2015-22 Rui Wang)

(E39) Hope all of you are well. (2015-31 Jie Chu)

Another type of small talk was holiday wishes as the following examples show.

(E40) Merry Christmas in advance! (2015-09 Xianxian Liu)

---

[1] In Chinese, it is written as "闲话".

(E41) Happy Mid-Autumn Festival! (2013-06-02 Qingwan Li)

Christmas is the most important holiday in the West, and Yuanyuan Qiu gave her festival wishes at the end of her email in Example (40). In Example (41) Qingwan Li's targeted professor was a Chinese. Her move to share spring festival wishes symbolized a collegial tie with respect to a shared cultural scenario, to strengthen their cultural and affective bonding.

Idle talk is about irrelevant things to the topic and usually happens among people who are familiar with each other.

(E42) Congratulations on your coming baby. (2015-44 Yan Tang)

(E43) Spring has come to Beijing and *** campus is now full of blossom. (2014-10-03 Shunying Qin)

In Example (E42), Yan Tang knew her targeted professor a little bit from her supervisor in China. The congratulation on the professor's coming baby serves as a kind of idle talk, which seems to put the email correspondents into an "acquaintance" relationship. In Example (E43), Shunying Qin told the professor that the campus was full of blossom, which could be a casual talk among acquaintances because of their alumni relationship. And she further explained in the interview.

(I9) "Because he graduated years away from my university too, I thought, you

182

see, the season now here is quite beautiful. How about yours? After all, I still feel that I should have said something courteous, but I don't know what to say and how to say it. Therefore, though it appears a little far-stretched, I said that. I assumed that he knew what's like here. And he replied that there were a lot of cherry blossoms there." (Interview transcripts 2014-Dec. Shunying Qin)

An American professor whom I consulted appraised the usage of such kind of idle talk as "irrelevant" to the email theme and said that American students wouldn't do that under most circumstances unless they were acquainted with each other. The irrelevance indicates the "waffle" phenomenon (Chen, 2015) prevalent in the *Taoci* email writing, which violates the maxim of relevance (Grice, 1975) and therefore diffuses the illocutionary force of the major speech act in a sentence or text. However, it is an often-recognized rhetorical strategy adopted by Chinese to reach someone who they are unfamiliar with, though some research participants showed their concern about the need to "cut to the chess" with Americans.

The style of writing irrelevant things was criticized by scholars in L2 email research and was regarded as pragmatic inappropriateness. It deviated from the norms in the canonical Anglo-Saxon conversational principle (Grice, 1975) or politeness (Brown, Levinson, 1987). However, this deviation should be better framed in a critical way.

If taking a more constructivist approach, small talk attests the fact that Chinese people attach great importance to feeling (*qing,*情), an essential part of *guanxi*, which means they like to care about and show warmth to other people (Bi, 1996). Doing irrelevant speech acts, like greeting, asking about personal issues is a way to work on that *qing* between each other, which might be misrecognized as poking into other's privacy by westerners. Although the applicants were using English, which was supposed to follow the English norms, their deeply rooted *guanxi*-oriented habitus seeped through their linguistic behavior.

4.2.2.3　Articulating Previous Association

Previous association serves as a prior common ground. To get acquainted with an unfamiliar person, some applicants resorted to their previous encounter with targeted supervisors, for instance an encounter at an academic conference, auditing their courses, listening to their lectures, a past contact through email, etc., which more often than not never occurred to foreign professors' mind until they received the *Taoci* email. The explicit articulation of such kind of previous associations worked as a kind reminder of the existing common ground between them. "When such a relationship already exists, Chinese may try to exchange messages to bring the relationship closer and more intimate." (Chang, 2010: 55)

184

One prominent linguistic feature of claiming previous association was the demonstration of the pronoun co-occurrence of "I" and "You". For example, in Example (E44), Meng Li first showed gratitude to the professor's lecture, indicating that "I attended your lecture", and then reminded the professor that he was one of the audience who raised a question, indicating that "I talked with you". In Example (E45), Liang Zhang mentioned the specific name of the course that the professor instructed, showing that "I attended your course" before. The co-occurrence of "I" and "You" within one clause was a clear sign of the interaction between the two parties, "which helped to shape an involved relation and thus, shorten the distance between the writer and the professor" (Chen, 2001: 16).

(E44) Thank you for **the lecture** '***' given for celebrating 100 years of mathematics at ** University last week. So after the lecture **I asked you** how can we choose the suitable spaces for the energy functional ... (2015-38 Meng Li)

(E45) I **audited your EU Administrative Law course** as an exchange student at *** University, which impressed me deeply. (2015-42 Liang Zhang)

Another kind of linguistic output for the previous association was the use of pronoun "we". The plural "we" has been examined under the term of positive face (Brown, Levinson, 1987), solidarity (Scollon, Scollon, 2001) or rapport (Spencer-Oatey, 2007b). It signifies an emerging common ground (Kecskes, Zhang, 2009), which piles up along the communication process.

(E46) ..., actually we have met in *** city, China two years ago ... When you came to *** city, we had dinner together, you probably don't remember me. (2015-04 Feifei Hu)

(E47) **We**'ve been connected through Email before. (2014-10-04 Yunyang Liu)

In Example (E46), Daming Liao met the professor before and even dined with him. The plural pronoun of "we" indicated that there was a kind of previous association between them. Although the professor might not remember it as Daming Liao also said in his email, an explicit mention of the occasion in the email could help to bring the existing shared information into the professor's current mental state. Example (47) occurred in the fourth email of Yunyang Liu's email package with the targeted professor. Since they had several rounds of email exchange, it became an established fact that the two parties knew each other better and this fact could be reflected through the usage of "we". The emerging plural pronoun also echoed what Schiffrin claimed "what language thus allows us to do is represent what I and others have already said and done (or will say and do) in a textual world that can be reflected or acted upon, denied or supported, desired or dreaded, in the social worlds in which we are currently speaking and doing" (Schiffrin, 2006: 129).

The explicit articulation of previous association couldn't be counted as serious *guanxi*, since it usually takes a longer time to build up *guanxi* with people, not just a brief encounter, a dinner meeting or a lecture. Nonetheless, such pseudo-*guanxi*, resembling the function of pseudo-kinship terms, is employed as an improvised networking resource to function as *guanxi* capital, which draws the two sides into a kind of factual relation and create a chance to develop a fruitful relationship in the future. It testifies to the fact that "As the interaction among the participants progresses, additions and modifications in this initial informational state will of course occur" (Goffman, 1959: 10). Previous interaction paves the way for further interaction.

4.2.2.4　Soliciting Further Association

Such classical speech acts as urging, wishing, hoping, asking or even requesting can all be used as response solicitors under certain conditions for the pragmatic function of soliciting further communication. Chinese people pay great attention to the mutual-ness of interaction, in Chinese *laiwang*[①], i.e. to and fro, back and forth, or reciprocation. A smart applicant would leave open the chance for further contact

─────────────

① In Chinese, it is written as "来往".

with his or her recipient through skillful use of response solicitors. A question or a request, for example, would invite a probable response. Request occurred a lot in *Taoci* emails as applicants were petitioners for limited educational resources, and the counterparts were naturally positioned as resource allocators. These response solicitors (Bhatia, 1993) function as petition for further communication and initiate a new relation. It overlaps a lot with the speech acts under the meso speech act of negotiating entry, which will be elaborated on later. The following excerpts illustrate the linguistic features of response solicitors.

(E48) I wish to have your response soon. (2015-01 Zhi Gao)

(E49) I am looking forward to your reply. (2015-16 Ming Liu)

(E50) I will appreciate any feedback from you. (2015-02 Qi Xin)

(E51) If there is any problem, please feel free to let me know. (2015-10 Hong Cai)

Examples (E48) and (E49) above contain the mental verbs of wishing, in which the applicants expressed their eagerness to keep the contact on. Example (E50) is in the form of appreciating, showing the applicant's gratitude towards the professor's reply. The graduation term of "any" with "feedback" indicates that the applicant was open to negative, positive or constructive response, which places little imposition on the recipient and could invite a response. In Example (E51) is in the form of a direct speech act of request but accompanied by the politeness marker of "please". Using response solicitors is a strategic means to build up solidarity. As long as there is a chance to keep the communication on, the common ground is possible to be established. Only in continuous interaction will applicants have more opportunities to compete for their desired capital, the education offer.

4.2.2.5　Demonstrating Loyalty

Showing loyalty represents applicants' inclination to come closer to professors psychologically. Making promise is a linguistic realization of expressing loyalty.

(E52) ...if I couldn't be a visiting student in your group, I will abandon this programme. (2015-25 Xian He)

(E53) my hard work will never let you down. (2015-46 Guo Fang)

In Example (E52), the loyalty is delivered in a conditional sentence, in which the applicant said he would give up the opportunity if he couldn't receive the offer from the professor. It is a firm promise as well as determined loyalty—he would only choose the targeted professor and no one else. In Example (E53) the utterance "my hard work will never let you down" stipulates to the professor that the applicant was dependable due to his hard work. The usage of the mood intensifier "never" excludes all other disappointing possibilities. Another example is given below.

189

(E54) Since you are my top choice, I hope to study in your group... (2013-07-11 Huyang Long)

In Example (E54), Huyang's loyalty to his targeted professor is delivered through the upgraded appreciation term of "top choice", which means that the offer from his targeted professor has all priority. He recalled,

(I10) Actually, compared to last year's situation, I am a little more cunning this year. Actually at that time, I didn't make a firm decision to go there [accept the offer]. But I told him directly, that you are my top choice. (Interview transcripts 2013-May Huyang Long)

The loyalty shown through words might not be the applicant's real thought just as Huyang reflected that actually he didn't make up his mind yet to join the professor's group at that time. The "top choice" statement gave his words to the professor and if the professor had the same idea, an offer would be issued soon. In the latter part of interview, he mentioned that he received the offer very quickly after he wrote that the professor was his priority, which exhibits perfectly the perlocutionary force of demonstrating loyalty.

Loyalty also involves the affective dimension of a relation or *guanxi*. The move to show loyalty through linguistic expressions in *Taoci* emails was strategically intended to consolidate the affectionate bonding, particularly when professors were hesitating to make the final call about an offer in the later period of application. The loyalty delivers applicants' firm inclination towards a certain professor and thus has symbolic power to make the professor believe in the applicant's genuine and sincere application for his supervision or his research group. However, this speech act could probably risk professors' negative face to a great extent. It would drag the professor into an awkward position if there is a hard decision to be made, putting professors into an emotional dilemma.

4.2.2.6   Keeping Contact

Frequent contact leads to familiarity between interlocutors. By taking active turns during email communication, applicants can manage to keep the *Taoci* ball rolling with their supervisors. Turn taking is concerned about the procedural aspect of the participation domain in rapport building (Spencer-Oatey, 2007b). In the email data, a "turn" is defined as a battery of email contacts pivoting around a specific topic, which differs from the popular conception of "turn" in conversation analysis. In the *Taoci* situation, an applicant usually initiates turns more often than professors, and professors' word amount in email is far less than that of applicants. In the four full email packages, all of the four participants initiated more email turns than their targeted

191

professors. Take Huyang's case as an example. In Huyang's package of 25 pieces of email texts, 15 were from Huyang and 10 from the targeted supervisor, Professor Kiong. These are grouped into 9 turns, according to thematic relevance as Table 4.1 shows.

Table 4.1 Turn sequence in Huyang's *Taoci* package (F1 means the first follow-up action. F2, F3 likewise.)

Turn	Range	Topical Relevance	Who initiates?
Turn 1	Email 1–Email 4	Consultation about possible PhD position	Huyang
Turn 2	Email 5–Email 7	Follow-up about application status (F1)	Huyang
Turn 3	Email 8–Email 10	Updated resume	Huyang
Turn 4	Email 11–Email12	Possible offer	Kiong
Turn 5	Email 13–Email 15	Follow-up about accepting the possible offer (F2)	Huyang
Turn 6	Email 16–Email 18	Notifying about fellowship	Kiong
Turn 7	Email 19–Email 21	Follow-up about official offer (F3)	Huyang
Turn 8	Email 22	Notifying about confirming file	Huyang
Turn 9	Email 23–Email 25	Seeking help about visa interview	Huyang

Among the 9 turns, seven email turns were initiated by Huyang and only two were by the supervisor. There were three email follow-ups by Huyang, about his application status, about accepting the possible offer and about the official offer, when Huyang had not heard from the supervisor immediately. The asymmetry of email turn-taking showed that Huyang self-selected the turn more often, indicating that he was a proactive applicant with a strong desire to be acknowledged for his personal quality of "taking initiative" by the supervisor. Though the frequent initiation might inflict imposition on the hearer's negative face want (Brown, Levinson, 1987) or equity rights (Spencer-Oatey, 2007b), the action resulted in Huyang's more association with Professor Kiong and paved the way for solidarity. In other words, the contact itself was the very way of pulling *guanxi*. Once the contact was made, *guanxi* had a chance to be produced or reproduced. Huyang reflected on his behavior of keeping frequent contact.

(I11) "After that [positive feedback from the professor], I kept contact with him, or kept contact for the sake of contact, just that situation. It is also a kind of *Taoci*, because you keep giving him a signal, that you haven't sold yourself out, and you still want to go to his lab, that you are still my choice. And then certainly, he would put you in his waiting list." (Interview transcripts 2013-May Huyang Long)

To keep frequent contact with targeted professors is not all about exchanging new information. The contact itself is taken as the end, just like phatic communion, or the necessity to "say something even where there is hardly anything to say" (Malinowski, 1947: 316). It

193

works for the maintenance of the accumulated relationship snowballed in previous contacts. In the interview quote below, Qingwan explained why she also sent out emails during festivals, with no explicit concern about her application issue.

(I12) Qingwan: "Actually, at that moment, I did it on purpose. I'm not interested in their holidays, so I didn't send wish email. I only sent wish email on the festivals we Chinese have. Although some people may not take the Spring Festival, it is related to their research, related to the East Asia. Researchers in this field all know Spring Festival. The wish email is in fact like a reminder, a sense of self-existence, a reminder of my existence. And then, I thought quite a lot then."

Researcher: what do you mean by a reminder of self-existence?

Qingwan: Just to keep contact … The truth is that, after the completion of online application and submission of hardcopy materials, a long time has passed. What kind of ways should I use to tell the professor that I am still alive … The wish email, mid-autumn day and spring festival, to me is effective to tell my self-existence. (Interview transcripts 2014-Dec. Qingwan Li)

Qingwan described her keeping frequent contact as a way to prove her self-existence (*tell the professor that I am still alive*), which was regarded as the precondition to keep the relation. Applicants usually apply for more than one university and contacted several potential supervisors at the same time, which are also known by foreign professors. By alerting professors that they are still available

194

through frequent contact, to some extent, give professors a reference for their offer decision. Hence, in my understanding, the reminder of "self-existence" has another deeper indication—the applicant is still interested in the professor and available to be enrolled.

Traditional *renqing* usually develops through the exchange of gifts on such occasions as marriages, birthdays, and funerals (Hwang, 1988; Yang, 1994). However, in contemporary China, in particular in urban and metropolitan areas, *jiaoqing*[①] is often used in place of *renqing* (Chen & Chen 2004). Jiao literally means interaction or exchange, clearly capturing the ongoing interactive and reciprocal nature of *guanxi*. Therefore, frequent contact, like what Chinese applicants do in their *Taoci* email could facilitate *guanxi-building* as it nurtures the important element of *qing* (feelings) in *guanxi*. The accumulation of interaction will increase the closeness between each other and creates a chance for social capital of *guanxi* networking.

4.2.2.7   Switching Code

In *Taoci* emails, switching from English to another language that both parties know signals a bonding of a shared linguistic capital or a shared cultural background. Examples are given below.

---

① In Chinese, it is written as "交情".

(E55) Best regards,

　　Xiaoyun Fang

　　期待回复

　　方筱云

　　　　　　　(2015-07 Xiaoyun Fang)

(E56) Thank you for your attention! Joyeux Noel!

　　Sincerely Yours,

　　***

　　　　　　　(2015-39 Yuanli Jiang)

(E57)本当にありがとうございます

　　Best Regards,

　　Sincerely,

　　****

　　　　　　　(2015-44 Yan Tang)

In Example (E55), the applicant switched from English to Chinese at the end of her email to solicit response. From the addressing term used at the beginning and the content in the email body, it is known that the contacted professor was a Chinese or at least of Chinese origin. Changing to the shared Chinese language demonstrates not only the shared language but also probably the cultural common ground, which brings the two sides closer. In Example (E56), the applicant switched to French to express his gratitude, because he targeted a French professor in France. In the excerpt of (E57), the applicant shifted to Japanese to express her gratitude again. The targeted professor was a Japanese as the professor's name showed. The fact that applicants purposefully diverges from a particular code to another one displays their possession of multiple language capitals which might be necessary for their study-abroad education, and more importantly serves for the purpose of solidarity through indicating the fact of knowing the same language.

The occurrence of each speech act under the solidarity-oriented strategy in all *Taoci* email texts is given in Fig. 4.2. The category of keeping frequent contact is a textual level feature, so it is not calculated here. Nonetheless in all of the four sets of *Taoci* email package the participants played the role of starting each new turn. Calling for further association is the most prominent speech act, followed by introducing intermediary. Articulating previous association only occurs 12 times, which indicates that most applicants and their targeted professors are unfamiliar with each other. Switching code, partially demonstrating their common cultural background and partially their linguistic competence, occurs only four times.

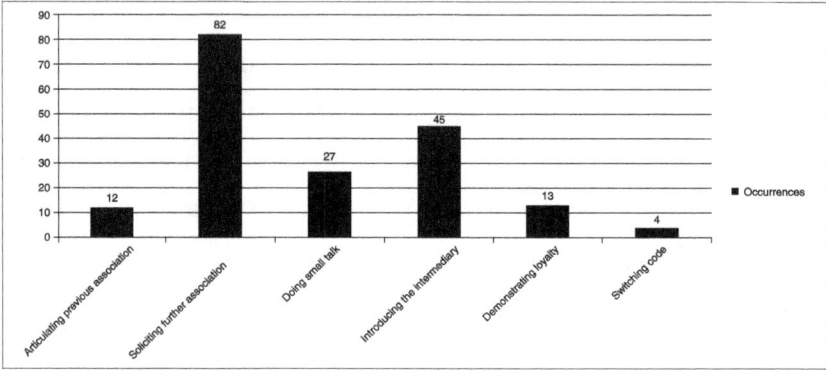

Fig. 4.2   Solidarity-oriented strategy distribution

4.2.3   Sectional Discussion: Investment with Social Capital

In the meso speech act of pulling *guanxi*, two broad types of strategy are distinguished: deference-oriented and solidarity-oriented, both of which include a spectrum of micro speech acts with rich linguistic instances. Pulling *guanxi* is used to invest in the social capital of building harmonious relationship with professors, which could be beneficial for the application issue.

The deference-oriented strategy shows Chinese applicants' appreciation and respect for foreign professors' authority, confirming their deferential relational identity constructed in intercultural student-

198

faculty email in Chen (2015) and deferential politeness in Huang (2015). It actually creates a great difference between applicants and their targeted professors, either in a self-abasing way or an others-raised way. The solidarity-oriented strategy engages applicants with foreign professors into the same group by drawing attention to the commonality between them. It emphasizes togetherness between the two parties. In this sense, the solidarity-oriented speech acts are complementary to the deference-oriented ones, which leads to an interesting phenomenon of the Chinese style of pulling *guanxi*: it can be either pulled towards "me" (closeness) or pushed away from "me" (deference), both of which could generate *guanxi* that will become pragmatically important for *guanxi* pullers.

Applicants' keenness to show deference to and closeness with their targeted professors derive from the latter's alluring capitals that applicants long for and compete for with international rivalries, for instance, the economic capital of research funding that professors could allocate to support applicants, the cultural capital or more specifically their academic capital of research achievement, even their social capital of being involved in the applicants' desirable academic circle. All of these capitals that professors then possessed contribute to the symbolic capital, i.e. gate-keeper power, authority, prestige, recognized by

199

Chinese applicants, which explains the fact that Chinese applicants spare no effort making compliment, showing loyalty, introducing their middlemen, etc.

The observation of the email content and interview transcripts shows that Chinese applicants are endowed with different amounts of social capital and linguistic capital. The social capital of having a middleman and previous encounters is an available resource to build up *guanxi* network based on existing relationship. The use of English to communicate demonstrates their linguistic capital. Switching to other codes not only boasts their multilingual ability, but also implies a sense or an understanding of shared cultural background. These capitals are strategically interwound through the uses of concrete linguistic forms to establish interpersonal bonding with foreign professors, and to invest in applicants' future and imagined identity of becoming international scholars, or researchers.

The deference-oriented strategy such as addressing formally, making apologies, humbling self, and exhibiting a formal style, are closely related to Chinese lower-status' maintaining structural *li* in front of the higher-status. In particular, the speech act of humbling self is often considered inherent to the Chinese spirit of being modest (Tyler, 1995; Chen, 1993). The solidarity-oriented strategy demonstrates

200

Chinese people's attitudinal warmth (Bi, 1996) and preference to keep a harmonious relationship with others so that this *guanxi* will become "useful" sometime in the future. For example, introducing the intermediary and articulating previous association are recognized as strong characteristics of the indigenous concept of pulling *guanxi* in Chinese society (Chang, Bolt, 1991; Chen, 2004), reflecting their sensitivity to counting *guanxi* as an instrumental networking resource and fitting the collectivism of construing self as connected and relational entity in Chinese traditional culture (Fei, 1948; Chang, 2010). Some speech acts may not be recognized as *guanxi*-pulling in its indigenous sense but as routine generic moves, such as addressing formally and showing gratitude. However, all of them are intended to nurture a harmonious relationship with professors, which would be helpful for application from the applicants' perspective. In this sense, we can understand the local concepts of Chinese *guanxi* and pulling *guanxi* as enlarged or lifted to a global register, accompanying the enregisterment (Agha, 1999; Dong, 2010) of the Beijing dialect *Taoci* into a national term among the community of international education application.

A specific form of speech act is inseparable from the speaker's habitus and identity, as Bourdieu argued "What speaks is not the utterance, the language, but the whole social person" (1977: 653).

201

Habitus provides a socially and cultural structured explanation for the formation of identity constructed through discourse. The ways of being polite through showing attitudinal warm, being modest and complimenting the higher-status are related with the *guanxi*-oriented habitus, which celebrates the traditional Chinese Confucianism of valuing interpersonal *li* and interpersonal *guanxi*, and its vestige is still observable in *Taoci* emails. For example, the hierarchical value of li between student and teacher was cherished as well as strengthened through such speech act as addressing formally, humbling self, and apologizing. The sensitivity to creating and/or maintaining good relationship with other people is represented through such speech acts as articulating previous encounter, showing loyalty and calling for further association. These features confirm that the East Asians would encourage deference and modesty to superiors in line with greater power distance and relationship-oriented values (Cheung, 2004).

On the other hand, the *guanxi*-oriented habitus and its generative linguistic forms are probably undergoing constant challenge from the self-promotion spirit advocated by the Western culture featuring competition and individualism. The Western style tends to encourage positive self-appraisal, assertiveness and independence even in front of authority, which is consistent with agentic and economic-oriented

202

values (Elliot, Chirkov, Kim et al., 2001), as self is construed as independent, separate and distinct entity in the individualistic culture, and a person is responsible for the main task of standing out or becoming distinguished from others through self-sufficiency and self-promotion. Due to the globalized competition and marketization as well as great pressure from the stereotypical criticism of Asian people's over-courtesy, humbleness and indirectness, the *guanxi*-oriented habitus is incongruent with its field or market (Bourdieu, 1991), the field of international offer hunting. Facing the delicacy of doing *Taoci*, Chinese applicants have also developed other discourse strategies to make convincing self-presentation in the high-stake competition, which is the theme of the next subsection.

4.3   Speech Act as Promoting Self

This section is about the meso speech act of self-promoting, in which linguistic analysis is concerned about how applicants demonstrate their personal competence to attract foreign professors' attention.

The meso speech act of promoting self, in particular their academic competence, is about applicants' intellectual readiness, professional and practical experiences for PhD programs, which represent their academic capital acquired slowly over a long time of education or training. Academic capital is a constituent of cultural capital, referring to any forms, embodied, objectified, or institutionalized, of capital that is related to a person's academic competence, ability and potential, for example skill, books, articles, awards, etc.

Following Pierre Bourdieu's argument of speech act as the encounter between linguistic habitus and linguistic market, if one wishes to produce discourse successfully within a particular field, one must observe the rules and formalities of that field. In the global offer hunting process, the field of international higher education, on the one hand, leans to the value of self-promotion advocated by the Western English-speaking culture, and on the other hand, forces applicants to promote themselves due to the fierce competition for rare educational capitals. Previous researches on the application genre reviewed in Chapter 2 are evidence of applicants' reconciliation between the norms of the field they participated in and the discourse features in their local cultures. With regard to the subject matter of *Taoci* emails, the speech act of presenting self-competence also testifies to speech act as a result of the tension between habitus and field (Bourdieu, 1991).

"In order to perceive and seize the potential opportunities, which is allegedly open to all, subjects have to possess a minimum amount of economic and cultural capital, constituting a key entry condition to a field" (Bourdieu, Wacquant, 1992: 124). For graduate programs, applicants' academic potential and competence are the minimum amount as well as the most convincing form of capital to persuade supervisors to recruit them. Hence, they would try their best to present them as competent as possible in order to get a position in the international higher education field. In the prize application genre in Hyland (2012), applicants are described to display a skillful adoption of a disciplinary value system, evaluation, research expertise and (or) self-aggrandizement in order to construct an academic competent identity. What Chinese applicants did in their *Taoci* discourse resembles that of the prize application discourse, but with subtle differences. Two broad strategies of Me-oriented and Us-oriented are abstracted and each with micro speech acts illustrated with specific examples. Here "Me" means Chinese applicants and "Us" means Chinese applicants and foreign professors as a dyad.

4.3.1   Me-oriented Strategy: Advertising Self

The Me-oriented strategy is all about a show of how competent Chinese applicants appear to foreign professors, i.e. advertising myself as a potential competent academia. It overlaps with Bhatia's move of self-appraisal in job application letters but subsumes richer details. This higher-level strategy is realized through such micro speech acts as

205

self-evaluating, introducing academic background, listing achievement, specifying research/experience, and forecasting, which are intermingled with the investment of applicants' existing and potential cultural capital.

4.3.1.1 Self-evaluating

"Self-evaluating" means that applicants resort to explicit evaluation-laden lexicon or structure to lay bare their skill and competence that would be helpful for obtaining an offer in the competition of global-offer hunting. Applicants' *Taoci* emails are imbued with different types of evaluative terms, but only those evaluations related to a competent candidate image are discussed below in terms of the appraised subjects.

(a) Positive Affect

Affect is about people's emotional status (Martin, White, 2008). It is to display likeness or dis-likeness, inclinational or disinclination, security or insecurity, satisfaction or dissatisfaction towards a certain subject. Two types of affect are generalized, contributing to applicants' claim for their competence.

(E58) But I am **willing to learn new stuff**... (2014-02 Ying Li)

(E59) I am also **passionate** about applications of psychology in real life. (2014-09-01 Pianhong Yin)

(E60) I **love** doing research, because only doing research can satisfy my curiosity.

(2014-08-04 Yunyang Liu)

(E61) And **I enjoy** the entire experience... (2013-05-01 Ran Xia)

Ying Li in Example (E58) claimed that she was willing to learn new stuff after she introduced her ideas about her future research, which revealed that she had a strong curiosity and motivation for new things. Pianhong Yin in Example (E59) said she was passionate about practical psychology and Yunyang Liu in Example (E60) expressed his love for doing research. Both "passionate" and "love" showed highly intensified inclination. Example (E61) is a little different. The mental verb of "enjoy" was used to deliver Ran Xia's happiness, which originated from his working experience. A person who could gain happiness from researches sounds like an internally motivated candidate with research potential. Although these affective appraisals only pinpoint applicants' emotional status instead of their capacity, it reveals that they possessed the fundamental temperament for doing research, i.e. their love for doing research.

(b) Self-credited Ability

Self-credited ability means that applicants appraise themselves as able or competent individuals by using explicit evaluation terms. Two major themes are appraised explicitly, their language ability and research ability, which constitutes the minimum amount of their linguistic capital and academic capital (Bourdieu, Wacquant, 1992) to be used for their investment in overseas education.

Most of our applicants went to English-speaking countries for their overseas education. Even among those who went to non-English-speaking regions, English was the lingua franca in their programs. Thus, English proficiency is directly related to the application issue as the preliminary requirement in order to join international programs in targeted countries. Foreign institutions set up specific standards for international applicants' language ability. English proficiency certificate is required in the official application portfolio. Still, some applicants specified explicitly how competent they were in command of English, by listing their embodied form or institutionalized form of language capital. Examples are given below.

(E62) I have taken a TOEFL test and scored 108 (total 120), so **I have the ability** to further my research in ***. (2015-04 Feifei Hu)

(E63) My English and German are both **fluent enough** to undertake research studies in your research environment. (2015-46 Guo Fang)

(E64) I am **able** to use English as a tool in writing and communication **proficiently**, and I've passed CET-6 (College English Test by the Ministry of Education), GRE, and TOEFL exams. (2015-13 Lan Luo)

208

In Example (E62), the applicant gave a specific score of his TOFEL test, 108 out of 120, which indicated an advanced level. The applicant added an explicit self-appraisal of "I have the ability" to emphasize that language would not be a problem for his further research in the foreign institution. Similarly, in Example (E63), the applicant was not only good at English but also German. His language was self-claimed "fluent enough" for him to carry out researches abroad. In Example (E64), the adjective of "able" and adverb of "proficiently" were two direct self-assessment of the applicant's language proficiency level. The succeeding clause further specifies it by listing a series of English examinations that he had passed: CET-6, GRE and TOEFL. The English proficiency certificates, and the institutionalized form of cultural capital, are invested as affordance in their application.

In addition to self-assessment of language ability, applicants also claimed that they were capable in doing research via explicit evaluation. The terms of "excellent research ability" in Example (E65), "a researcher with great energy", "strong self-study ability" in Example (E66) and "a competent researcher" in Example (E67) below contain strong self-credited values. With such intensification terms as "excellent", "great", "strong", the claimed ability is aggrandized. These appreciation terms boast their research capacity as Hyland's

(2012) prize applicants did in their application letters.

(E65) With **excellent research ability**, I am... (2015-14 Mei Li)

(E66) ...I am a researcher **with great energy**, broad interest **and strong self-study ability**. (2015-26 Yuan Zhao)

(E67) ...and my experience that accumulated during previous study may enable me a competent researcher. (2014-08-01 Yunyang Liu)

(c) Showing Skills

Relevant skills, like coding in computer science, doing a specific kind of experimentation, are especially indispensable for science major students. Skill is a sort of embodied cultural capital (Bourdieu, 1977), engrained as body hexis over a long time of training and practice where habitus could be formed in this process. In *Taoci* emails, applicants' skill is manifested either through explicit evaluation or an implicit way.

(E68) I am also **very skilled** in programming (I am in charge of all the simulation work in my current research group). (2014-08-04 Yunyang Liu)

(E69) With the training in Ph.D. program at *** School, I have **good programming skills** and understanding of marketing models. (2015-10 Hong Cai)

(E70) Over the years, I feel that I have **gained many essential professional skills** ... am **familiar** with some geological software like Petrel, Discovery, CorelDraw, and GeoFrame. (2015-13 Lan Luo)

In Example (E68), Yunyang Liu claimed that he was "very

skilled in programming" and he added that he took charge of the simulation work as a piece of evidence to support his skillfulness in programming. In Example (E69), Hong Cai said he had "good programming skills" and in Example (E70), Lan Luo used the phrases of "many essential professional kills" and "familiar with". The skills were not only presented but also intensified through such up-scaling terms as "very", "good", "many" to emphasize the amount and quality of the embodied capital that they possessed, which is welded as their investment affordance to impress foreign professors.

(E71) During this time, I have already managed **some skills** such as Linux commands, Shell Scripts, Eclipse, SVN, Putty, Google GWT and Java, C languages. (2014-04 Zhou Zhou)

The example listed above differs a little from the previous discussion in that Zhou Zhou used the phrase of "managed some skills". The graduation term of "some" is usually located at the down-grading scale of amount. However, in the rest of the sentence, he had a long list of the software skills he grasped: Linux commands, Shell Scripts, Eclipse, SVN, Putty, Google GWT and Java, C languages, which actually overturn the de-evaluation term of "some". This could be related to the value of modesty advocated by Chinese students in front of higher-status professors. It is similar to the micro speech act of humbling self, but the two differs functionally in that the former was oriented to academic self-presentation while the later to pulling *guanxi*.

(d) My Experience

"Evaluating my experience" means to show what applicants have gained from their learning/working/research experience, also a kind of embodied capital, which could be beneficial for their imagined future as overseas students.

(E72) I **benefit a great deal** from the study of both physical mechanism and computational skills. (2013-05-01 Ran Xia)

In Example (E72), Ran Xia asserted that he obtained a lot of benefits from the learning experience. The word "benefit" indicates a positive evaluation towards this experience, while the phrase of "a great deal" serves to boost that benefit.

(E73) Besides what I mentioned above, I have **a lot of practical experiences** on doing scientific research. (2014-08-04 Yunyang Liu)

(E74) In addition, I received **extensive training** in sequence stratigraphy and depositional systems analysis during my graduate studies. (2015-13 Lan Luo)

In Example (E73), "a lot of practical experiences" indicates that the applicant had accumulated research experience useful for his future work, and "extensive training" in Example (E74) shows the applicant's plentiful training as embodied capital shaped during his graduate education. The intensifier of "a lot of" and "extensive" upgrades the amount of their experience or training and amplifies how competent the applicants were in doing research work.

(E75) While there, I acquired much **valuable** experience, **not only in** outdoor exploration like regional geological survey in Zhoukoudian, Beidaihe, and Inner Mongolia, **but also in** laboratory affairs such as the proximate analysis of coal, coal facies analysis, and the organic geochemical experiment of coal. (2015-13 Lan Luo)

In Example (E75) contains an evaluation of the quality of the applicant's experience. The appreciation term of "valuable" appeals to the worth of "my experience". This worth is further specified by the conjunction term of "not only ... but also" to show that the applicant had experiences in different research areas.

(E76) Through my **active participation** in a number of research projects and programming, I have gained **some working experience** in these areas. (2014-06-01 Liguo Zhao1)

In Example (E76), Liguo Zhao appraised himself as an active participant by using the expression of "my active participation" and he continued with the expression of "gained some working experience". Similar to Zhou Zhou's case, the down-scaling usage of "some" dims Liguo's working experience.

(e) My Knowledge

Applicants usually claims they have a good command of the knowledge in their research fields. For example, in Example (E77) below, the terms of "solid" and "comprehensive" intensified the applicant's educational background in geology. This solidness and comprehensiveness derived from both his education and his professional training, which became habitus inculcated in his disciplinary identity. In Example (E78), the applicant claimed that he had profound knowledge in the subject of chemistry, which would be convincing because his targeted professor did interdisciplinary research of chemistry and engineering.

(E77) I have a **solid and comprehensive background** in geology which was gained not only from my academic studies, but also from my professional career in an oil company. (2015-13 Lan Luo)

(E78) …that I, as a non-chemistry majored student, have **a relatively profound knowledge** on Chemistry. (2014-08-01 Yunyang Liu)

The five themes of love for research, research ability, skills, experiences and knowledge showed that applicants resorted to various self-evaluation vocabularies or syntactic constructions to represent their cultural capital, and their potential as competent academics or researchers. Moreover, the self-evaluation discourse has the dominant "I"-fronted sentence structure and upgrading evaluation forces,

214

notwithstanding some exceptions of downscalers, which displays Chinese applicants' confidence as well as their agency in making a convincing self-presentation. This counters the popular argument that Chinese students were reticent, reserved, and passive when they communicated with authorities. The bold thrust of personal worth in front of higher-status professionals poses a stark contrast with the traditional self-efficacy value cherished and still practiced by Chinese people. Situated in the global competition pool for better educational resources, the new generation of study-abroad applicants has developed new ways of communicative strategies and practices, which are the reflection of the newly engrained dispositions of habitus of being self-expressive characterizing the western individualism.

4.3.1.2   Introducing Academic Background

Academic background tells about applicants' information in terms of their institutional education (including major, program, degree), research interest, and taking courses. Most of these are in the form of plain statement, without obvious evaluative modifications. The introduction of academic background, according to the timeline, can be divided into three parts in terms of timeline, present, past and near future, indicating their existing and potential academic capital, and their present and imagined identity.

(a) Current Position: "Who I Am"

"Who I am" refers to an applicant's current position in a Chinese educational institution when s/he makes the application, for example, major and education program, the name of their affiliated departments or universities. The simplest form, exemplified in the following two instances, is to declare the name of their currently affiliated institutions, which was used in every initial email.

(E79) I'm ***, from *** University, China. (2015-14 Mei Li)

(E80) My name is Zhi Gao, from *** University. (2015-01 Zhi Gao)

Some applicants would specify their major for their education. The structure of *my major is …* and I *major in …* is the dominant form. The various majors exemplified below in Example (E81), (E82), (E83) and (E84) (*pure mathematics, quaternary ecology, jurisprudence, constitution and administrative law*) showed applicants' identification with their respective discipline and specific academic community.

(E81) …and my current major is pure mathematics. (2015-36 Zhen Fan)

(E82) My major is quaternary ecology. (2015-46 Guo Fang)

(E83) I am majoring in jurisprudence… (2015-14 Mei Li)

(E84) I major in constitution and administrative law. (2015-20 Xun Jin)

More complicated expressions expand the content with a

216

combination of the name of project, department, major, and/or grade.

(E85) Currently I am a student working for the degree of Master of Philosophy (Mphil) in the department of *** of *** University. (2013-01 Qiang Miao)

(E86) I am a Chinese second-year graduate student majoring in theoretical and evolutionary ecology of Beijing *** University. (2014-02 Ying Li)

(E87) My name is Nan Wang, a third year Ph.D. candidate (five years straight towards Ph.D.) (2015-06 Qing Huang)

Qiang Miao in Example (E85) pointed out his current status as graduate student by saying that he was "working for the degree of Master of Philosophy (Mphil)", and added the name of his affiliated department. Ying Li not only mentioned his major but also his grade in Example (E86). In Example (E87) the applicant even specified that her PhD project was "five years straight towards Ph.D.". Actually, for foreign professors, they might not fully understand what was implied in the phrase of "five years straight toward Ph.D.". When I was in the USA, I consulted two American professors about this expression, and both of them felt a little confused at the first sight of it. In China, only excellent undergraduate could be enrolled in the so-called "five years straight towards Ph.D. project" immediately after they graduate with a bachelor's diploma. The connotation of excellence in this kind of expression hasn't been delivered successfully.

The institutional affiliation relation is also realized through other relational verbs rather than copula verbs, such as the verb of "enrolled", which should be "am enrolled" in Example (E88), and "come from" in Example (E89) below.

(E88) Currently I am enrolled (am enrolled) in *** majoring in legal philosophy and legal methodology… (2015-15 Yi Wang)

(E89) I come from the Department of Political Science, School of Government at *** University. (2015-22 Rui Wang)

Most applicants were then enrolled as students at university. Nonetheless, a small number of them just graduated from school and worked for a while. Their working status was only transitional as they were still working on their application for overseas education programs.

(E90) I am … currently working at *** as a research assistant. (2013-04-01 Chu Gao1)

(E91) …, and also a member of the Key Laboratory of Mathematics, Informatics and Behavioral Semantics, Ministry of Education, *** University, Beijing China. (2015-27 Panpan Wei)

(E92) …and I am the post-bachelor research assistant… (2013-02 Si Chen)

Chu Gao claimed to be a research assistant at *** institute in Example (E90). The applicant in Example (E91) said he was a member of the Key Laboratory affiliated to the Ministry of Education. The role of research assistant and key lab membership was a convincing credential for application, a kind of symbolic capital. Example (E92) was a little different. Si Chen used a creative term of "post-bachelor" to modify "research assistant", which incurred doubt about whether there existed a "post-bachelor" position in real. According to the interview, she explained that she just graduated from A University that summer and she didn't want to look for a job immediately because she still had the dream of going abroad. Therefore, she stayed in her supervisor's lab to do some research and prepared for the application next year. The term of "post-bachelor research assistant" gave her a symbolic title to use for her application like Chu Gao's institutional position of "research assistant" and the membership of "the Key Laboratory of Mathematics, Informatics and Behavioral Semantics, Ministry of Education" in Example (E91). These titles were turned into symbolic capitals for applicants to use as affordances for their imagined future of studying-abroad dream.

A majority of students also detail their research interest. "introducing my interest" is distinguished from the strategy of "claiming shared interest" in the later discussion in that the former was more about "what I am interested in" while the latter focused on "what we are instated in". In addition, "my academic interest" is an inherent

219

part of an applicant's major.

(E93) My interests are distributed system, parallel computing and data mining etc. (2014-04 Zhou Zhou)

(E94) My academic interests mainly lie in the area of computational physics in materials with novel properties and device design based on first-principles calculation. (2013-05-02 Ran Xia)

In Example (E93), Zhou Zhou listed his interest in "distributed system, parallel computing and data mining", which were all related to his "computer science" major. In Example (E94) Ran Xia specified his interest of "computational physics in materials with novel properties and device design based on first-principles calculation". Showing what they were interested in was another way to demonstrate their academic ability. The passion for and interest in research is the source of academic achievement. Academic interest, like knowledge and skills, is integrated into their disciplinary disposition of habitus to become academics or researchers in their own disciplines.

(b) Educational Experience: "Who I Was"

Applicants also resort to their previous educational experiences to establish credentials by specifying their received degree and relevant courses taken. In particular, a bachelor's degree or master's degree represents the institutionalized cultural capital earned from their previous professional training.

(E95) Before studying in A University, I received **the degree of Bachelor** of Science in EE department of W University, China. (2013-01 Qiang Miao)

(E96) I **got the bachelor's degree and master's degree** in computer science from Beijing *** University and *** University respectively. (2015-10 Hong Cai)

(E97) I **achieved my Degree of B.S of Biology** in *** University in 2007, due to the performance in undergraduate study I was admitted to the Graduate School of *** University **without examination**. (2014-02 Ying Li)

Yu Miao in Example (E95) and Ying Li in Example (E97) told professors about their completion of bachelor's program at a famous university, and the applicant in Example (E96) obtained his bachelor's and master's degree then. The achieved degrees guaranteed that the applicants had gone through comprehensive and essential intellectual training in a certain discipline and were ready to continue further higher education in the next stage of graduate program. What is interesting, Ying Li added that she was exempted from the graduate entrance examination of her current institute. In China, if students want to be enrolled in a MA or PhD project, they can either be recommended by their undergraduate schools or take the entrance examination. Only those outstanding students will be recommended and exempted from such competitive and selective examinations. Therefore, by telling the foreign professor that she didn't take the exam, Ying Li tried to impress the professor how excellent she was. However, to her targeted foreign professor, this strategy might not be that effective especially under the condition that he had no idea of the Chinese MA or PhD enrollment policy.

(E98) I was **an exchange student** at *** College last semester and I took the Cognitive Process **seminar**. (2014-09-01 Pianhong Yin)

In this example, Pianhong[①] proclaimed one of her educational experiences as an exchange student in an American college and she took a relevant seminar concerned about the psychology program that she was then applying for. She also mentioned the seminar professor's name, a famous figure known by her targeted professor too. Hence, the exchange program she attended demonstrated her credential and became a part of her academic capital as investment affordance.

(E99) To prepare for this plan, I ... have attended **a winter school** for earth system modeling held by Professor *** from LSCE and Professor *** from W, and have taken **some advanced statistical and physical courses** in related fields. (2013-04-01 Chu Gao1)

----

① Pianhong Yin was the only research participant who ever went abroad for a short-time program before her PhD program application.

222

(E100) In the latest two years, I am (was) **studying** on classification using spatio-temporal information and Markov random field (MRF) is adopted. (2015-05 Ling Xu)

In Example (E99), Chu Gao was narrating the courses he had taken related to the research direction of earth environment he set up for himself. The winter school about earth system modeling was directly linked to his research topic, and the advanced statistical and physical courses were useful for the research method. In Example (E100), the applicant claimed that she spent the past two years studying on "classification using spatio-temporal information", which showed that she had developed adequate knowledge and credential for the research.

(c) Educational Experience: "Who I Will Be"

For the application for a PhD program, obtaining a bachelor or master degree in their affiliated domestic universities is one of the prerequisites for being enrolled by foreign institutes. After telling their past and present educational background, some applicants would estimate the time of their graduation. It also delivered the message of the time "when I am available for my imagined future".

(E101) I will graduate this summer. (2013-03 Zhi Yu)

(E102) Since my current project started in 2009 when I was a sophomore, I will obtain my degree of M.S of Ecology in advanced in June, 2013. (2014-02 Ying Li)

(E103) I will get my master's degree this year. (2014-03 Lin Jiang)

In Example (E101), Zhi Yu didn't specify what degree he would receive, but the email co-text told the professor that he would get his MA degree that summer. In Example (E102), Ying Li claimed that she would have her degree in advance because she started her project earlier when she was still a sophomore. Lin Jiang would also get his master's degree in Example (E103), which would not be a problem for his enrollment into the foreign university. Compared to the PhD program application, applicants for visiting position rarely mentioned their graduation time, perhaps inasmuch as foreign professors had no strict time frame to expect their arrival and no requirement for their degree-achievement in the foreign institutes. But there was one case mentioning about the time to accomplish his doctor degree in Example (E104).

(E104) I will receive my doctor degree in 2016. (2015-21 Yao Sun)

To wrap up this subsection briefly, introducing educational background involved the use of applicants' cultural capital of education and degree, was employed as affordance to invest in the imagined study-abroad identity. To be more specific, the names of Chinese universities are usually associated with the ranking of universities in the nation's higher education system. All of the four universities, from which the

224

research participants came, enjoy well-recognized prestige not only domestically but also internationally as Chinese higher education has been catching up and becoming better known to the world. Therefore, these university names have become symbolic affordances for the applicants' self-presentation. So is the symbolic power embodied through major, department, interest, exchange experience and course-taking activities. To specify one's college education credential is to posit one's intellectual ability, even academic advantage in the fierce competition of global offer hunting. Their education, training and course-taking experiences have sedimented into academic habitus varying across disciplines, and endowed them with the symbolic capital that they could manipulate for investment into their future international education and imagined identity.

4.3.1.3   Elaborating on Experiences

In addition to just mentioning their research or experience, applicants specify in great detail what researches they have done or what experiences they have accumulated to further exhibit their academic competence.

(a) Specifying Research Field

In the foregoing subsection, applicants' interest is ascribed to their academic background. The research field is separated because "interest" was what applicants' subjective choice, while the research field refers to applicants' ongoing or past project, which they are either truly interested in, or required to carry out by their supervisors. "Research field" is usually realized through the grammatical component of subject. By contrast, "interest" is more often realized through the ideational component of complement participant (Halliday, 1992) within the "I"-fronted clause structure, which to some extent indicates the difference of agency in the two categories.

(E105) **My research concentration** was put on the study of millimeter wave devices, such as tunable RF MEMS filters and radiation pattern reconfigurable microstrip antennas. (2014-01-01 Nan Zhou)

In Example (E105), Nan Zhou detailed his research concentration on the study of millimeter wave devices by illustrating the wave devices of "tunable RF MEMS filters and radiation pattern reconfigurable microstrip antennas".

(E106) But in fact, **my field of research** during Master study, as a RA in Institute of Computing Technology (ICT), China Academy of Science, was Localization-Based Service, especially indoor location algorithm. (2014-05 Wei Hong)

(E107) **My research field** is in enterprise innovation, focusing on innovation and Performance: Evidence from China's industrial enterprises, which is also the subject of my research proposal. (2015-35 Fang Xi)

(E108) **My research area** is experimental geochemistry, mainly about Hydrothermal Diamond Anvil Cell (HDAC) and micro Raman spectroscopy. (2015-02 Qi Xin)

In both Example (E106) and (E107), the subject of "my field of research" is used with respective specification of the research details: "Localization-Based Service, especially indoor location algorithm" and "focusing on innovation and Performance: Evidence from China's industrial enterprises". Another type of specifying research field is the synonym of "area" in Example (E108), detailing the experimental geochemistry by using "mainly about Hydrothermal Diamond Anvil Cell (HDAC) and micro Raman spectroscopy".

In addition to the synonymy cluster of "research field", other ideational expressions like "dissertation topic" and "efforts of research" respectively in Example (E109) and (E110) give an explicit elaboration on their research topics.

(E109) **My doctoral dissertation topic** is mainly about the production, circulation and regulation of copper resource, like ore ingot and copper ware between the South and North of China in Shang and Zhou dynasty. (2015-04 Feifei Hu)

(E110) **My primary efforts of research are**: Cooperative Dynamics on Complex Networks, Evolutionary Game Theory (population dynamics, evolution of ecosystem, and mechanisms in maintaining biological diversity), Social Behaviors (cooperation, conflict, punishment, and retaliation), and Big Data Sets (human mobility pattern, infectious diseases, voting behavior, and financial systems). (2015-25 Xiao He)

There are also instances of using verbal predicate to introduce the research details, such as the expression of "focusing upon" in Example (E111) and "working on" in Example (E112) below, the former of which specifies the applicant's research concentration of "unconventional geology, sequence stratigraphy, and basin analysis" while the second of which shows that he participated the research project of "Integrated Land Use Planning for Resource-Saving and Environment-Friendly Society in Central China" with a specification of the research method "systems dynamics, CLUE and CA model".

(E111) At the present time, I ... **focusing upon** unconventional geology, sequence stratigraphy, and basin analysis. (2015-13 Lan Luo)

(E112) Currently, I am **working on** a project named "Integrated Land Use Planning for Resource-Saving and Environment-Friendly Society in Central China" through systems dynamics, CLUE and CA model. (2015-33 Xi Cui)

The expatiation of "my research field" gives more details about their specific research area. The usage of professional terms demonstrate their research focus instead of giving a general description of their interests and constitutes a part of their academic capital and a more

228

convincing evidence of their qualification for application.

(b) Detailing Research Experience—the Reporting Practice

A more complex way to demonstrate applicants' research ability is to report the details of their research experience, such as what they did, what role they played in the team, what expertise they were in command of. Four types of linguistic resources are categorized by referring to Hyland's (2002, 2012) analysis of academic discourse.

Highlighting researcher's agency. There is a high frequency of the structure of "I+Action" when applicants specified their working experiences, which implicated a strong sense of agency. Hyland (2002) classified three types of activity in reporting verbs: Research (Real-World) Acts (e.g. *analyze, calculate, assay, explore, plot, recover*), Cognition Acts (e.g. *believer, conceptualize, suspect, assume, view*) and Discourse Acts (e.g. *ascribe, discuss, hypothesize, report, state*). The research acts represent experimental activities or actions carried out in the real world, which is the most prominent category discovered in the present research. The action is about the real-world research procedures that applicants took in their research or experiment.

(E113) **I joined** the lab of our institute in September 2010 and **began to do research** on the design, fabrication and testing of a carbon nanotube Pirani vacuum gauge. **I used** the Dielectrophoretic (DEP) method on assembling CNTs between electrodes without the aid of Focused Ion Beam (FIB) and **used** SEM to observe the assembly result. I explored the releasing technique making CNTs suspended over the substrate beneath alone, which greatly enhanced the performance of the vacuum gauge. (2013-07-01 Huyang Long)

(E114) **I have done** some research on the climate feedback of forest decline. I **have done** research in validating the cooling effect of forest decline by combining modeling result and paleo data of vegetation and ecological in North China for my undergraduate research program. (2013-04-01 Chu Gao1)

In Example (E113), there are five instances of the "I+Action" structure: *I joined the lab, I began to do, I used, I used, and I explored*, which explain the applicant's joining the lab, and research method as well as research subject. In Example (E114), the applicant listed the research topic in his research by using the form of "I have done" and "I have done", and an embedded action of method usage of "by combining". The person behind these first-person pronouns is the one who carried out various steps in the course of research, which indicates a high degree of agency. Therefore, the structure can be regarded as representing "how a meaning-less sign 'I' is coagulated into a meaning-full subject in the properties that are predicated on it" (Chiang, 2009: 268). Hyland (2012) also argued that the application of first person was not a casual or neutral choice. It represents a claim

230

for subjectivity. The pairing of first-person pronouns with material process verbs (Halliday, 1994) and with the past tense suggests a kind of professional competence since things could have been done otherwise. The agency embedded in such high-frequency syntactic structures also demonstrates the applicants' identity as initiative researchers.

Displaying expertise. In reporting research experiences, *Taoci* emails are usually imbued with professional and disciplinary terms, which serves as a demonstration of academic competence and an embodiment of disciplinary habitus. One cluster of the specialized terminologies is the usage of shortened forms.

(E115) Now I'm doing service work on **JetMET** trigger, collaborating with **CERN**. Moreover, I'm learning and researching analysis work on Wgamma-Plus-Jets and Zgamma-Plus-Jets, cooperating with Fermilab. During last three months, I worked on hardware work of RPC at CERN. (2015-11 Tao Feng)

(E116) I utilized multimodal techniques to analyze the signals in CPW and slot line. Also, conformal mapping was used to calculate the characteristic impedance of some non-standard transmission lines. Our group also introduced **RF MEMS** switches into a single antenna element to alter the physical dimensions of antenna, hence changing the radiation pattern. (2014-01-01 Nan Zhou)

In Example (E115), there are four abbreviations used, JetMET, CERN, RPC and CERN to report the applicant's "doing service work". These are technical terms used among computer technology researchers. In Example (E116), two shortened forms of "CPW" and "RF MEMS" were used. To the people who are involved in the same or similar field, these short terms are just jargon. Applicants' familiarity with these terms implies that the previous researches they did help enculturate themselves into their own disciplines and demonstrate their disciplinary expertise.

(E117) In the last two years, I am studying on classification using **spatio-temporal information** and **Markov random field** (MRF) is adopted. So far, I have carried on two main researches. One is about the comparison between MRFs using **pair-site/multi-site cliques**. The other is to improve the potential function by considering **spectral similarity**. (2015-05 Ling Xu)

(E118) Currently my work focused on using **microsatellite markers** to determine the male fitness of *Aconitum Kusnezoffii*. And on the whole I am working on the **sex allocation** issue of this plant and the microsatellite is the final part of my project. Since I studied the **male-biased sex allocation** of *Aster ageratoides* since I was working on isolating microsatellites *of Delphinium glaucum* and *Aconitum Kusnezoffii*. (2014-02 Ying Li)

(E119) Now we are reading the **Verañjakaṇḍa**, which I found a few terms possibly not based on the **theravāda** tradition. Take the division of the three worlds (**saṅkhāra loka, sattaloka, osākaloka**) as an example. It shares a lot of similarities with the cosmological theory of *Abhidharmakośa* which belongs to

Sarvāstivādin tradition. (2015-16 Ming Liu)

In Example (E117), the applicant mentioned several terminologies of the used research method in the major of physics like "spatio-temporal information" and "Markov random field" with the addition of its acronym, "pair-site/multi-site cliques", and a term of the research parameter of "spectral similarity". Example (E118) shows that the applicant specialized in botany, so there were some Latin names of different plants like "Aconitum Kusnezoffii", "Aster ageratoides", "Delphinium glaucum". His research method was "microsatellite markers" while the research subject was "sex allocation" and "male-biased sex allocation". In Example (E119), the applicant studied Sanskrit and Buddhism. Verañjakaṇḍa is a classic piece of Sanskrit literature. "theravāda" and "Sarvāstivādin" are about two traditions of Buddhism. Saṅkhāra loka, sattaloka, osākaloka are divisions of the three worlds in the literature of Verañjakaṇḍa and *Abhidharmakośa* is about a cosmological theory. Each discipline develops its own semiotic system of nomenclature, and the contractions as well other specialized terminologies as presented above, displayed applicants' socialization into, or in Hyland's term "proximity" to their respective discipline. "The control of these disciplinary resources and knowledge of in-group terms, concepts and celebrities not only represent specific understandings, but display considerable expertise." (Hyland, 2012: 85) And this expertise is inculcated into the applicants' implicit propensity as a part of their habitus. The skillful usage of professional terms, originating from their possession of various academic capitals, is turned into symbolic affordances to persuade foreign professors of their competence.

Exemplifying teamwork spirit. Being a member of a research team also demonstrates the quality of being a researcher since important projects are usually accomplished through concerted efforts rather than a solo show. The usage of the plural pronoun "we" is a symbolization of teamwork spirit.

(E120) I've already done some preparation work for my doctoral dissertation, including the excavation in Tongling city, *** province which is one of the major copper production places in the Shang and Zhou Dynasty. **We** have some exciting finds (findings) during this excavation. **We** found two primitive furnaces for copper production, both of which belong to early period of the Zhou Dynasty. The size of the furnace is very small, considering the information of the archaeological sites nearby, we began to realize that the copper production in this region is not like what **we had in mind** before. Besides the furnaces, we also collected some slag samples in this area and done some archaeological survey work. (2015-04 Feifei Hu)

(E121) To do this **we** used the process we developed in the first attached paper. It turns out that we no longer do microcantilever-based biosensors but are developing some new techniques that we have not yet published. The reason we moved away from microcantilevers is contained in the 2nd attached paper. (2014-01 Nan Zhou)

In Example (E120), the applicant was engaged in archeological studies. Excavation, as an indispensable part of fieldwork in this major, was a routine practice for archeologists and usually needed teamwork to finish. In this excerpt, the plural pronoun "we" is used five times to describe the detailed research experiences. In reporting this piece of research experience, three research acts (*found two primitive furnaces, collected, had exciting findings*) and two cognitive acts (*began to realize, had in mind*) are used. In Example (E121), "we" are used five times, in which four research acts (*used the process, developed, no longer do microcantilever-based biosensors, moved away from*) and one discourse act (*have not yet published*) are used to describe the research team's cooperative work. All of these reporting actions are combined with the plural agent of "we", which amounts to say that the applicants joined the teamwork during the whole research cycle from carrying out step-by-step research procedure, conceptualizing the research result and finalizing the research activities through verbal expressions.

The repeated usage of "we" indicates a collective agency. It further shows that as a member of the team, the applicants respected teamwork value. Otherwise, he or she could have just used such "I + Action" structure as "I had exciting findings". The joint effort embedded in the pronoun of "we" presented in this narration of research experience displays the applicant's alignment with his or her research group as well as acknowledgement of other team members' hard work. The spirit of teamwork is built into their disciplinary habitus, which would generate a sense of practice (Bourdieu, 1977) in their future academic career.

Recounting research experience. The "recounting" aspect of research experience is actually not a parallel with the previous discussions because recounting is on a textual level while technical terms, usage of pronoun are on the lexical level. We add this part to emphasize that some applicants would narrate their research experience like a story to make the whole research experience more vividly presented, hence more convincing to foreign professors. The narrative tone adds to the authenticity by means of showing the timeline of each detail and demonstrates applicants' overall research ability. In Example (E122) as quoted below, Ran Xia recounted his research experience of studying "Bi2FeCrO6", a kind of perovskite material in physics. There is an obvious time frame of his experience, propped by the temporal conjunctions of "after", "after", "in order to", "when" and "now".

236

The change of verb tense from the past to the present further testifies to the development of Ran Xia's experiment, which navigates from the past to the present. The recounting tone also discloses a rational and logical academic mindset.

(E122) **After** [I obtained] obtaining some basic knowledge of the use of packages like WIEN2k and VASP, my advisor suggested me study the structure of double perovskite with a host of materials of this kind, among which he selected Bi2FeCrO6 for me. **After** reading the inspiring paper First principles study of the multiferroics BiFeO3, Bi2FeCrO6, and BiCrO3 published in 2005, I was amazed by the versatile properties of multiferroics—it magically combines ferromagnetism and ferroelectricity together and becomes the most potential candidate in the future device design ... **In order to** figure out the sheer difference in a quantitative approach, I did a series of calculations with the package WIEN2k. **When** estimating Tc, I wrote a program in C language myself, within the framework of Monte Carlo method and Heisenberg model. The work is **now** still in process and it turns out that the results correspond fairly with the experimental data. (2013-05 Ran Xia)

In the course of detailing their research experiences, the applicants have resorted to such linguistic resources as professional terms, "I+action" structure, and plural pronoun as qualification for being a researcher. The acronyms and specialized terminology are used as academic capitals to show their disciplinary training, the "I" plus action verbs indicates their strong agency while the "we" form declares their value of teamwork spirit. The recounting tone used in detailing a "research story" boosts the trustworthiness of their research work. The four types of linguistic means and the applicants' academic capitals contribute to creating the subtext that "I am academically attractive, so hire me".

4.3.1.4 Listing Achievement

Publication in journals, books and conferences, prizes and patents could be the most ostensible proof of one's research competence, which was credited as their "hardware" or "dry stuff" as the interviewee Huyang Long mentioned. Academic achievement constitutes a part of applicants' cultural capital, which can be objectified into article, books, or institutionalized as certificate and patent certificate, and a symbolic capital of their academic potential. Applicants usually just list rather than evaluate their achievement.

Research paper is a common achievement that many applicants present in their *Taoci* emails. To introduce their paper publication, different applicants go from the simplest mentioning to the most complex detailing. The simplest mentioning means applicants just state the preposition to deliver the message that they have publications. As they add such specific information as research topic, publication time, journal's name, and journal grading, they adopt the complex style of detailing.

(E123) **I had written one paper** in this area. (2014-04 Zhou Zhou)

(E124) My CV and **published papers have been attached.** (2015-34 Feng Huang)

Example (E123) and Example (E124) only contain the barest information of "I have publication", without information other than the publication itself. Although Zhou Zhou phrased it as "written one paper", he said in the email interview that he actually wanted to say that he had one paper published in this area. The applicant in Example (E124) didn't write anything about his papers until the end of his email, reminding the professor that he had papers published.

(E125) **I published two papers** [3] and [4], as **a Second Author and a Third Author**, respectively. (2015-31 Jie Chu)

(E126) At this stage, I **have one first-authored international conference publication and several co-authored conference and journal publications.** (2013-01 Qiang Miao)

The above-listed two examples provide more details about the publication. Example (E125) adds authorship of "second" and "third" author to his publication. Example (E126) specifies both authorship (first-authored and co-authored) as well as some general information about the publication sources (conference, journal).

(E127) I have **two papers about** the protoporcelain which **will be published**

recently... (2015-04 Feifei Hu)

(E128) I ... **published one paper** using classic methods to compare the male and female reproductive function,... (2014-02 Ying Li)

These two examples enrich the publication details with specific research content. Example (E127) mentions about his two papers concerned about protoporcelain, while in Example (E128), the applicant detailed its research method and the purpose of using this method, "compare the male and female reproductive function".

(E129) ...and I've already **published three SCI papers** as first author or co-first author. (2015-26 Yuan Zhao)

(E130) I have published **two SCI papers** (one as first author and the other as second author) based on my previous research. (2015-33 Xi Cui)

The publication mentioned in Example (E129) and Example (E130) above is specified with its journal ranking. Publication on high-ranking journals speaks aloud for academic capital. SCI refers to Science Citation Index, one of the three major (the other two are EI, ISTP) retrieval systems of science research in the world. In the Chinese academia, publication on SCI journals has been considered high-level or first-class work. Therefore, the term of "SCI" contains as strong symbolic power under this circumstance. SCI publications are not only objectified capital, but also become symbolic capital, and whoever owns it is taken as academically competent. The applicant in Example (E129) claimed that he had three SCI paper as first author and co-first author, and the applicant in Example (E130) had two SCI papers as first author and second author respectively, which not only specified the quality of his publication, but also the volume of it, i.e. the type and volume of their academic capital.

(E131) My paper "Single-walled carbon nanotube pirani gauges prepared by DEP assembly" submitted to **IEEE Transactions on Nanotechnology** was accepted yesterday. (2013-07-05 Huyang Long)

(E132) In one study, the HHT is applied to the study of low-level jets in the atmospheric boundary layer which was published in the **Boundary Layer Meteorology**. The other accepted by the **Acta Meteorologica Sinica** (in Chinese) is the basic discussion about the application of HHT in the boundary layer turbulence. (2015-12)

(E133) Based upon this research, I completed my English thesis, "Six Properties Assessment" as a Key Method in Evaluating Shale Gas "Desserts": A Comparison of Marine Shales in China and the United States, which is now under reviewed by the *Journal of Earth Science*. (2015-13 Lan Luo)

In the three examples, the applicants not only specified their thesis topic, but also named the journals, which gave readers an accessible source to retrieve these papers. In Example (131), Huyang Long claimed his paper was accepted by the journal of IEEE Transactions on Nanotechnology. In Example (E132), the applicant had two papers published separately in *Boundary Layer Meteorology and Acta Meteorologica Sinica*. He further noted that the latter journal was in Chinese. In Example (E133), the applicant hadn't yet had his paper published, but under review by the famous *Journal of Earth Science*, which exhibited his research potential.

(E134) And I have a paper for the field which was **published in a workshop of** Ubicomp 2011. (2014-05 Wei Hong)

(E135) I have submitted my finished paper to **2013 ICIS (accepted) and 2014 HICSS (accepted) and 2014 ECIS (final notification will come out in March, 2014)**. (2015-07 Xiaoyun Fang)

Some applicants also make their publication more retrievable by adding the time of publication. For example, in Example (E134), Wei Hong specified the publication occasion of workshop of "Ubicomp" and mentioned the year of "2011". In Example (E135), the applicant listed the year of 2013, 2014, 2014 for the three papers respectively accepted by ICIS (International Conference of Information and System), HICSS (Hawaii International Conference on System Sciences) and ECIS (European Conference on Information Systems), which were all top-level conferences. In the computer science area, top-level conference publication sometimes is often regarded of more academic value than journal articles as the interviewee Zhou Zhou, a computer major student, told me. Although many applicants used a wrong structure "I have published or I published...", instead of "I have ... published", the message of "I have publications" was still successfully delivered.

There are some other achievements to validate applicants' cultural capital they possess. For example, in Example (E136) and Example (E137) Yunyang Liu mentioned the prize he won and a patent that he was in charge of in the following examples.

(E136) Moreover, I won the First Prize of National Chemistry Competition for High School Students, the highest level Chemistry contest in China, in 2009. (2014-08-02 Yunyang Liu)

(E137) And a patent ([5]), of which I am the Lead Author, is under processing. (2014-08-01 Yunyang Liu)

Publication is an important criterion for foreign professors to judge whether an applicant had the ability and potential to start and accomplish a PhD program, just as Huyang reflected in his interview.

(I13) You need to show him the "dry stuff", and don't say something useless... I feel that he would definitely recruit me this year, because I had another paper published this year. Before, I had a second-authored paper. This year, I had a first-author paper, I wrote it, not co-authored, I wrote it. So, for an undergraduate student, it's very difficult to have a first-authored paper and the paper is published

——"套磁"话语实践研究

on an international journal. Supervisors attach great importance to research ability. Going abroad for a PhD program is just doing research for the supervisor. If you have published paper, it means you are able to do the research. Just that simple. (Interview transcripts 2013-May Huyang Long)

Academic achievement, in particular publications represents applicants' cultural capital. Many applicants want to pursue an academic career. Otherwise, they would probably not apply for PhD programs. The academia circle is mainly producing knowledge through different forms of publication as "we are what we write" (Hyland, 2012: 25). Starting to publish one's research is a way to join his/her imagined scholarly community through specific words.

4.3.1.5 Forecasting

The previous four speech acts are mostly about a past or present self, who have various types of and volume of cultural capital as affordances to compete with international applicants. Moreover, applicants "forecast" their future research direction to cast an imagined "self" in the academic field, resembling the move of Stating Goal reported in Ding (2007). Forecasting is about what applicants would like to do in the near future or in the long run. It could be a specific move about their research practice, or an aspiration for future careers.

(a) Specific Move

(E138) In future, I will **learn Myanmar** in order to make good use of the Myanmar version and the P ā li- Myanmar Dictionary. (2015-16 Ming Liu)

(E139) In the near future, I plan to **refine the models** from case studies and conduct empirical tests based on a large sample of Chinese high-tech companies, including Tencent, JD, Alibaba. (2015-07 Xiaoyun Fang)

(E140) In the following years, I would like to do researches **on computational methods of Monte Carlo radiation transport and radiation transport and its applications like reactor shielding and design**. (2015-18 Yanli Ge)

These examples are all about what applicants were planning to do in the near future. In Example (E138), the applicant's research is related to Myanmar literature. Hence, she claimed that she would learn the language so that she would make a good use of that literature. Examples (E139) and (E140) are about the two applicants' research plan. The applicant in Example (E139) claimed that he would refine the models and conduct empirical tests, while the applicant in Example (E140) conceived a longer-term plan, to "do researches on computational methods of Monte Carlo radiation transport and its applications like reactor shielding and design".

(b) Future Career

Some applicants would write about their aspiration for future career. It indicates their imagined identities and imagined community to move into and signifies the benefits that they expect from their study-abroad education.

(E141) My academic aspiration is to be a **first-class scholar** on *** at home. (2015-19 Feng Li)

(E142) But I find that I need to **take a more advanced study** in computer science, **not just work as a coder**. (2014-05 Wei Hong)

In Example (E141), the applicant claimed that he desired to be a first-class scholar in China on the research subject he mentioned. The academic aspiration symbolizes applicants' imagined identity of his future academic career. This imagined identity is to be achieved with the help of having the chance of visiting the foreign professor's institution. In Example (E142), Wei Hong presented a contrast of what he wanted to do and what he was doing. He claimed that he didn't want to work just as a coder, a technician, but wanted to take more advanced study in computer science, i.e. researcher, which was a step-stone for his future academia career. "It is in the realm of the imagination ... imagined identities that learners are able to express this desire ... Imagination allows learners to re-envision how things are as how they want them to be." (Darvin, Norton, 2015: 46) The concrete imagined identity as "first-class scholar" and "computer science researcher" in the two examples motivated the applicants to invest through their *Taoci* practice.

(E143) I have always wanted to make my research results helpful to learning in real-life settings. (2014-09-04 Pianhong Yin)

(E144) Also, personally speaking, I think water photolysis is a great job for human being. Beijing, where I lived now, is one of the most polluted cities in the world. The pollution is primarily come from the steam power plant and car exhaust. If one day solar fuel generation is applicable to our daily life, there would not be that much pollution. I wish I could contribute my power to **this great job**. (2014-08-06 Yunyang Liu)

In the two examples listed above, the imagined identity is more general, without specification of a certain career or social position. In Example (E143), Pianhong Yin claimed that she wanted to make her research results in psychology helpful to real-life learning. In Example (E144), there was a long pre-sequence for Yunyang's aspiration to contribute to "this great job". He first appraised that water photolysis was a great job for human being, then introduced one of his real-life case—the polluted city of Beijing. One solution to the pollution could be the application of solar fuel. The applicant's wish was to make his contribution to this great job, which was related to the whole human being.

(c) Liaison

There is only one case in the present research relating about applicants' imagination of being liaison of two institutions.

(E145) Meanwhile, I can try my best to **bridge potential cooperation with *** University, or maybe with Chinese academia** in future. (2015-24 Lan Yang)

Instead of specifying their aspiration for their own future work, the applicant in Example (E145) imagined that he could become a liaison between the Chinese university and the targeted foreign institution, or even the Chinese and the foreign academia.

As Norton and Toohey (2011: 415) commented, "A learner's hopes for the future … are integral to language learner identity." The email content reveals that the Chinese applicants' imagined community is not only the target language community to learn or to improve their English proficiency, but also their academic or disciplinary community to become a researcher, scholar, or liaison. Various capitals are integrated into speech acts to invest in their study-abroad education and academic future. The expected return from such investment is supposed to offer more possibilities for advanced educational and academic resources to forward themselves in their disciplinary profession.

In brief, under the Me-oriented strategy, the five speech acts of self-evaluating, introducing academic background, listing achievement,

248

specifying research/experience, and forecasting work for the advertising of an academically capable image. The occurrence of each speech act is presented in Fig. 4.3. Introducing academic background and specifying research/experience account for the dominant share, while listing achievement the least share, which is understandable as most of the applicants were still green-hand researchers and that was why they wanted to pursue a PhD degree or receive more training in foreign universities. Evaluating self is not prominent but still significant in that it indicates the alignment with explicit self-promotion characterizing the "Western" style in application genre (Bhatia, 1993; Li et al., 2007).

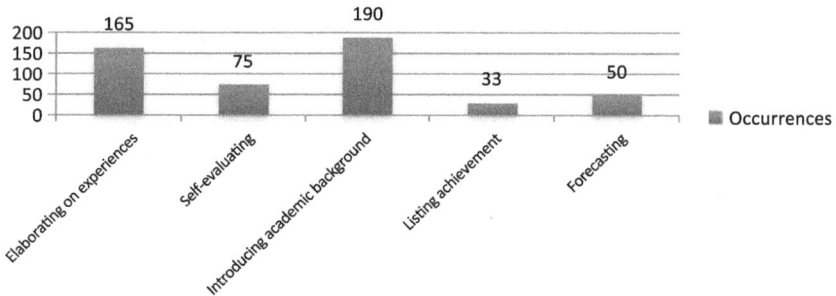

Fig. 4.3   Me-oriented strategy distribution

Contrary to boosting foreign professor's magnetic attraction in the deference-oriented strategy under the meso speech act of pulling *guanxi*, the Me-oriented strategy stresses applicants' advantages to magnetize applicants to draw professors towards them. Therefore, various types cultural capitals are invested or sold as affordances (Darvin, Norton, 2015) on the offer-hunting market, such as the embodied form of language competence, knowledge, and skill, institutionalized form of degree, and objectified form of journal publications and books. All of these also constitute symbolic power to impress and to get acknowledged by their targeted professors in order to win their favor in the candidature contest.

4.3.2 Us-oriented Strategy: Striking up Academic Bonding

Promoting self is far more than a solo show of self. The Us-oriented strategy aims at striking up academic bonding with overseas professors in term of shared interest and a chance to speak out legitimately as a researcher.

4.3.2.1 Sharing Academic Interest

Sharing the same academic interest with targeted supervisors can be regarded as the most crucial common ground that applicants try to demonstrate through *Taoci*. As some interviewees commented, the "match" (i.e. my interest matches yours) was a fundamental prerequisite. Mutual academic interest could be verbalized explicitly, like the speech act of articulating previous association, so as to pull the two parties into the same disciplinary community. The shared interest is sometimes general but more often than not specific so that the supervisor's discipline is squarely targeted.

(a) "Match" Claim

"Match" means fit, not necessarily the same or the best, but fitting each other. Applicants would make an explicit claim that they match with targeted professors in terms of research interest. This "match" claim is usually in the form of evaluation.

(E146) I believe my former education and research experiences, which **match your research direction quite much**. (2015-18 Yanli Ge)

(E147) I notice that my ideal research direction **matches yours pretty well**. (2014-07 Xiaoyun Fang)

(E148) …you are interested in **the same** topic and have done some wonderful research work in ***. (2015-04 Feifei Hu)

(E149) Had noticed your project, "Accelerating Data-Intensive Applications", which **has many in common with** my interests. (2014-04 Zhou Zhou)

(E150) I have read some papers from your team and I am very happy to find that our opinions reach a concensus to a large extent. (2015-42 Liang Zhang)

In Examples (E146) and (E147), both applicants used the word "match" to declare that their research direction fit the professors'. The terms of "quite much" and "pretty well" intensify that their interests matched to a great extent. In Example (E148), the expression of "be interested in the same topic" conveys the idea of the shared interest between the applicant and the professor. Example (E149) contains the formulaic expression of "has many in common with" to match the professor's project of "Accelerating Data-Intensive Applications" with his own interest. Example (E150) describes how the applicant found they matched each other and used a more serious lexicon "consensus". These match claims are voiced from applicants' point of view.

(E151) I discussed with Doctor Nazul about my research interest, and he also **agree** that my research interest **fits well** the work of your lab. (2014-04-01 Chu Gao1)

Some applicants resort to external voices to make the "match" claim. For example, in Example (E151) above, Chu Gao introduced the opinion of Doctor Nazul, a researcher that both the applicant and professor knew. According to the applicant, Doctor Nazul "agree[d]" that his interest "fits" the supervisor's lab well. The conjunction of "also" indicates a concurring opinion while the graduation term of "well" upgrades the degree to which their interests fit each other. The externally attributed locution and an embedded concurring voice are combined to stress the "fit" between the applicant and the professor.

(b) "Interested in" Claim

"Interested in" claim is the most frequently used form to demonstrate the shared interest. Some applicants phrase the interest claim in a direct manner while others take some preparatory steps to the point.

(E152) I am very interested in your researches. (2015-25 Xiao He)

(E153) I am interested in research of your group. (2014-10-01 Shunying Qin)

(E154) I am very interested in your research area of "natural disaster science"... (2015-40 Dong Wang)

(E155) I'm very interested in your research about combination of the paleoecology and genetics approaches. (2015-43 Shuang Xia)

Example (E152) is the most concise way to express the "interested in" claim by saying "I am interested in your research". In Example (E153), Shunying claimed that she was interested in the research carried out in the professor's group. Although her expression was a little problematic ("interested in research of your group" sounds like she was interested in researching the professor's group), she successfully had her idea conveyed since there was no misunderstanding in the ensuing email exchanges from the recipient. Examples (E154) and (E155) are more specific about the shared interest as the applicants mentioned the specific projects "natural disaster science" and "combination of the paleoecology and genetics approaches" that the foreign professors were working on.

Many applicants state specific reasons why they are interested in foreign professors' work. The commonplace preparatory move is applicants' coming across professors' research works.

(E156) I find it really interesting **after learning about the realm** you are devoted to. (2013-05 Ran Xia)

(E157) In previous research and course **I read some your works** which are about friction and contact dynamics or simulation control publicated on Siggraph and TOG and I'm interested in these works. (2013-03 Zhi Yu)

(E158) **After I look through your research publications**, I found that I am really interested in it... (2015-46 Guo Fang)

In Example (E156), Ran Xia claimed that he found it interesting after learning about the professor's research realm. Zhi Yu in Example (E157) said he had read the professor's work and then became interested in it. The applicant in Example (E158) mentioned that he read the professor's publications. These pre-sequences bring in the concrete occasion when applicants became interested in the professors' work, demonstrating their knowledge about professors' work and posing a convincing claim of sharing an interest. This overlaps a little with the strategy of "knowing about professors' work" in the next subsection, but a difference will be articulated later.

254

A more sophisticated way to deliver the interest claim needs the recipients to make a little induction. In Example (E159) below, Si Chen first listed her own interest and then made the assumption that such interest was what the professor's group was interested in, which generated the conclusion that they were interested in the same topic. Example (E160) works the other way around. The applicant first presented the professor's work and then claimed he was interested into it, so they shared the interest. There is no explicit claim of the shared interest, but hearers could work out that point based on a little induction.

(E159) Generally, **I am interested** in questions related to functional and phylogenetic patterns in a large spatial scale and that how they change over time, which, I guess, is also **the research interest of your** group. (2013-02 Si Chen)

(E160) On your website, I notice that **your research interests** include MEMS and electromagnetic analysis and design of optical structures, which **I am very interested in**. (2014-01-01 Nan Zhou)

The previous examples have showed applicants' firm interest in the professor's work, a less firm claim of sharing the same interest was an assumption of the professor's interest in the applicant's work in the following example.

(E161) I have tried to write an email to professor Holms, unfortunately in his reply he told me that he is no longer accepting applicants for positions, but he also informed me that you are actively involved in researches ... as **you might be interested in my** research topics. (2015-24 Lan Yang)

In Example (E161), the applicant didn't come to the conclusion of "I am interested in your research", but "you might be interested in my research topics". Professor B was his targeted professor. In his email, he had a story to tell about how he got in touch with Professor B: he contacted professor A before, but that professor didn't take visiting students anymore and recommended professor B who did some similar researches in the applicant's field. Therefore, the applicant assumed that the professor might be interested in his work. The term of "might", a weak modalization of possibility, entertains alternative opinions and imposed less on the professor. When applicants show their interest in professors' work, they often upgrade it through such intensifiers as "really" and "very" like Example (E157). However, when the reversal is claimed, i.e. the professor's interest in applicants' research, the tone is substantially softened through assumptive forms. The speech act of "claiming shared academic interest" is the first step to involve "us" together. Upon this basic common ground, applicants have more discursive space to breed the closeness. Some applicants also emphasized this in their interviews as follows.

(I14) Doing *Taoci* is mainly to let the two parties of student and professor know each other's research interest and what areas they are good at. This is quite important for the following five years' learning and research. (Email Interview 2013 Liu Guo)

(I15) I feel it is necessary to, if you write to, to introduce yourself, your qualifications, you research interest, at least you have to let the professors know that your research direction matches each other ... With regards to personal interest, you certainly need to drag yours close to the professor's. Yes, otherwise, what are you going to do there? If the professor's work is not relevant to yours, he cannot supervise you, and you will end up doing nothing. Eh, actually, research interest and direction is the main thing, the main thing. Sometimes when you are interested in this and he is also interested but he changes to another interest suddenly and you don't know. Or you are doing something different the professor's but what you're doing is very helpful for him. This is also a kind of match. If you didn't *Taoci* with the professor, you will definitely have no idea about this. (Interview transcripts 2013-Apr. Si Chen)

(I16) In general, the best situation for application is that you need each other, just like one radish one hole. You find your best hole to fit, no matter it is due to alumni complex or your research interest. (Email interview 2013 Qingwan Li)

Taoci helps an applicant to check personally with foreign professors that they do share the same research aspiration for a specific field, which might not have been displayed well in the application portfolio submitted online and by mail. The confirmation of sharing the same interest serves as the starting point for a possible cooperation between institutional student and supervisor. It engages, from the applicants' perspective, the two sides into the same disciplinary membership, i.e. resulting in alignment with a specific community (Hyland, 2012).

4.3.2.2　Knowing about Professor's Work

To impress targeted professors, applicants express that they have read the former's research papers or are their academic followers. This is only about "knowing" professor's work, instead of understanding professors' work deeply and initiating an academic discussion. The most explicit expression is stating the "reading" activity itself.

(E162) I've read lots of your published paper and the profiles in the *** website. (2015-24 Lan Yang)

(E163) I have read some articles of yours in English. And I am reading almost all your books, and now I'm working on the translation of your latest book *Philosophy of Law* (it will be published by *** University Press later this year). (2015-15 Yi Wang)

In Example (E162), the applicant claimed that he had read many papers written by the professor, so he might know the professor's research work very well. In the next example of (E163), the applicant listed what he had read authored by the professor—articles as well as books. The rest part describes another strong bond between the

258

applicant and the professor: the applicant was then translating the professor's latest work, to introduce the professors' work into the Chinese academia.

(E164) I have read your paper "Unitary, Executive, or Both?" (2015-20 Xun Jin)

(E165) I read a series of work form your group, such as, "Analysis of velocity fluctuations and their intermittency properties in the surf zone using empirical mode decomposition"(2009), and "Multifractal description of wind power fluctuations using arbitrary order Hilbert spectral analysis"(2013), etc. (2015-12 Xu Liu)

Another way to show that "I know your work" is to name professors' publication or summarize the content in the articles. In Example (E164) above, the applicant wrote down the name of the professor's research paper "Unitary, Executive, or Both". In Example (165), two of the professors' research articles were listed with a specification of publication year. The detailed information about the publication implies a dependable source and sounds sincere about the reading activity.

(E166) After reading your papers and visiting your web site, I find that you have been working on Chinese law for several years. (2015-17 Rong Chen)

(E167) I have paid a close attention to your information on web page for a long time, and I have known that the synthesis and energy application of microporous carbon materials in your recent research interests ... After browsing your website, I

259

understand that you are working on synthesis and energy application of microporous carbon materials. (2015-21 Yao Sun)

Some applicant makes a brief summary about targeted professors' work. In Example (166) above, the applicant showed his understanding about the professor's research filed of "Chinese law". In Example (E167), the applicant claimed that he followed the professor's personal website and he knew the professor's research interest and area of "synthesis and energy application of microporous carbon materials".

Following targeted professors' work may have connotation of power difference between an academic green-hand and an academic expert, since it is applicants who read professors' work, not the other way around. Some applicants would attach their own research publications as reference at the end of the email, which to some extent balances the power difference between them. Reading the professor's work is more oriented toward the goal of showing that "I know your work" to emphasize the shared knowledge of a specific research area. The shared interest and knowledge are demonstrated for applicants' pursuit of the same disciplinary membership with foreign professors. It also establishes the platform for further academic communication, i.e. the academic dialogue discussed in the next section.

4.3.2.3   Dialoguing Academically

The micro speech act of dialoguing academically refers to the action that students discussed research questions with professors in their *Taoci* emails. It usually happens after a positive reply received from targeted professors. Only in *Taoci* packages could we retrieve their dialogue sequences with professors, so the majority of examples used in this section are extracted from those partial or full email packages.

Dialoguing academically enables applicants' engagement in particular research positioning with regards to targeted professors, as an interactive way to establish academic rapport with foreign professors, because it may usher in new round of exchange and generate more common ground between each other. Applicants' dialoguing activity could be divided into three prominent discourse acts: commenting, questioning and proposing.

(a) Commenting

Commenting means applicants' making evaluation or voicing an opinion about a certain topic, either the professors' work or anything that both of them are interested in. The content of "commenting" is often led in by meta-pragmatic utterances and imbued with evaluative vocabulary.

(E168) I read one of your papers, "Single-sided inkjet functionalization of silicon photonic microcantilevers", to gain the concept of bioMEMS. **For my understanding** of bioMEMS, the molecules to be detected interact with reactants on the cantilevers, hence changing their physical dimensions, which would reflect in the change of photonic signals, or electric signals in other cases. However, **I also have some incomprehensions**. For instance, the method in this article is based on small enough droplets that only wet the top MCL surface. However, MEMS cantilevers are always bent upside or downside, due to residual stress releasing. (2014-01-01 Nan Zhou)

In Example (E168), there was a preparatory step of "knowing the professor's work", from which he knew about the concept of bioMEMS. The engagement term of "For my understanding of bioMEMS" introduces the applicant's understanding on this topic, which is an agreement. The conjunction of "however" and the clause of "I also have some incomprehensions" (the word of "incomprehensions" should have been "miscomprehensions") open another lead of commenting, i.e. his disagreement with the professor. Nan Zhou claimed that "the method in this article is based on small enough droplets that only wet the top MCL surface", in which the downscaling graduation term of "small" and the contracting term of "only" deliver his doubts about the method used in the professor's research. In the next clause, the word "always" indicates that even though the method was not perfect

262

the result was the same, which caused another doubt of the professor's research.

(E169) **I have a little thought on** the combination of data from eddy covariance tower and remote sensing after reading the soft protocol of RECCAP. Flux towers are **accurate but scarce**, while carbon emission derived from CASA GPP is less accurate but abundant; with a significant relationship found between these two measurements (for AVHRR and MODIS separately) of similar spatial resolution, maybe it's possible to calibrate the interpolation of carbon emission measured from flux towers, at least on a regional scale. **I recalled a similar work by Nagler et al., in 2005**, on Remote Sensing of Environment, in which a linear relationship built from EVI and maximum daily air temperatures was used to predict ET measured from flux towers and was used on the estimation of river evapotranspiration. (2013-04-02 Chu Gao2)

In the above-quoted episode from Chu Gao's second partial email package, the meta-pragmatic marker of "I have a little thought on" indicates that he was going to express his ideas about "the soft protocol of RECCAP", a research topic in the professor's group. The contrasting pair of appreciation terms in "accurate but scarce", "less accurate but abundant" expresses his critical understanding of the conflicting relationship respectively in "Flux towers" and "carbon emission derived from CASA GPP". This relationship was considered "significant" by Chu Gao in the following clause. After making a proposal (to be discussed later), Chu Gao introduced a piece of reference as a supporting evidence for his argument by saying "I recalled a similar work by…" so as to make his comment endorsed. The precise citation form of the authors ("Nagler et al."), time ("2005") and the article title (Remote Sensing of Environment) reveal a reliable source and at the same time show a scientific mindset cultivated in the academic discipline, a part of his academic habitus.

(b) Questioning

Usually after making comment on professors' work, applicants would raise some questions about professors' work to show their critical thinking ability and to lead to further communication. While commenting implies applicants' implicit doubt about professors' work, questioning is a direct way to challenge professors' research.

(E170) I wonder how did you guarantee the cantilevers in your fabrication were flat. PS: Is it because the fabrication process in U.S. is mature enough, and that is not a problem anymore? (2014-01-02 Nan Zhou)

(E171) Actually, I have some questions about the results. Do you have any measurements to make sure subjects in retrieval and imitation practice (e.g. IQ)? (2014-09-04 Pianhong Yin)

In Example (E170), Nan Zhou raised three questions in his email. He started his doubt with the engagement term of "I wonder"

264

and continued with the question content of "how did you guarantee the cantilevers in your fabrication were flat". This sounds like an accusation of the professor's failing to make enough "guarantee". The second question is in a yes-no form, related to the previous one about fabrication process. And the last one is a question in an assertive form. The three consecutive questions, though perhaps threatening the professors' social face as a professional, might attract the professor's interest to think about Nan Zhou's criticism and to continue the academic dialogue. In Example (E171), Pianhong Yin phrased her question after the meta-pragmatic marker of "Actually, I have some questions about the results". Her doubt about the research result of the professor's work starts from the engagement term of "actually", often indicating disagreement. Her real concern was about "measurements to make sure subjects in retrieval and imitation practice".

Questioning professors' work is a highly face-threatening speech act. Therefore, the question marker of "I wonder" and the meta-discourse clause are used as a transition to the main question and to soften the accusative tone implicated. Another linguistic device to alleviate the potential threat is the employment of plural "we", a solidarity marker.

(E172) Do **we** use clusters to do simulation works? My current group is using a cluster with 10 nodes and each of them has 8 cores (which is not a big one). (2014-10-02 Shunying Qin)

(E173) But can **we** find any picture of buildings in present-day South India and Sri Lanka or from archeological sources which corresponds to the feature of addhayoga described in both atthakathās and tikās? (2015-16 Ming Liu)

In the two examples above, both applicants used the plural pronoun of "we" to raise their questions. Shunying in Example (E172) asked about whether clusters were used to do simulation works while the applicant in Example (E173) inquired about the possibility to find "any picture of buildings in present-day South India and Sri Lanka or from archeological sources". With the co-text, the "we" in Example (E172) refers to the inclusive "we" (the speaker and the listener, and the listener's group), since the professor showed his interest in Shunying's application. Let's call it "the narrow inclusive we". In Example (E173), which was extracted from the first email, the pronoun of "we" is also used as an inclusive term, but it could be extended to all the researchers, including the speaker and the hearer, and whoever interested in the topic. Thus, it could be termed as "the wide inclusive we", a representative of a specific academic community. The usage of plural pronoun symbolizes applicants' active involvement into the same discipline with professors, building up their academic bond.

The questions discussed here should not be mixed up with the questions subsumed in the strategy of "calling for further interaction" in pulling *guanxi* and the speech act of requesting in negotiating institutional entry, since these questions are oriented to academic issues and aimed at both promoting applicants as critical researchers as well as striking up an academic conversation with foreign professors in order to accumulate more common ground.

(c) Proposing

Applicants would propose some solutions or plan for future research to supplement the comment or critique they made. "Proposing" displays applicants' academic potential as constructive researchers, and paves the way for the solidarity of being involved in the same discipline.

(E174) **Have you thought of using** more complicated material in this paradigm? For example, **instead of** using words appeared in the training, the final test can also test some words that relates to the trained words in some way. Or maybe **grammar rules** have similar effect. (2014-09-03 Pianhong Yin)

In the above-listed example, Pianhong proposed her suggestion by using the interrogative form of "Have you thought of using...". On the surface it is questioning, but it is more of her own understanding about how to improve the professor's current research. The expression

267

of "Instead of using words" indicates that Pianhong Yin would propose to use other testing materials, like the words "related to trained words" and "grammar rules" she mentioned later. Rather than using a directive form, such as "you can use more complicated material in this paradigm", the questioning form makes the proposal sound less imposing, not offending the professor who might have his own consideration of designing a new research.

(E175) …**maybe it's possible** to calibrate the interpolation of carbon emission measured from flux towers, at least on a regional scale … **Is it possible to interpolate** the carbon emission data from flux towers and adjust it by the relationship between measurements from flux towers and AVHRR/MODIS? (2013-04-02 Chu Gao2)

In Example (E175), Chu Gao proposed to "calibrate the interpolation of carbon emission measured from flux towers" and the idea of "interpolate the carbon emission data from flux towers and adjust it by the relationship between measurements from flux towers and AVHRR/MODIS". The entertaining engagement term of "maybe", "it's possible" and the questioning form of "Is it possible to…" soften the possible impingement of making a proposal to a professional. There is another example, (E176) below, from Gao Chu's another partial email package. The meta-pragmatic clause of "I am considering a potential research project that I would like to discuss with you" usher in the coming proposal. The "I+Action" structure used in "I am thinking about..." show that it was his idea and emphasized his agency, and the left part of the email text is all about that idea. This proposal is accepted by the professor, as the latter wrote back "I am very happy to hear your ideas for projects with me. We are actively engaged with using these kinds of measurements in modeling, so this might fit in very well".

(E176) **I am considering a potential research project** that I would like to discuss with you. **I am thinking about** parameterizing individualbased forest models through the observations in Amazon, and to simulate the future biogeochemical consequence in different climate and social scenarios. (2013-04-03 Gao Chu1)

Chinese people usually resort to the indirect or implicit rhetoric to make comments or raise a request in order not to hurt hearers' feeling or face (Bi, 1996: 58). This is a well-recognized value attached to the collectivism society and low-context culture (Hall, 1976). It is particularly true when the lower-status speaks to the higher-status. However, as the foregoing examples showed, these applicants were rather direct, though using softeners and downgraders, when they discussed academic questions with unfamiliar foreign professors. The academic green hands commented, proposed and questioned, which was a kind of challenge to those academic professionals. Their mindset of being a peer to comment, question and propose must have been cultivated through previous education and training, invisible and hidden from daily observation. It is sedimented as a part of their cultural capital or disciplinary disposition. This cultural capital is actively put into verbal display and secures their symbolic status of being a competitive applicant. However, this kind of academic *Taoci* strategy usually poses a high requirement for applicants, as it is pertinent to how much and what types of academic capital they really have in command of. The following quote from Bourdieu captures this point:

> "And the structure of the distribution of the different types and subtypes of capital at a given moment in time represents the immanent structure of the social world, i.e. the set of constraints, inscribed in the very reality of that world, which govern its functioning in a durable way, determining the chances of success of practices." (Bourdieu, 1986: 46)

This point is also testified by two research participants' reflection in their interviews as follows.

(I17) Before doing *Taoci*, it is necessary to read extensively about the professor's and his/her research group's paper, to know about their research direction and the latest development. And then you show explicit interest in a specific area, so that you can shoot the arrow at the target when you carry out a discussion about research issues with the professor. (Email interview 2014 Nan Zhou)

(I18) Perhaps for me, I would make some academic communication with the professor on purpose, that is to say, to demonstrate purposefully that I know his research to quite an extent, and I'm able to propose some of my own ideas... some teachers, oh, that is, you can feel that he is interested in you. Some supervisors didn't reply me that enthusiastically, though it doesn't mean that he was not interested in me. I mean, if he replies to me very enthusiastically or request, and his research work is very close to mine, then I would probably read some of his papers, then, I can raise some, just, some, detailed questions, like why did you use this paradigms like that, why did you do that, and then whether you feel that this result might be generated by some other factors. Then, or, to like such more macro questions, have you ever thought of how to carry it. Anyway, I want to show him, that I'm interested in his work and I am an intellectually capable person. (Interview transcripts 2014-Dec. Pianhong Yin)

Carrying out academic dialogues with foreign professors in *Taoci* email requires applicants to read their research work extensively and intensively. Otherwise, the dialogue would not be fruitful. Dialoguing on the one hand helps keep the communication on, and on the other hand, demonstrates applicants' academic qualification. We have seen the Chinese applicants' initiative to think critically and make constructive proposal, behaving like academic peers, but we could still feel their tentativeness and great care, such as the frequent use of softeners, in commenting, questioning and proposing, which rests on the power difference between academic green-hands and experts. Another possible interpretation would boil down to the teacher-student hierarchy discussed in the speech act of pulling *guanxi*. The fact is that Chinese students' enculturation is more oriented towards a hierarchical relationship with their teachers, rather than a peer relationship. Perhaps this disposition of traditional cultural habitus still penetrate or perpetuate hard into applicants' hexis even if they resorted to the more western style of self-promotion, which also exemplifies the subconscious dimension of speech act investment.

4.3.2.4　Claiming Personal Value

Claiming personal value to professor is concerned about applicants' articulating their ability and potential with regards to foreign professors. It appears similar to self-evaluation in the Me-oriented category but differs from it essentially in that the evaluated value here is directly related to the professor's benefit. The evaluative terms underscore the affinity that applicants try to create with foreign professors, instead of putting on a solo show about applicants themselves.

(E177) I think that my experience of software development would be **helpful**. (2014-05 Wei Hong)

(E178) I am learning DFT, which is **useful** in researching the strongly correlated electrons. (2014-06-01 Liguo Zhao1)

In Example (E177), Wei Hong claimed that his experience of developing software could be helpful for the targeted professor's research in the future. It is an explicit self-judgment about the applicant's value to the professor. In Example (E178), Liguo Zhao said the skill "DFT" that he was then learning would be useful in the research of "strongly correlated electrons", which was the professor's research topic. Although the word of "useful" is an appreciation term of the DFT learning, the person who was doing the DFT learning was simultaneously evaluated.

(E179) I think my research background on optics and photonics **can facilitate** the SPs research **a lot**. (2014-08-05 Yunyang Liu)

(E180) I will **surely bring my understanding of *** Theory to your class**. (2015-19 Feng Li)

In Example (E179), the modality verb of "can" indicates ability while "facilitate" captures the applicants' worth in that his research background could make the SPs research much easy and the SPs research was the professor's research theme. The future-tense action of "facilitate" is intensified by the upgrading term "a lot". In Example (E180), the applicant proclaimed that he would bring a different understanding about "*** Theory" to the professor's class. It indicates a possible contribution to the diversity of classroom discussion, which could be helpful for the professor's lecture. This assertion is contracted and upgraded by the usage of "surely" to emphasize the applicant's confidence in doing this. These applicants' claim imagined value serve as offering future incentives (Bhatia 1993) to the professors if they were admitted to the programs and also indicate their quality of competent candidature.

In brief, under the Us-oriented strategy, the four speech acts of claiming personal value, dialoguing academically, knowing about the professor's work and sharing the same interest are intended to create more academic bonding with foreign professors. The occurrence of each speech act is given in Fig. 4.4. Dialoguing academically is the most prominent speech act. Sharing the same academic interest and knowing about the professor's work ensue. Claiming my value to professors is the least, which might indicate that Chinese applicants are still uncomfortable with explicit self-enhancement.

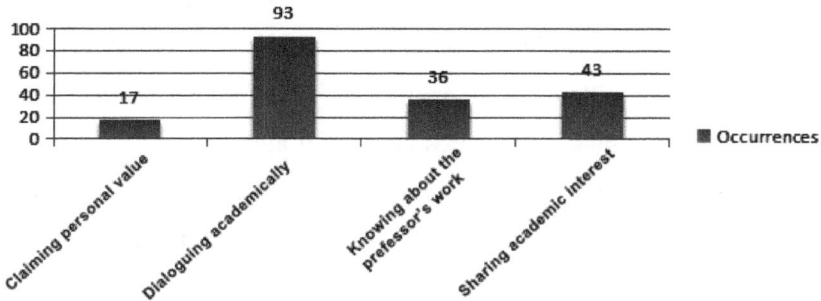

Fig. 4.4   Us-oriented strategy distribution

4.3.3   Sectional Discussion: Investing with Academic Capital

The meso speech act of presenting academic competence is divided into two broad strategy types: Me-oriented strategy and Us-oriented strategy. The former refers to applicants' self-advertising while the latter striking up academic solidarity. Both strategies work for the effect to attract professors' attention through explicit or implicit self-promotion, which would add to their stakes in the offer wrestling.

The analysis of email content and interview transcripts reveals that Chinese applicants possess a repertoire of cultural capital: the embodied state, for example their knowledge, critical thinking ability, their acquired programming skills, and English proficiency and

275

other language competence; the objectified state of research articles, conference publication, books, and awards; and the institutionalized state like TOEFL and GRE certificate, bachelor degree or master degree. These capitals have been cultivated and accumulated over a long time of education and training, which might be imprinted into their mind and body, forming different kinds of disciplinary habitus and guiding their performance of doing researches as well as their communication with academics.

These capitals are distributed unequally among applicants in terms of type and volume. Some of them are used more frequently, such as the institutionalized cultural capital of interest, education, knowledge, degree and language certificate to invest in their imagined future, which are counted as the minimum capital requirement for applicants to compete in the global education market. The objectified capital of publications and books appears the least since the majority of these applicants are still taking the first steps towards the academia.

In order to obtain more desirable capitals and achieve imagined identity as a researcher, a scholar or a scientist, the capitals that applicants already enjoyed are invested as affordances and transformed into what is regarded as more valuable in the international offer hunting field. In the speech act of promoting self, it is revealed that the majority of Chinese applicants are ready and confident to present themselves, in terms of showing themselves, evaluating themselves positively, demonstrating their value and dialoguing with authority directly, etc. This feature diverges from the traditional Chinese Confucianism value that the lower-status should display modesty and self-efficacy in front of the higher-status, but instead comes closer to the agentic self-promotion that is found particularly strong in individualistic countries (Kurman, 2001). Self-promotion has been reported less prominent in South-East Asia than in North America and Western Europe (Heine, 2003), so the speech act of presenting individual competence forms a stark contrast with the popular view of Chinese students being reserved and mild, underselling themselves, or having difficulty impressing their audience reported, for example, in Xin (2004). The young generation of Chinese applicants seems to be taking in and moving towards the individualism of the "western" culture, which indicates that their habitus is undergoing slow and subtle transformation. The Chinese "mildness" is on its way approaching the western "wildness". This fact could be probably related to the English learning heat in China in the past decades, which brought prominent change of positive self-confidence due to English learning (Gao, Jia, Zhou, 2015). Increasing intercultural communication with the outside world both in and out

277

of classroom have exposed the young generation to the influence of western value, ideology and belief. In the high-stake competition for study-abroad offer, they are rivaling with competitors from all over the world and this field still follows the dominant self-promotion style characterizing the "western" individualism. Their discourse practices are accordingly adjusted in the tension between their own linguistic habitus and the market of global higher education.

Nevertheless, we could still glimpse the great carefulness and modesty seeping through applicants' *Taoci* textual lines when they discussed academic questions with foreign professors. Even though some of them made a sharp point in criticizing the authority's research work, they did it very tentatively through using a bunch of softeners and downgraders. These linguistic features indicate their awareness of behaving appropriately in the Chinese way, i.e. being humble, being cautiously polite, in front of such authorities as experts and professors. Just as the speech act of humbling self in the discussion of pulling *guanxi*, this disposition seems to lurk and linger on, alluding to the subconscious dimension of investment. At the same time, applicants' current identities such as research beginners or experienced coders, academic starters, proficient English users, equal academic peers and imagined identities of ambitious scholars, promising professionals or

278

international liaison are constructed through discourse, which attests to identity as "a struggle of habitus and desire, of competing ideologies and imagined identities" (Darvin, Norton, 2015: 45).

To summarize, in the speech act of promoting personal competence, Chinese applicants have used various speech acts to convince foreign professors of their excellent candidature. Its working force differs from the speech act of pulling *guanxi*, which stresses professors' attraction to applicants. Instead, the self-presentation is supposed to create applicants' magnetic force to attract professors. The reverse working force of this speech act demonstrates the appearance of individual-competence-oriented habitus taking shape among young Chinese applicants.

4.4 Speech Act as Negotiating Entry

The last meso speech act to be discussed is negotiating institutional entry, which is to negotiate applicants' identity of moving from a domestic institution to a foreign institution. Becoming a PhD student or visiting scholar at foreign universities is the applicants' imagined identity in which they invest with great efforts through doing *Taoci*.

"Institution" in its simplest definition refers to workplace, like hospital, school, and court operated on the basis of a set of habitual

279

or routine practices (Sarangi, Roberts, 1999; Drew, Heritage, 1992). However, it is not necessarily physical. Agar (1985: 164) defined institution as "a socially legitimated expertise together with those persons authorized to implement it", which emphasizes legitimation and authorization indicating the nature of power in institution. Smith used the term "to identify a complex of relations forming part of the ruling apparatus, organized around a distinctive function—education, health care…" (Smith, 1987:160), highlighting the relation element. The power difference and relational positions are two most prominent features in institution (Benwell, Stokoe, 2006), which also characterize the institution (discussed in the present study.

Chinese applicants and their foreign professors are affiliated to different universities before the applicants are officially enrolled. Chinese applicants assume the role of student in a given university, say, Institution A in China, while foreign professors assume the role of professor or supervisor of, say, Institution B in America, British or other foreign countries. These are termed as the factual institutional roles, which preexist before the application, but find their ways to be re-presented through *Taoci* emails. However, when Chinese applicants perform *Taoci* with targeted professors, they place themselves at the student rank instead of "colleague", and their interlocutors are naturally imposed with the teacher position. This constitutes the imagined student-teacher dyad only legitimate from applicants' perspective, often considered illegitimate from supervisors' perspective.

On the other hand, when applicants start to prepare for their application and reach targeted professors, they engage themselves in the application system constituted by the two parties of "applicant" and "the applied PhD program" provided by foreign universities. Let it be defined as the remote "applicant-applicantee"[①] relation, with no identifiable physical setting thanks to the modern network and computer technology. The application institution involves habitual practices (e.g. a series of rules and policy, regular time frame, required documents, etc.) recognized by both parties. More importantly, there exists an inevitable power contrast between them with foreign universities as the powerful "employer", institutional representative or gatekeeper, and applicants as the passive "employee". In this mechanism, "supervisors can perform the role of gatekeepers to the discipline and qualification of a postgraduate research degree" (Miao, 2012: 10) and "professors represent their institution that grants them the positional power to

---

① Applicantee is a word coined by the present researcher to refer to either the applied professor or the applied university. It is used to capture its institutional role in opposition to "applicant".

perform professional actions upon students" (Chiang, 2009: 258). To help enroll suitable PhD candidates is one of the institutional responsibilities that professors undertake for their own department. However, once official offer is decided or letter of acceptance is issued to applicants, the dyad of Chinese students and foreign supervisors becomes institutionalized.

Compared with the meso speech acts of pulling *guanxi* and promoting self, the meso speech act of negotiating entry "cut to the chase" of the offer request—the ultimate goal of being enrolled—moving from a Chinese university to a targeted academic institution. However, these entry-negotiation requests exemplify different degrees of directness (or indirectness) at the micro linguistic level. Since institutional negotiation of entry is in essence about the offer request, this subsection classifies micro speech acts based on request content in accordance with the application timeline in order to capture what applicants perform discursively in their *Taoci* emails.

4.4.1 Inquiring Availability

The first and foremost thing is to make sure that the targeted foreign professors will recruit PhD students or provide funds for the program, which has been bantered as "door-knocking" on online *Taoci*

282

forums. After knowing that there is a vacancy or position, further entry-negotiating strategies would ensue.

The linguistic outputs of this request speech act are quite direct. Applicants have to behave bold-on-record about the availability of a position in the targeted institution, i.e. a request for information, even though the inquisition could get in the way of foreign professors' freedom. Some requests are phrased in direct forms, but applicants employ various strategies to alleviate that imposition.

(a) Imperative Form

There are only very few occurrences of imperative direct request in the data. Even when a direct request has to be made, it is alleviated through the use of politeness marker and conditional clause as Example (E181) shows.

(E181) If you have available funds and are interested in any applications from graduate students next fall, please let me know. (2014-03 Lin Jiang)

The main request is phrased in a directive form of the mood-derivable of "let me know", which could have, if used alone, greatly threatened the recipient's negative face. However, two linguistic devices help lessen the imposition: the fronted conditional clauses (*if you have available funds* and *if you are interested in any application*) and the

283

usage of the politeness marker of "please". The two conditional clauses prepare the email reader for the grammatical object of the sentence "let me know": funding and position. The usage of "any application (s)", instead of "my application" further lowers the imposition weight of the direct inquiry. Therefore, the preparatory moves lead to a smooth transition to the succeeding request, offending the recipient as least as possible.

(b) Statement Request

Another form of direct request is realized through stating the explicit performative action that applicants are then undertaking, or their intention, desire or feeling, corresponding the Blum-Kulka and Olshtain's (1984) explicit performative and scoping statement. However, they are put in one category because they are realized through the statement form. The typical linguistic outputs of such kind of performatives inlcude "asking", "wanting", "hoping", "wondering".

(E182) Therefore, I am here to ask if there is a Ph.D. position open for 2014 fall admission. (2014-01-01 Nan Zhou)

In Example (E182), Nan Zhou was performing the verbal action of "asking" by articulating his inquiry of "a Ph.D. position" explicitly. Although it is counted as a direct request, it appears not that imposing for the following reasons. First, there is no clear sign of involving the professor in this request since it is phrased as "there is a Ph.D. position open for 2014 fall admission", which gives a sense of objectivity and removes the possible imposition. Second, the conjunction of "Therefore" indicates that Nan Zhou paved his way to come up with the request, which actually he did according to his email content.

(E183) I was wondering if you are taking any new Ph.D. student next year. (2014-09-01 Pianhong Yin)

The word of "wondering" in Example (E183) is a mental verb about the applicant's cognitive processing and it is in a past tense. The structure "I was wondering..." is often used as a formulaic lead-in to the request locution. It also serves to lessen the imposition of that request.

(E184) **I want to** ask about whether you have any enrollment plan for the autumn term of next year. (2013-06-01 Qingwan Li)

(E185) **I hope** that you may reply me if there would be any opening position that you may encourage me to apply for. (2014-05 Wei Hong)

The "wanting" action in Example (E184) is about desire while "hoping" in Example (E185) is about expectation. The two inclination verbs, diverting from the cognition of "wondering" in Example (E183), are laden with applicants' emotion and disclosed a clear desire towards a positive feedback to the request.

The statement request has some feature of conventionally indirect speech in that the main information-seeking proposition is intact (e.g. *whether you have any enrollment plan...*). However, it seems much closer to the non-conventionally indirect request, in that by "stating what I am doing at that moment", it aims at "requiring you to do something for me", which goes astray from the conventional indirect speech act.

(c) Interrogative Request

The majority of the request action of the metaphorical door-knocking is in interrogative form, fronted with such modality verbs as "could" or "would" (reference to ability and willingness) and containing a complete proposition, which is a type of conventionally indirect request to lessen the possible impingement on the hearer. Examples are listed below.

(E186) **Could you tell me** if you have available PhD positions in the next academic year? (2013-3 Zhi Yu)

(E187) **Would you please** tell me how many doctoral students do you plan to enroll during this coming year? (2014-06-01 Liguo Zhao)

(E188) **Would you please** offer me some information, such as how many doctoral students you plan to enroll, and whether you plan to enroll international students? (2014-08-01 Yunyang Liu)

In Example (E186), the modalization form of "could" fronts the sentence. "Could" is an inquisition about the ability to carry out a task, i.e. questioning the felicity condition of preparatory condition (Searle, 1975). It is even more indirect than its present tense of "can". This form of request is highly conventionalized in English to convey the illocutionary force of "do it for me". The action required is "informing": telling me whether you have or you haven't available PhD positions in the next academic year.

The two examples of (E187) and (E188) all begin with the modulation term of "would". "Would" is concerned about "willingness", and conventionally more indirect than its present form of "will", which is supposed to deliver more politeness. The word of "would" is used together with the politeness marker of "please", which further helps decrease the potential imposition incurred by consulting information. As many of the inquisition requests start with "would" tailed by "please", the formulaic expression of "would you please" becomes a situation-bound utterance among Chinese applicants framing their request. Although there are some grammatical problems in these sentences, e.g. "tell me how many doctoral students do you plan" in Example (E187) should have been "tell me how many doctoral student you plan", the request for information is delivered successfully in spite of the formal blemish as applicants receive feedback email informing them about the inquired availability.

The speech act of inquiring about position availability appears either at the beginning or at the end of the email, and none of them are posed in the middle of an email text, which fall into two types of textual unfolding: inductive and deductive. For the inductive, applicants pull *guanxi* and/or presented themselves and then come to the key question about enrollment, a typical oriental rhetorical style (Kaplan, 1966). For the deductive, availability checking is put at the beginning and the rest part served as supporting evidences to convince recipients for a positive feedback, a typical western logic. It is interesting that the deductive logic takes a dominant share among the email text data. As we understand it, the language used—English—might have some influence on this tendency, as English is more analytical and Chinese English learners are more often than not taught or even reminded to follow this kind of rhetoric logic in classroom or other settings. The change of rhetorical style may indicate a change of linguistic habitus due to the learning of English.

4.4.2 Asking for Offer

Compared to the information request in the act of inquiring availability, the offer request is more heavily imposed on recipients. Even in the very initial email, applicants may start to bid for the offer request for an invitation letter, recruitment, chance, position, etc. The following analysis is made based on the dichotomy of implicitness and explicitness. Implicitness and explicitness are adopted instead of indirectness and directness because the latter dichotomy is often described in terms of continuum while the implicitness and explicitness are distinguished by me based on the appearance of a cluster of semantic meanings of "offer". Undoubtedly, there exists a degree of explicitness and implicitness in light of the degree of interference into recipient's freedom.

4.4.2.1 The Explicit Category

The explicit request for offer is realized through mentioning the offer itself. The explicitness is scaled into intensified request, plain request and mitigated request.

(a) Intensified Request

Intensified request refers to instances that the request is not only brought forward directly, i.e. bald-on-record in Brown and Levinson's

289

(1987) terms, but also intensified through the sentential structure. Bold-on-record means doing an act boldly, the most clear, direct, unambiguous and concise way.

(E189) Now what I need is a chance offered by you. (2014-08-04 Yunyang Liu)

(E190) What I need from you is an invitation letter… (2015-07 Xiaoyun Fang)

In Example (E189), "a chance" refers to a chance to be recruited by the targeted professor's research team. This request was made in the fourth email written by Yunyang Liu, who was then undergoing great pressure confronting with no funded offer coming. Example (E190) raised the offer request of invitation letter for a visiting position. In both cases, the sentences are structured into the appositive complex form ("What I need…"), which means the position of subject and complement is interchangeable. This emphatic structure indicates the two applicants' strong desire to obtain the offer. In particular in the first example, the time adjunct "Now" sounds like "time is pressing", and the authority of the professor is also underlined through the passive structure ("offered by you"), which implies that the professor has the power to issue an offer. Such kind of intensification could leave a strong impression that the applicants were urging the professors to make a decision and actually infringed the latter's autonomy. However, it might also convey the applicants' strong loyalty to the professor, which overlaps a little with the *guanxi*-pulling strategy of "showing loyalty".

(b) Plain Request

Plain request means that there are no obvious evaluative terms and the tone sounds mild. It is realized through statement expressions as the following examples show.

(E191) ...I am looking for a PhD position on MRI in *** Uni. (2015-30 Ningfu He)

(E192) I am writing to apply for the Letter of Acceptance. (2015-46 Guo Fang)

(E193) ...I am writing to ask for an invitation letter for my application of studying one year in your department as a visiting student. (2015-10 Hong Cai)

The explicit statement of purpose for "a PhD position" in Example (E191), "the Letter of Acceptance" in Example (E192), "an invitation letter" in Example (E193) is not modified with other terms, creating a sense of distance between the two parties. Thus, it is a request, but the statement passes over no strong interference into the professors' action, because applicants were just stating their own behaviors and professors were free to make their choices to give either positive or negative reply, or neither.

(c) Mitigated Request

Mitigated request is concerned about requests that are mitigated through different linguistic devices, thus lifting up the burden of imposition for a while.

(E194) I am writing to you about **the possibility** of studying and researching in your group as a visiting scholar. (2015-27 Panpan Cai)

In Example (E194), the use of the modality noun of "possibility" gives the impression that the applicant was not intending to make any positive presupposition about the offer. It treats "studying and researching in your group as visiting scholar" as a matter of possibility to negotiate, instead of some preexisting fact as the previous examples have shown. In other words, the applicant could claim that he was just making the move of consultation rather than making the request. Thus, the embedded imposition can be reduced to a great extent.

(E195) I'll **appreciate greatly** if you could kindly offer me a letter of invitation. **I do not need any credit from your university**. (2015-24 Lan Yang)

In Example (E195), the mitigator is reified through two forms: showing gratitude and giving a reason. The gratitude is delivered through a formal expression of "appreciate" together with its intensifier of "greatly" served as a comfort to the imposition. The upcoming explanation of "I don't need any credit from your university" means that "I won't bother you in the institutional course matter, so you don't have institutional responsibility for me", functioning as a disclaimer for the offer request of invitation letter. The two mitigators alleviate

292

the face-threatening volume.

(E196) **He [Chinese supervisor] asked me to contact you** for the reason that I have strong desire to become a visiting student of *** University. (2015-04 Feifei Hu)

Attribution, as an engagement device, is to attribute the claim to some external source (Martin, White, 2008), thus externalized the proposition. In Example (E196), the applicant claimed that his Chinese professor asked him to contact the foreign professor for the issue of overseas visiting position. There could be two ways of interpretation. The first is that the applicants ascribed his strong desire to become a visiting student in the professor's institution to an external voice, so it was not solely his own idea. If there was any feeling of impingement from the professor, the responsibility for such imposition could be split and accordingly it was lessened on the applicant's side. The other explanation could be the strategy of introducing the intermediary (the Chinese professor's name) in the solidarity-oriented strategy.

4.4.2.2   The Inexplicit Category

In the situation of inexplicit offer request, the "offer" itself does not appear and email readers have to make some inferences about it. Different degrees of cognitive effort are required for hearer to process these requests. Three types are distinguished based on the email data content: showing willingness to work for the professor, wanting to have the professor as supervisor and discursively pregnant request. The first two are achieved within a grammatical sentence, while the third is made at the discourse level.

(a) Having You as My Supervisor

(E197) I would be so happy if I could have you as my PhD supervisor. (2014-08 Zhijing Xiang)

(E198) I am writing to ask whether you are willing to be my hosting foreign supervisor from *** 2014 to ***, 2015, 12 months in total. (2015-35 Fang Xu)

In Examples (E197) and (E198), both applicants expressed their expectation to have the targeted professors as their supervisors. Becoming someone's supervisor means having the person enrolled or recruited into the institution. This type of request is the closest to explicit request. Still the action of asking for the offer itself is absent and an inference is called for on the recipient's side: "Since I want you to be my supervisor, can you give me the offer?".

(b) Willingness to Work with Professor

(E199) ...and hope that I could have the chance to study and work in your lab. (2013-04-01 Chu Gao1)

(E200) if I am admitted to your program, I am more than willing to work with

294

you. (2013-05-01 Ran Xia)

(E201) I would like to explore the possibility of doing research with you. (2014-03 Lin Jiang)

In the above-listed three examples, Chu Gao claimed to hope to work in the professor's lab, Ran Xia said he was willing to work with the professor, and Lin Jiang wanted to look for a chance to do research with the professor, all three of which demonstrated that they were willing to work with/for the foreign professors. The inference works like "Do you have any position available in your team?" "Since I want to work with you, I want to have you as my supervisor, so can you give me the offer?" There is one more step needed in the processing, thus more implicit than the previous one, "having you as my supervisor".

(c) Pregnant Request

Pregnant request means that the action of request for offer is not explicit and it had to be deciphered at a discourse level. Two examples are provided below.

(E202) I'm writing this email is about the PhD program in your research group... I want to pursue a PhD in the next year. (2014-04 Zhou Zhou)

The first half of Example (E202) was the beginning sentence of

Zhou Zhou's email and the second half was the ending. The first half was only about his consultation about the PhD program instead of "checking available position". The second half showed his intention to study for a PhD degree, but failed to point out his purpose to study for a PhD degree in the professor's program. There was no other clear sign of offer request and the professor had to make the inference at the whole textual level: *You want to know about my program, you want to pursue a PhD degree, and you wrote this email to me, so I assume that you want to work on the PhD project in my group, so you are asking for an offer.* Apparently, this inference costs much more efforts than the previous two implicit requests.

Another example of (E203) is given below.

(E203)

1 Dear Prof. **,

2 Thank you for the lecture "Defects in materials and their mathematical description"

3 given for celebrating 100 years of mathematics at *** University last week. I was

4 amazed by the example which the functional have different minimizer in different W1,p,

5 so after the lecture I asked you how can we choose the suitable spaces for the energy

6 functional when facing the real material. I want to know more about the mathematical

7 description of defects. **Could you please send me the PPT you used in the lecture or**

8 **other materials**?

9 I received my bachelor degree in Information and Computing Sciences from ***

10 University. Now I'm a second year graduate student of *** University in China, and

11 my current major is pure mathematics. But I also realize that we are in the real world

12 and we should do something for our society not just the empire of mathematic itself.

13 My ultimate goal is to be an applied mathematician who can solve problems rises from

14 practical demands. To do so, solid foundation of basic mathematic is indispensable,

15 that's why I choose pure mathematics as my graduate major at *** University. After a

16 year's study I think I have equipped with strong mathematical basis and it's time for

17 me to turn to applied mathematics. **So I want to apply *** University's mathematics**

297

18 **and I have an intense desire to do something closed to our life and nature.**

19 Thank you very much!

20 Best regards!

21 *** (signature)   (2015-36 Zhen Fan)

   The email text begins with a respectful addressing term and continued with a gratitude for the targeted professor's lecture given in the applicant's institution. The applicant mentioned that they had some previous association (*guanxi*-pulling strategy) and then posed the only explicit request speech act occurring in the email in Line 7, where he asked the professor to send him the lecture material. In the second paragraph, he was detailing his academic background (Me-oriented strategy) and expressed his imagined identity of becoming an "applied mathematician" in Line 13 and what he had done for this goal. In Line 17, he mentioned that he wanted to apply for mathematics in the professor's university in order to "do something closed to our life and nature". There is a long series of preparatory sequence to arrive at his desire to "apply *** University's mathematics". Nevertheless, even read closely, there is no literal signal to the hearer that the applicant wanted to get an offer from the professor or his institution except the "want"-request in Line 17. The inference processing effort for the professor seems much more enormous: *you attended my lecture and*

298

you showed interest in my topic by asking for my PPT; you aimed at becoming an applied mathematician and you did a lot of preparation for this ambition; you show intention to apply for my university and I am a mathematician professor in our institution; and you are writing to me, so you may want to have me as your supervisor and want an offer from me.

As observed, the pregnant request for offer is behind the skin of textual lines, just like we know there is a baby in a pregnant woman's belly, but we could see no part of it at all. To wit, the applicant is beating around the bush and falls into the stereotyped oriental rhetorical style (Kaplan, 1966). This kind of writing style might echo that "Chinese indirectness in polite requests is manifested **at the discourse level**, through a series of supportive moves, rather than syntactic structures at the sentence level" (Chen, 2001: 4, bold added by the present author).

The speech act of offer request demonstrates Chinese applicants' straightforward move to fight for an offer, though some of them detoured discursively through preparatory moves or using softeners. The ostensible action of asking for an offer to some extent diverts from the traditional Chinese value of being indirect in front of the higher-status. However, the local value of behaving subtly cannot function well under the competitive global context, dominated by English-speaking countries' norms and ideologies. Therefore, "…their [learners'] styles and registers are measured against a value system that reflects the biases and assumptions of the larger sociocultural context" (Darvin, Norton, 2015: 45). In this process, the local is moving towards the dominantly global, which probably contributes to the change of the cultural and linguistic habitus of the Chinese young generation.

4.4.3 Informing Application Status

Informing application status is to state the "applicant" role in the institutionalized overseas application system. Applicants state explicitly in their email that they are applicants or they have submitted application files. Thus, the linguistic realization consists of two forms based on the action content: being an applicant and submitting an application.

(E204) I am an **applicant** to *** University computer science PhD program in fall, 2013. I completed the steps in the application system about 10 weeks ago. (2013-3 Zhi Yu)

(E205) I'm Wei Hong, **an applicant** for ECE in **U (Applicant ID: ****). Now my application status is admissible. (2014-05 Wei Hong)

(E206) I have **applied** to the Ph. D. program of your department. (2013-01 Qiang Miao)

In Example (E204), the noun of "applicant" declares Zhi Yu's application status. This role is further supported by the subsequent clause, which indicates the time when he was officially engaged in the application system (*I completed the steps in the application system...*). In Example (E205), Wei Hong told the professor her application ID of applying for the targeted university. The ID number represents an authoritative censorship of her application. Furthermore, she told the professor that her application was then admissible, and she then needed to look for an advisor as well as funding. In Example (E206), being an applicant is reflected through the verb of "applied". Although Hui Miao used the wrong collocation of "applied to" as the correct expression is "applied for", he could still be understood as a prospective applicant.

(E207) ..., so I **submitted applied** to EEB Program at U**. (2013-02 Si Chen)

(E208) I **submitted the application** just now and mentioned your name in my Personal Statement (2013-07-02 Huyang Long)

(E209) I have just **submitted my application** of *** 2014 Fall Ph.D. Enrolling programe. (2014-08-03 Yunyang Liu)

(E210) **My information are submitted** to Ms SATO and she told me that she would send you my material soon. (2015-44 Yan Tang)

The four examples all resort to the action form of "submit application" to describe them as "applicants". Si Chen in Example (E207) mentioned specifically her application for "EEB Program". In Example (208) Huyang pointed out that he added the professor's name

301

in his personal statement, which indicated he wanted the professors as his supervisor. Yunyang Liu specified his application status for the "2014 Fall Ph.D. Enrolling" in Example (209). Example (E210) shows the applicants' information submitted to the enrollment secretary. There are some grammatical mistakes in the expressions. "Submitted applied" should have been "submitted my application" in Example (E207), and "my information are submitted" should have been "my application is submitted" in Example (E210). Nevertheless, readers would not mistake the message: the email sender was an official applicant in the application institution. In other words, the speech act of "informing application status" shows that applicants are working their way out, from the domestic/local talent identity to the international/ global sojourner identity.

4.4.4　Following up Application Status

If there is a positive answer from professors to the previous discussed requests and it means the door of the application institution is kept ajar for applicants though they are still outside. In the rest of *Taoci* process, applicants would seize the optimistic signal and follow up their application status closely. It is a way to maintain contact with professors to inquire about the application progress, and has some overlapping zone with the strategy of "keeping frequent contact". The only difference is the contact content: review progress, research funding issue, and offer release time. This kind of speech act is abstracted from applicants' *Taoci* email packages because it only occurrs in the rest of communication after the initial contact.

4.4.4.1   Tracking Down Progress

(E211) I want to ask about the status of my application, cause I really want to join your group in the coming fall semester. (2013-07-03 Huyang Long)

(E212) Since it's been a while when I submitted my application to the psychology department, I am wondering how the review process is going. Will there be an interview soon? (2014-09-04 Pianhong Yin)

In Example (E211), Huyang was checking about his "status of application" in his third email to the professor and added the reason that he really looked forward to joining the professor's group. According to his interview, it was then February, when the application was still under review and no offer decision came out as the professor replied "Your application is currently under review". Huyang mentioned in his interview that he tried to contact the professor once a month, neither too less nor too frequently so as to keep the professor informed that he really wanted to go to his group and he was still available. He added that it was not only checking his own application status but also keeping contact for the sake of contact. In Example (E212), in her fourth email, Pianhong Yin asked about the review progress and the interview issue. This email was sent in January when the review progress didn't start yet and the professor replied "*** University's PBS grad programme will be having a recruitment/interview weekend in late February for prospective students". Knowing about the interview time frame, Pianhong could better set up her own schedule, such as arranging her winter holiday, writing her graduation thesis, and making better preparation for the admission interview in late February.

4.4.4.2 Consulting about Financial Issue

Funding source (e.g. scholarship, fellowship, research assistantship, teaching assistantship) couldn't be more important, especially for PhD program applicants who couldn't afford the expensive expenditure in overseas study. Therefore, they would try hard to figure that out before they made a decision to accept an offer.

(E213) May I know about the RA if I get the offer from you? (2013-05-04 Ran Xia)

(E214) Actually I am concerned about the financial issues. Since my family isn't wealthy enough to support my phd work, I am wondering if I am gonna receive financial support from ***. Do I need to apply for some kind of scholarship? (2014-09-02 Pianhong Yin)

In Example (E213), Ran Xia asked about the RA (research assistantship) in his fourth email by using a conventionally indirect form. In Example (E214), Pianhong consulted about whether she would receive financial support from the targeted university and if there wasn't whether she needed to apply for other funding sources. She gave a reason (*my family isn't wealthy enough to support my phd work*) as a pre-request move to validate her questions. If given an admission without funding resource, many applicants would like to give up and find another way out, like the interview informant Qingwan Li said,

(I19) "It is so expensive to study in America. Only the tuition fee, will burden out an ordinary Chinese family "breathless". If there is no money [scholarship], who would like to come here to study for a PhD degree? Of course, for those rich families, it is not a problem." (Interview transcripts 2014-Dec. Qingwan Li)

As we can observe from the interview excerpt, economic capital plays a crucial role in the PhD program application. By doing *Taoci*, applicants want to seek the economic capital that would afford their study-abroad expenditure. Therefore, applicants have to confirm the funding sources if they're going to attend foreign schools, especially when foreign professors do not initiate the funding topic. However, such kind of consultation about financial support never appears in the first email or the beginning of an email, which might be due to the following reasons. First, the financial issue is usually taken into consideration after the admission notice. Second, it would sound too

305

direct and even weird for the Chinese students if the "money" issue is talked at the beginning as one participant reflected as follows,

(I20) "I remember once I sent an email to a professor in *** University. Actually I wanted to ask about the money issue, that is, I wanted to ask him that I had admission and do you have money to support me. But I felt it is too strange to ask that directly. Just think about it, if you are a professor and a student asks about the money issue at the very beginning of communication, why should I give you that money?" (Interview transcripts 2014-Dec. Shunying Qin)

In Shunying's mind, talking about money was not regarded as a proper topic with professors. She also mentioned in the interview that she finally tried to ask her foreign supervisor about the money issue in the later phase of her *Taoci* period, but she could not do it and at last she said something else in Interview (I21) below.

(I21) Oh, about asking about how is it going in *** city (the professor's city). Actually in that email, I had planned to ask him about the funding issue, the money. However after give it a second thought, I still decided to say something else, the flowers. (Interview transcripts 2014-Dec. Shunying Qin)

It seems that money is a taboo, particularly when the lower-status student communicates with the higher-status professor. Money should be put behind the scene. This might be related to the Chinese value of stressing renqing instead of material when people are trying

306

to build up *guanxi*. Still many applicants try to address this important financial issue directly with their foreign professors, just like doing business in the western style.

4.4.4.3   Chasing the Final Decision

Taoci comes to a halt when the application season ends. Naturally, at the later stage of the *Taoci* process, applicants would like to know exactly their application result: accepted or rejected.

(E215) When can I get the final official offer? (2013-07-11 Huyang Long)

(E216) So I wonder if the admission committee have made their decision about my application to the PhD program. (2013-04-03 Qingwan Li)

(E217) I was just wondering how the review of applications is going on in *** University. I received an offer the other day but I really like your program and it's my top choice right now. (2014-09-06 Pianhong Yin)

Example (E215) is extracted from Huyang's eleventh email (15 emails in all), Example (E216) is Qingwan's fourth email (6 in all) and Example (E217) Pianhong's sixth email (9 in all). All of them are concerned about the final result of their application. In detail, Huyang wanted to know the "final official offer"; Qinwan wondered the committee's decision about her application; Pianhong tried to make a decision about where to go based on her application in *** University. Compared to Huyang and Qingwan, Pianhong seemed to have more options, because she mentioned that she had received an offer from another foreign institute. It resembled the move of "Using pressure tactics" in Bhatia (1993), when job applicants felt they had much higher stakes than the employer and negotiated the offer from position of strength. As Bhatia also noted such kind of move was only occasional on the competitive market, in my data, Pianhong was the only case I encountered. Whatever stakes Pianhong had in her hands, she still regarded *** University as her dream school, so it was justifiable for her to know about *** University's review result.

In the system of overseas application, applicants have no power at all on the control of committee review progress, financial issue and offer decision. They are supposed to "sit and wait" for any decision made by foreign universities. However, the examples given above, to some extent, demonstrate applicants' active involvement in following up their application status instead of being informed at the last moment. If they know more about their own application progress, at least they could have choices. For example, if the chance of getting the offer from one university seemed bleak, applicants could invest more on another university by making more communication with the professor in that university. If all the overseas programs turn them down, at least they could look for a job at home, or take into consideration doing graduate programs in domestic universities. Following up application status actually manifests applicants' agency and resistance against being kept waiting.

4.4.5　Asking for "Illegitimate" Favor

Asking for illegitimate favor refers to the situation when the requested help or information actually goes beyond foreign professors' institutional responsibility as a gatekeeper of the application system or a representative of their universities. Following Bourdieu's argument that "'legitimate' and 'illegitimate' speakers are distinguished by their differential 'rights to speech' or their 'power to impose reception'" (Bourdieu, 1977: 648), the legitimacy of requests raised by applicants as not necessarily acknowledged by the latter. Therefore, the question of legitimacy and illegitimacy of utterance boils down to whether speakers are on the right position to impose his speech act in that "speech always owes a major part of its value to the value of the person who utters it" (Bourdieu, 1977: 652). The legitimacy of the speaker's utterance is inseparable from the social structural positions. In the *Taoci* situation, applicants' positional value is attached to the applicant role with regards to the representative applicantee of foreign professors in the application institution. Therefore, an utterance is regarded as legitimate and could be taken by recipient if it matched such an institutional dyad. The examples of request in the previous four subsections fall into foreign professors' routine duty to answer questions from and solve problems for prospective international candidates. The illegitimacy is divided into two types based on the exchanged content: information and help, or in Halliday's (1994) terms "questioning" and "commanding". Before we venture into illegitimate request, I would like to further the discussion on what legitimate request looked like.

(a) Legitimate Questioning

(E218) And about the program, I have read the Ph.D. Degree requirements on the department website. Do students take most of their required courses in their first year? (which is a common case in my current department). (2014-10-04 Shunying Qin)

In Example (E218), Shunying was inquiring about whether PhD students needed to finish all the required courses in their first year and she gave a reason for her question "which is a common case in my current department". This question is concerned about course-taking, which is usually individual preference and within the duty the requirement of graduate program. Supervisors would give advice on taking courses, but how and when candidates took them was out of their duty. Therefore, this question makes the foreign professor deal with some administrative business and could be regarded as illegitimate question. However, if the context of this email is examined, the illegitimacy would vanish. This email was sent after Shunying was told by the professor that "I have informed the department that I would like to offer you a position in my group" and "In the meanwhile, please feel free to contact me if you have any questions about your future research plan, our phd program, career plan, or living in the US or ***University". Although Shunying didn't get the official offer at that time, the professor had the power to nail down her institutional membership in his research group and gave her the permission to get in touch for any problems, including course-taking in his PhD program. Hence, her information request about course-taking turns out legitimate with the professor's empowerment, i.e. she had the "power to impose reception" (Bourdieu, 1977: 648).

(b) Legitimate Commanding

(E219) Could you please send me a more detailed resume? (2013-07-14 Huyang Long)

In this example, Huyang asked the professor to send him a more detailed resume because he needed it for his visa application. This was a request for help, i.e. commanding, because then Huyang had been informed by the professor saying "You'll receive the letter within this month. You'll get fellowship, and on top of that, 0.5 TAship". Although

Huyang hadn't received the official letter of offer, the professor gave his words to Huyang's admission and scholarship and considered him a legitimate PhD candidate in his research lab. As a result, Huyang's asking for help with the visa processing was accepted as legitimate imposition, i.e. he got the right to impose reception.

However, if offers hadn't been bid to applicants (officially or personally), or professors didn't give applicants the power to ask for help or information, the request would turn illegitimate. That is where we depart for illegitimate request in the next subsection.

4.4.5.1　Illegitimate Questioning

(E220) A Tier-4 VISA needs the CAS (Confirmations of Acceptance for Studies) number provided by the university, so do you think it's possible that I can get the number? (2015-04)

Example (E220) is drawn from the applicant's first email to his targeted professor. The applicant was asking whether he would get the CAS number for Tier-4 VISA application. This occurred in the very first contact when no agreement of acceptance was reached yet. Dealing with students' visa application is not within the duty of the professor, so it is illegitimately addressed to the professor.

(E221) Would you please tell me ... whether it is possible for me to be enrolled? (2014-06-01 Liguo Zhao)

(E222) <u>Do you think I am a competitive</u> candidate among all the applicants? (2014-08-03 Yunyang Liu)

(E223) Finally, <u>I want to ask about your attitude toward my application</u> to be your PhD student. (2014-08-06 Yunyang Liu)

The three examples are all about soliciting personal opinion about their application issues from targeted professors. Liguo Zhao in Example (E221) asked whether it was possible for him to be admitted. Yunyang Liu in his third email as shown in Example (E222) and sixth email in Example (E223) asked whether the professor thought him competitive and required the professor's attitude towards his application. As we know, the enrollment system in America is a complex mechanism involving graduate school, department decision and committee board. All applications will go to enrollment committee for panel discussion. Hence supervisors have no absolute power to give an offer to an applicant, though they can argue for their desirable candidates. Before committee convenes, professors usually have no final say about offer decision. It is safer for professors not to reveal their preferences during the early application phase because if there were anything unexpected, a biased attitude would lead to possible troubles or awkwardness. Therefore, the questioning about professors' attitude in the three examples could be regarded as "illegitimate" because they were addressed not at the appropriate time as well as to the inappropriate personnel. Luckily for Liguo Zhao, he received a promising response from the professor stating "while it's hard to guarantee that I will hire student, certainly the chance is high". However, Huyang Liu didn't get any response to his two questions, which further proves the illegitimacy of his requests.

4.4.5.2 Requiring Illegitimate Help

(E224) Would you recommend something more to help me successfully get a position in your group? (2014-06-02 Liguo Zhao)

(E225) Besides, since I have relatively insufficient experience on your field, would you please list some elementary reading material for me? (2014-08-02 Yunyang Liu)

In Example (E224), Liguo Zhao asked the professor to recommend something to help him obtain the PhD position. In Example (E225), Yuyang Liu asked the professor for a reading list in the professor's academic direction after he received a positive feedback from the professor in which the professor encouraged him to apply for the position. Liguo received a reply from his professor saying "Just keep up the good work" instead of recommending what Liguo wanted, while Yuyang heard nothing from his targeted professor. The two applicants seemingly intended to construct an imagined student-advisor dyad from the applicants' perspective. Both applicants had received promising replies from their respectively targeted professors, so they naturally placed themselves into the student spot. In China, teachers are usually expected to assume not only institutional duty but also hold parent-like responsibility to take care of students as one's teacher is on a par with one's father under the influence of the Confucian doctrine and the Five Codes of Ethics. Here the foreign professors were also mistaken as caring professor who would help them with whatever concerned about study. However, such questions infringed foreign professors' autonomy in particular under the situation where the applicants were not yet admitted. Therefore, the applicants were not endowed with the power to impose and their requests were not legitimate.

4.4.5.3   Flipping the Illegitimate into Legitimate

The imagined student-advisor dyad could be transformed into a real one during *Taoci* process if professors volunteers to engage him/herself in the applicant's imagination. Qingwan's case is used to illustrate this point.

(a) Applicant Asked for Information and Professor Gave Information

(E226) I write to ask as an international student if I need a GRE score for application? The website information points out the domestic student must get one, but doesn't make it clear whether the international student have to. (2013-06-03 Qingwan Li)

(E227) I was packing application materials to mail them but I found two different addresses to send application, and I would like to ask which one should I send application materials to. (2013-06-06 Qingwan Li)

In Example (E226), Qingwan asked whether she needed to provide her GRE score for the application. English proficiency certificate was an officially required document in the application portfolio. Consultation about institutional requirement should be addressed to the administrative personnel dealing with the application processing, like secretary, not the professor. In Example (E227), Qingwan was concerned about the mailing address because the given addresses mixed up. This question was also beyond the professor's duty to solve. It should have been sent to administrative staff. Although the questions are perceived illegitimate by most foreign professors and might be totally ignored without any response, its legitimacy was acknowledged by the professor's positive engagement in helping tackle these problems. To Qingwan's first concern, the professor replied below.

(E228) I believe that all graduate students will need to have a GRE score. Let me know if you have other questions. (2013-06-03' Qingwan Li)

The first part of Example (E228) is a direct solution to Qingwan's question while the second sentence a voluntary offering for help in a directive tone. It shows the professor's willingness to deal with Qingwan's questions and discloses a bearing of being a helpful advisor, which has encouraged Qingwan's following illegitimate moves. To Qingwan's second concern about the mailing address, the professor wrote back in Example (229) below. The professor even contacted her colleague in the administration to clarify Qingwan's confusion and gave her the correct address.

(E229) Below is my colleague's response for the correct address. (2013-06-06' Qingwan Li)

(b) Applicant Commanded Help and Professor Offered help

The help that Qingwan sought from the professor related to the issue of writing her personal statement and study plan, which led to four email rounds. These email texts present a kind of supervisee-supervisor relationship.

(E230) By the way, I am not very satisfied with this version of statement and I want to revise it again. Would you mind giving me some advice about how to revise it? (2013-06-07 Qingwan Li)

(E231) I wondered if I should cut the background part and say more about Chinese archaeology, or the details about the object I would like to investigate on. If so,

317

how specific should I describe it? (2013-06-08 Qingwan Li)

(E232) Would you mind taking a look at the new version? I added some information about "why choosing UI" and a general study plan. Considering the word account limitation at the website page, the study plan may be a little short and it's only a general description instead of a precise plan. Shall I specify it more? (2013-06-10 Qingwan Li)

In Example (E230), Qingwan said that she was not satisfied with her personal statement and needed the professor's advice on it. In Example (E231), she asked about the content in her statement and the degree of specificity to describe the background part. In Example (E232), she asked for a favor for a final check on her personal statement before she sent out the application package to the applied university. To each of her concern, the professor answered in great details and made constructive suggestions as follows:

(E233) I did some editing changes. Most of the changes are not about right or wrong. It is more about clarity, remember that your readers are mostly people who know a lot about *** but not *** in China. (2013-06-07 Qingwan Li)

(E234) I think that it is fine to keep the background part. However, for your research question and study interest, it is better to be as clear and specific as possible. For example, you can talk about what you would like to understand based on the analysis of settlement pattern? Do you plan to study Yangshao settlement pattern or Sichuan? How would you plan to do that? Who at IU can potentially

318

work with you regarding what you plan to do? (2013-06-08' Qingwan Li)

(E235) <u>I did some editing in this version</u>. I think this version is much better than the first one. If there is a word limitation, then don't go over it. Still, be as concise as possible! (2013-06-10' Qingwan Li)

In Examples (E233) and (E234), he commented on Qingwan's writing that "Most of the changes are not about right or wrong. It is more about clarity" and "I think this version is much better than the first one", playing the role of an evaluator. In Example (E235), he raised several consecutive questions for Qingwan to reflect on her writing, acting like a guider, and he offered the advice of "it is better to be as clear and specific as possible", behaving like an advisor to coach. In Examples (E233) and (E234), he used direct speech acts to guide Qingwan's writing "remember that your readers are mostly people who know a lot about *** but not *** in China" and "If there is a word limitation, then don't go over it. Still, be as concise as possible!" The tone in these sentences sounds like a supervisor performing his role of advising students' thesis. This kind of interaction fits what Dong (2012) generalized about the identity relation between Chinese students and British supervisors during thesis supervision session, e.g. professor as the evaluator and student as the evaluated, professor as the questioner and student as the answerer, professor as the advisor and student as the advisee. The professor's active "supervision" in helping Qingwan to enhance her personal statement and research plan legitimatized all Qingwan's illegitimate request, turning the illegitimate reception imposition into a legitimate one. Qingwan also seemed to couch on the student spot comfortably to accept the professor's kind help. However, it didn't mean that the professor had the total power in deciding her application, as he pointed out in his later email reply, "At the same time, you should also apply for other graduate programs. Because of funding issue, my department may admit fewer students this year than before."

Qingwan reflected her *Taoci* email communication with the professor in the interview:

(I21) I didn't expect that he was so nice. He helped me to revise my personal statement. You can just imagine that, I would not even have thought about it. I was just so lucky. I basically, he volunteered to look at my personal statement. And he reminded me of not only applying for *** University and that's very risky. He was very considerate. The key point is that, he knew my teacher (Chinese supervisor). He is genuinely considering that for me. Another point, perhaps, another layer of *guanxi*, we are actually alumni because he graduated from my university more than ten years ago. Perhaps because of this *guanxi*, he also wanted to guide and support (*tixie*, 提携) me as the younger school-sister, so he offered to help me with the PS issue. I felt I was just so lucky, soooo lucky,

320

luck strikes me. (Interview transcripts 2014-Dec. Qingwan Li)

As the interview content revealed, Qingwan entered the *Taoci* process endowed with a dependable social capital: the networking of alumni, supervisor as intermediary and schooling sistership. However, she only knew that she had this capital available to invest as affordances after she contacted the professor, because later she knew the targeted professor contacted one of her course teachers in her department. Therefore, the social capital of *guanxi* was only lurking until it was invigorated or "embezzled" into the actual *guanxi*-building process in the international PhD program application. The networking resource facilitated Qianwan's successful application much. However, without *Taoci*, as Qingwan mentioned, she would have never known the capital she could use and would have probably received no offer from the professor. In the similar vein, due to the activated *guanxi* capital put on the global offer hunting market, Qingwan's illegitimate requests were all turned into legitimate ones by the professor's helpful support in the following email exchanges. Close to the end of the *Taoci* course, Qingwan had the professor as her social capital too, since when the panel convened for review, the professor argued for her candidature revealed from her interview transcripts.

Chen (2006) appraised that Asian students may show a high level of deference to teachers (e.g. using formal address terms, honorifics, and indirect moves) while taking for granted their rights to ask for teachers' help. Chinese applicants feel safer to place themselves at the "student" position instead of "colleague", and their interlocutors naturally are imposed with the "teacher" role. It is probable that applicants adopt this traditional "teacher-as-parent" cultural habitus with or without self-awareness. This constitutes the imagined student-teacher dyad only effective from the applicant's perspective. If recipients barely respond to illegitimate requests, the imagined dyad of student-advisor would go totally disillusioned. On the contrary, if the request, however illegitimate it sounds to outsiders, solicits a promising feedback, the illegitimacy will be dissolved at least between the interlocutors and applicants are handed over "the power to impose reception" (Bourdieu, 1977: 648). L2 learners can create new opportunities to interact with English speakers by drawing on and activating their multiple as well as potential identities (Norton, 2000). As the subject is both positioned by relations of power and resistant to that positioning, he or she may "set up a counterdiscourse [illegitimate questions and commands] which positions him or her in a powerful rather than marginalizes subject position" (Norton, 2000: 16), just as what Qingwan Li has turned those illegitimate requests into legitimate ones to help her achieve her study-abroad dream.

The occurrence of the five micro speech acts of negotiating institutional entry has been calculated and is presented in Fig. 4.5. Asking for offer has the most prominent, which matches the assumption of *Taoci* as request email at a macro level. Informing application status comes next since most applicants tend to tell potential professors about their application plan at the very beginning of *Taoci*. Following up application is the least probably because it happens in the middle of *Taoci* and the email packages are not enough in the data pool.

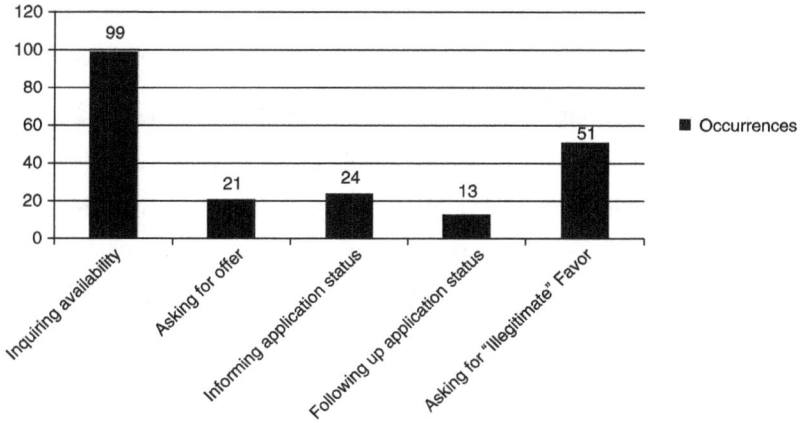

Fig. 4.5   Entry-negotiating strategy distribution

323

4.4.6 Sectional Discussion: Investment for Imagined Identity

The meso speech act of negotiating entry is mainly request, direct or indirect request, request for information or offer, illegitimate or legitimate. It represents applicants' initiative investment in their future institutional identity in foreign education universities.

Once the applicants decide on their application issue, they acquire the international "applicant" role. As they contact their targeted professor, this role could undergo constant evolution from the beginning of "being an applicant" to the end of "turning into an official member in a foreign university", i.e. a change of institutional identity from domestic to international. The application system amounts to a transitional institution to tide applicants over into their desired future of becoming internationally (or interculturally) educated. The institutional entry is not only part of their imagined identity, but also symbolizes all forms of capitals, social, cultural, economic and symbolic, which drives applicants to invest the capitals they have enjoyed as affordance (Darvin, Norton, 2015) in order to occupy new spaces (physically moving the foreign countries) and acquire new material and symbolic resources.

In the entry negotiating process, applicants' agency seems to be restricted as the discovered strategies are more often than not falling into my anticipation: asking for information and raising the offer request. However, these are signs of applicants' refusing to totally subscribing to the institutional power through performing discursive speech action, such as tracking down their application status, raising illegitimate requests, assuming imagined institutional identities, turning illegitimate requests into legitimate ones. The speech act of request itself demonstrates Chinese applicants' agency in fighting for their imagined institutional identities, and desirable social and cultural capitals in the international higher education field. The directness of asking for something from higher-status also implies the new individual-competence-oriented habitus in self-presentation occurring to the young Chinese applicants.

4.5   Discussion and Summary

This chapter has depicted the overall picture of macro speech act, meso speech act and micro speech act in *Taoci* email discourse. The hierarchy of speech acts in our *Taoci* email data is streamlined in Fig. 4.6 below.

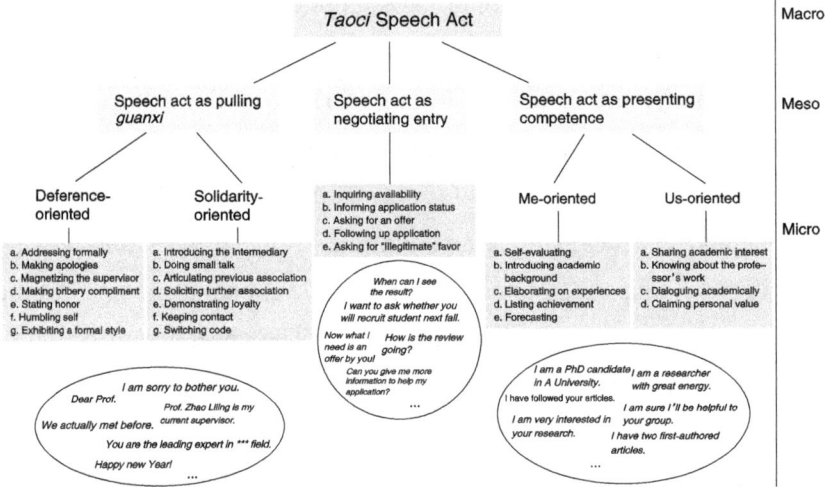

Fig. 4.6   Speech act hierarchy in *Taoci* discourse

As is illustrated, *Taoci* as a generic whole is taken as the macro speech act. The strategy types are placed at the meso level. The concrete speech acts and their linguistic realizations (in italic forms at the bottom) are put at the micro level of speech act. The overall distribution of the five strategies of deference-oriented, solidarity-oriented, Me-oriented, Us-oriented and entry-negotiating is calculated and illustrated in Fig. 4.7 below. Among the five, Me-oriented strategy to create applicants' attraction to foreign professors was the most frequently used, representing the dominant share of 38%. Deference-oriented strategy accounts for 19%. On the whole, the speech act of presenting competence (Me-oriented and Us-oriented) takes the dominant account amounting to 52% of all, pulling *guanxi* comprises 33% of the total, and entry-negotiating a share of 15%.

Overall distribution of strategies

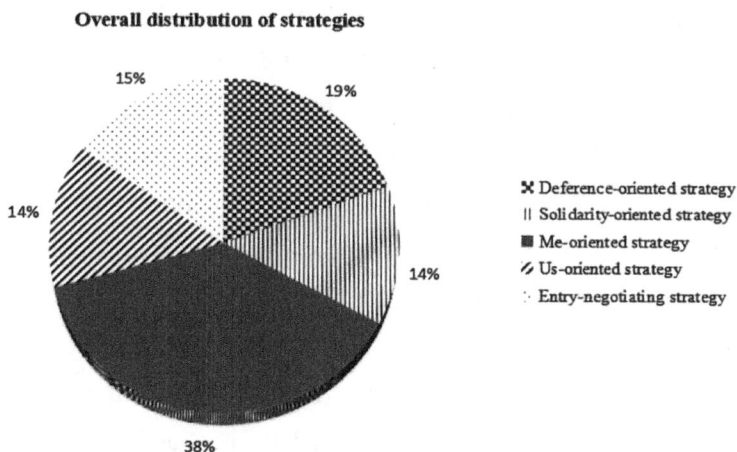

Fig. 4.7   The overall distribution of different meso speech acts

Chinese applicants are endowed with different amounts of social capital and cultural capital when they start their global offer application. The social capital of middleman and previous/potential association with targeted professors is used as direct networking resource to build up *guanxi*. The use of English demonstrates their linguistic capital and switching to other codes shows their multilingual ability. In addition,

327

they possess different forms of academic capital: the embodied state of programming skills, the objectified state of research articles, books, and patent, and the institutionalized state like language certificate, diploma and degree. Their skills, research ability, knowledge, critical thinking ability, and vision are accumulated over a long process of education and training. Moreover, the different forms of capital are used, turning into symbolic capital through the realization of speech acts, to convince foreign professors that they are competent for a PhD program or visiting position. To forage educational capitals on the international education market, Chinese applicants are confident in self-presentation such as showing their advantages, evaluating themselves positively, and dialoguing with authority directly in their email texts, represented by the dominant share (52%) of presenting competence speech act. They have to present themselves, in strategic ways, for their study-abroad education and imagined future academic career, because they are wrestling with competitors from all over the world and this world still values the western style of self-promotion in an assertive and direct way. Perhaps under the influence of increasing exposure to "Western" value, ideology and belief, their habitus undergoes slow and subtle transformation. It seems that the dominant *guanxi*-oriented habitus not only mixed with the competence-oriented habitus but the latter has become a focus in self-presentation (52%), which further confirms the individualism-based self-promotion as "new wine in an old bottle" added to the original sense of *Taoci* discussed by Xiao and Gao (2015).

By teasing out the hierarchy of speech act, in particular, the meso and micro speech acts with rich linguistic realizations, we have answered the sub-question of "What speech acts were used in *Taoci* email texts?". By diving into the email content and Interview transcripts in relation with the usage of various speech acts, it has revealed that Chinese applicants had different types and volumes of social, cultural and economic capitals, and these capitals were invested as affordances (Darvin, Norton, 2015) to compete with international rivalries for their imagined identity and imagined future of study abroad, which addressed the second sub-question of "What and how capitals were served as affordances for applicants' application for overseas education?" in the second big question. What is more, through analyzing Chinese applicants' speech act behaviors in their *Taoci* practice, it further revealed the fact that the more *guanxi*-oriented habitus rooted in Confucianism is moving towards the individual-competence-emphasized habitus under the influence of western individualism in the competitive offer-hunting field. This has addressed the sub-question of "Through

329

the investment of different speech acts in what way did the Chinese young people's habitus undergo changes perceived through their *Taoci* practice?".

As is mentioned, engaged in the field of global offer hunting, different applicants enjoy different types and amount of capital, which they could take advantage of as affordance to invest in their imagined overseas programs. Some applicants have more networking resources to exploit such as intermediary, previous association; some applicants choose to present more of their academic capital via self-presentation of academic achievement, ability or potential; for those who have less academic capital and social capital, they would try to create favorable *guanxi* relationship through frequent contact. Therefore, different applicants have their own trajectory of *Taoci* investment in terms of speech act categories, to pull *guanxi*, to present competence, to negotiate entry, or the mixture of three. What is more, under different phases of the application process, capitals as affordances would be used in different ways varying along with the change of speech acts. That is what the next chapter tries to address— "How were the speech acts employed across situations in the application process?".

Chapter 5

Writing to Act: An Individual Investment Trajectory

Speech acts and linguistic features could vary across application stages. For example, the speech act of "dialoguing academically" is more often employed after a positive response to the request of "inquiring availability" comes back. This chapter focuses on one applicant, Yunyang Liu's *Taoci* journey, to depict how *Taoci* speech act investment looks like in an individual's application process, from his first *Taoci* contact to receiving an offer. Therefore, this chapter will supplement a vertical description of Chinese applicants' speech act investment in their *Taoci* discourse.

5.1   Case Data

A few words, about why Yunyang is selected as the subject of case report, are necessary to repeat before we go further. First, Yunyang's email package included all email contacts between him and his targeted professor with no email missing in between, so it is possible for me to observe and analyze the complete picture of an individual's *Taoci* journey through email texts. Second, his email is a perfect example to exhibit the mixture of pulling *guanxi*, presenting academic competence and negotiating institutional entry, varying across the situations he was confronted with, which will be demonstrated later. Third, Yunyang's targeted professor was an American Caucasian, who could be regarded as a representative of "western" professors. Therefore, his *Taoci* discourse may represent the typical communication between a Chinese applicant and a western supervisor.

In April 2014, I sent Yunyang Liu (a pseudonym) a brief online message on the BBS of A University about whether he had written any *Taoci* with foreign professors and whether he would be interested in participating in our *Taoci* project. Actually, I didn't know anything about him then except his web ID and his successful application from his post. He replied my message instantly and sent an email to me. Since then, we communicated through personal email.

At first, Yunyang shared with me his initial *Taoci* emails. After having a quick reading through his email data, I asked whether he would like to join the interview part. He gave me a positive reply soon, and we made a schedule to meet in May 2014. Back to our first meet, he had accepted the offer from an American university (hereafter W University) for fall admission and his supervisor there was a Caucasian, renamed as Professor Smith. After the first interview, Yunyang was generous to share with me all his email contacts with his foreign advisor from the first email to the offer notice. Yunyang went to America in August that year. In December 2014 during my visiting program in the USA, I travelled to Yunyang's city and had another interview with him. We have kept in touch till now.

Yunyang was then an undergraduate majoring in information technology at A University in Beijing. He was enrolled in A University in China without taking the National College Entrance Examination because he had won a gold medal of the national chemistry competition and had excellent school performance, which meant that he was an outstanding student. He was first enrolled in the major of environmental technology. One year later, he found himself not interested in it and decided to transfer to information technology.

From Yunyang, we collected a set of *Taoci* email package from July 2013 to April 2014. There was in all 16 emails, among which 9 pieces from Yunyang and 6 responses from his targeted supervisor, one from institution enrollment secretary. I had two face-to-face interviews with him. The first interview was taken in May 2014 in China and covered topics about his English learning and *Taoci* experience. The second interview was carried out in December 2014 in America and covered themes about "why study aboard" and *Taoci* email writing. The interviews were intended semi-structural to solicit as much information as possible, but specific questions were asked when it was necessary to check with him. Each interview lasted about one hour and was recorded with his consent before we started and later transcribed by the researcher. Interview transcripts was used as a scaffolding material for the textual findings and provided an insider-view about his application process. All of his data is presented in Table 5.1.

Table 5.1   Yunyang Liu's data

Data	Access time	Words/characters
Taoci package	April 2015	1,993 English words (16 email texts: 9 from Yunyang and 5 from Prof. Smith and 1 from the enrollment secretary)[①]
Interview 1	May 2014 (transcribed in June 2014)	9,590 Chinese characters
Interview 2	December 2014 (transcribed in December 2014)	10,013 Chinese characters

Doing *Taoci* with targeted supervisors is a matter of process just as building up interpersonal relationship takes time. Applicants usually contact their desirable professors before an application season begins in order to check whether there is any enrollment spot. Once they receive a positive response, they try to keep email correspondences with foreign supervisors probably until the announcement of offer result.[②]

[①] Emails from the professor and the enrollment secretary had been anonymized by Yunyang before he sent them to me.

[②] *Taoci* is also regarded to continue by applicants even after they receive their dream offers. Hence, some applicants would still keep email contact with their professors before they arrive at the destination countries and consider that *Taoci* as well.

335

Foreseeably, as email interaction moves on along with relationship built up little by little, the speech acts used may exhibit situational adaptability along with the involvement of different capitals used as affordance.

According to the application timeline from applicants' perspective, three procedural stages are identified. The *door-knocking* phase refers to the initial exchange (s) when applicants conjure up *Taoci* emails to foreign professors to make self-introduction and inquired about any enrollment plan before they start their official applications. Each PhD program has its standards of applicant qualification and supervisors are one of the gatekeepers. The phrase of door-knocking captures the inquisitive sense of asking about the enrollment possibility from the gatekeepers. If applicants receive encouraging responses from professors, they will proceed to the pending phase. The pending phase refers to the period when applicants make further communication with targeted professors in the course of the official application. It is pending because supervisors make no commitment to applicants' request and the application result is still on its way. The resolution phase as the final stage happens when applicants accept the offer, either notified by supervisors or enrollment secretaries. It signifies the establishment of an official membership in a foreign university[①], the end of the "applicant" role. For the current topic, the first two sessions are of major concern due to the fact that applicants' studious doing *Taoci* with potential supervisors mainly occurs before an offer is finalized.

5.2   Speech Act Varying Across Application Stages

The three meso speech acts of pulling *guanxi*, promoting self and negotiating entry are employed in each of Yunyang's email, but with subtle variations of micro speech acts and their linguistic features across different phases. In the door-knocking phase, Yunyang was mainly checking the availability of PhD positions in foreign professors' institutions and introduced himself generally to all potential professors. As *Taoci* moved to the pending phase when Yunyang felt fraught with anxiety from the no offer situation (Yunyang Liu5), the speech act of pulling *guanxi* featured the discourse. When Yunyang Liu was confronted with the application deadline but still stuck in the dilemma of having admission without funding, the speech act of managing

---

① Although the more technical membership in foreign institution only takes effect after applicants go abroad and get officially registered, the notice of an official offer still means the change of institutional membership.

a competent face was the focus of investment. The following part will explicate the prominent features of strategy change across the three critical situations for Yunyang Liu: the initial contact in the door-knocking phase (the email of Yunyang Liu1), facing increasing anxiety with no offer (the email of Yunyang Liu5) and dealing with the approaching deadline (the email of Yunyang Liu7) both in the pending phase.

5.2.1 The Door-knocking Phase: Overriding Self-promotion and Less *Guanxi*-pulling

Yunyang's door-knocking situation involved one round of email exchange with Professor Smith. When the first email was sent, Yunyang was then a junior student at A University and was busy preparing for his TOFEL, GRE examinations and other application tasks. The official application season of W University spans three months from November to January, during which international applicants fill out online application and submit paper materials by mail. At that time, Yunyang felt quite easy about the application issue and was "casting a wide net" to inquire about PhD positions in American universities. Since he didn't aim at a particular professor, all the emails turned out quite similar, with only a minor change of addressee. The first email sent to Professor Smith was one of these and Yunyang recounted its background as follows.

(I1)① I had a study-abroad service agency to help me with my CV, sample essay, personal statements, filling online application forms. The agency recommended this professor to me. I checked his online website and he said he welcomed prospective candidates to contact him. He seemed quite nice. So I sent him the first email... For *Taoci*, I did it myself. I didn't refer to the model email on websites. They [study-abroad service agency staff] just gave some guidance and advice. I know that the best way to do *Taoci* is to talk about the content in foreign professor's papers as my fellow students often talked about. But I was too lazy to read it. My way is to go to their homepage and get to know what they are researching, learn a few key words from their articles. I didn't read their papers thoroughly. Just to say that I'm interested in your research, your field, by writing on those key words... (Interview transcripts 2014-May Yunyang Liu)

(I2) Actually he was the first professor that I contacted. I also wanted to have a try, to try what's like to communicate with foreign professors and to know whether they will understand my English writing. For the other emails, I just changed the name and sent it out. (Interview transcripts 2014-Dec. Yunyang Liu)

Yunyang had a studying-abroad service agency to help him with the application documents, for which he had to pay a large sum. In the earlier application season, he took advice on *Taoci* email from

---

① All the examples quoted from the interview transcripts and email texts are renumbered for readability in this chapter, starting from (I1) and (E1).

the agency and he also heard about writing academic *Taoci* emails from his peers. Table 5.2 gives an overview of the speech acts used in the first contact.

Table 5.2   Speech acts in the first contact

Meso Speech act	Pulling *guanxi*	Promoting self	Negotiating entry
Micro speech act	Deference-oriented: Addressing formally; Exhibiting a formal style	Me-oriented: Evaluating self; Introducing academic background; Listing achievement; Specifying research experience	Inquiring availability information request
	Solidarity-oriented: Magnetizing professor; Using response solicitor	Us-oriented: Sharing the same interest; Knowing about your work	Informing application status

The most prominent features in this phase are the overriding usages of micro speech acts of presenting competence and only sparse usage of speech acts of pulling *guanxi*. The following discussion will concentrate on the two aspects.

5.2.1.1   Overriding Self-presentation

The speech act of presenting personal competence takes more than half of the email space. There are six micro speech acts used to manage

340

a competent candidate image: evaluating self, introducing academic background, listing achievement, and specifying research experience under the Me-oriented strategy, and sharing the same interest and knowing about your work under the Us-oriented strategy.

(a) Me-oriented: Self-promotion Mingled with Self-devaluation

Introducing my academic background. There are two occurrences of speech act, in which Yunyang introduced his educational background and his academic interest, as Examples (E1) and (E2) show. By mentioning the name of A University at the very beginning, he asserted his personal strength. The articulation of "A University" contains a strong symbolic power since A University is a very prestigious institution not only in China but also in the world.

(E1) I am an undergraduate student from A University, China, majoring in Electronic Engineering. (2014-08-01 Yunyang Liu)

(E2) I am interested in mathematical modeling in optical problems as well as practical experiments... (2014-08-01 Yunyang Liu)

Listing achievement. Yunyang listed his research papers, patent and a first prize won in chemistry competition in high school as Examples (E3), (E4) and (E5) show below. These are the objectified forms of his cultural capital to validate his candidature.

341

(E3) I published **two papers** [3] and [4], as a Second Author and a Third Author, respectively. (2014-08-01 Yunyang Liu)

(E4) And **a patent** ([5]), of which I am the Lead Author, is under processing... (2014-08-01 Yunyang Liu)

(E5) Moreover, I won the **First Prize** of National Chemistry Competition for High School Students, the highest level Chemistry contest in China, in 2009. (2014-08-01 Yunyang Liu)

Specifying research experience. Yunyang mentioned that in his undergraduate years, his research focused on the area of "photonic crystal fiber and its dispersion, nonlinear properties, and post-processing" and he participated in the project of "Fiber Laser Frequency Combs for Astronomical Observations" in Example (E6) below. The technical terms, such as "photonic crystal fiber", "dispersion", "nonlinear", "post-processing", "Fiber Laser Frequency Combs", indicate the discipline with which he aligned. Doing research took time and brooded a certain kind of disciplinary habitus, and accumulated cultural capital, just as Bourdieu argued, "The ability or talent is itself the product of an investment of time and cultural capital." (Bourdieu, 1986: 50)

(E6) During my undergraduate study, I **did some research** focused on photonic crystal fiber and its dispersion, nonlinear properties, and post-processing, and **participated** in the building of Fiber Laser Frequency Combs for Astronomical Observations. (2014-08-01 Yunyang Liu)

342

Evaluating self. There are three occurrences of explicit self-evaluation as Examples (E6), (E7) and (E8) demonstrated below. The evaluative vocabularies of "skilled", "competent" and "profound" are laden with positive judgment. "Skilled in programming" shows Yunyang's embodied cultural capital. The top-tier mastery of chemistry knowledge is also part of the cultural capital he possessed. The positive evaluative terms not only promote Yunyang as a competitive candidate, but also deliver his strong confidence in himself.

(E7)...I am ... and **skilled in** programming. (2014-08-01 Yunyang Liu)

(E8) ...**my experience** that accumulated during previous study **may enable me a competent researcher.** (2014-08-01 Yunyang Liu)

(E9) I, as a non-chemistry majored student, have a **relatively profound** knowledge on Chemistry. (2014-08-01 Yunyang Liu)

The identity of an intellectually and academically competent applicant is thus constructed through these linguistic resources. However, if examined closely, there are some nuances about the way Yunyang presented himself. The downgrading adjective "some" in Example (E6) implies that the amount of research work that he did was not much. The modal verb of "may" in Example (E8) indicates a lower possibility and compromises the belief in being a competent researcher. The adverb of "relatively" preceding "profound" in Example

(E8) indicates that his knowledge on chemistry was just satisfying, not that "profound". The three examples of de-evaluation could have been phrased into Examples (E6'), (E8') and (E9') below, which would be preferred by westerners in their self-promotion in job application (Bhatia 1993).

(E6') I did **much** research focused on photonic crystal fiber and its dispersion.

(E8') ... my experience that accumulated during previous study **enables** me a competent researcher.

(E9') I ... have a **very** profound knowledge on Chemistry.

Actually, Yunyang did have rich research experience even though he was an undergraduate. He started to work in the lab from his third year as he told me in the first interview and had two academic papers published, which is an exceptional accomplishment for an undergraduate. He was also a genius in chemistry, since winning the first prize of National Chemistry Competition in China bespeaks the top level of chemistry knowledge as he mentioned in the second interview.

(I3) I was originally enrolled in the environmental department of A University without taking the college entrance examination because I won the gold medal in the national chemistry competition ... For example, for a subject called inorganic chemistry, I had twentyish books on it back at home, published by different presses. And for the other subjects in chemistry, almost all the teaching materials sold on the market, I have one at home ... I studied that department for one semester. I knew so well the chemistry taught there and I don't need to study it anymore. So I decided to transfer to my present major. (Interview transcripts 2014-Dec. Yunyang Liu)

The interview content shows that Yunyang's family had made economic investment in his study of chemistry since buying so many textbooks cost a sum. He also worked hard on it (he used the word "painful" to describe that experience) and finally won the gold medal. To such a competent candidate, even Professor Smith gave him a promising reply by saying that "I'm convinced you would thrive here".

The self-promotion in Yunyang's first email is done in a less explicit way or even a downgrading manner, as there are only a few attitudinal terms about self-acknowledgement, but more like an objective listing of facts: his previous research work, his papers, his awards and his patent. This only flags his research ability and undersolds himself as a competitive candidate. The comparatively low-profile exhibition of ability might still pertain to the self-efficacy value cherished by Chinese, so that Chinese students are usually not willing to thrust themselves in front of high-status professors. However, this kind of downplaying feature, as we will see later, disappears in later situations.

(b) Us-oriented Strategy: Creating Academic Bonding

There was no previous academic bonding between Yunyang and the professor and the first contact was intended to create it.

Sharing the same interest. There are two occurrences of sharing the same interest with Professor Smith in his first paragraph in Example (E10) and in the third in Example (E11). Sharing the academic interest constitutes the basic common ground for Yunyang and Professor Smith to work together in the future.

(E10) ...and find myself very interested in your project. (2014-08-01 Yunyang Liu)

(E11) I am quite interested in your research areas. (2014-08-01 Yunyang Liu)

Knowing about the professor's work. Yunyang mentioned that he had read the professor's work and listed the professor's publications at the end of his email in Example (E12). However, there was no deep discussion about the professor's research. Even the academic solidarity that he tried to build up was softened by the graduation term of "by chance" in the example. He read the professor's work only out of accident instead of on purpose, denoting a sense of aloofness.

(E12) I read some of your recent papers, such as [1] and [2] by chance...(2014-08-01 Yunyang Liu)

5.2.1.2　Less Speech Acts of Pulling *Guanxi*

Compared to the display of academic competence, the micro

346

speech acts of pulling *guanxi* are less used in terms of both quantity and category. There are three deference-oriented strategies: addressing formally as shown in Example (E13), showing gratitude in Example (E14) below, following a formal format (the email is in a complete epistolary form with addressing, body part and closing as well as signing).

(E13) Dear Prof. Smith (2014-08-01 Yunyang Liu)

(E14) Thanks a lot for your time. (2014-08-01 Yunyang Liu)

The solidarity-oriented strategy includes showing magnetic attraction as shown in Example (E15) and using response solicitor in Example (E16) below to invite further communication. The affect term of "appealing" in Example (E15) reveals the applicant's strong inclination towards the cultural capital of the professor's academic achievement. Example (E16) indicates Yunyang's wish for further association. These two strategies are used for building up solidarity-building Professor Smith.

(E15) I find it appealing to me. (2014-08-01 Yunyang Liu)

(E16) I am looking forward to receiving your reply. (2014-08-01 Yunyang Liu)

5.2.1.3 Request of Negotiating Entry

As to the speech act of negotiating entry, inquiring availability is realized through a conventionally indirect speech act together with the politeness marker of "please" as Example (E17) shows. The offer request is realized through an implicit expression of "intend" in Example (E18). The information request is very clear while the offer request is indirect. There is an instance of the act of "informing my application status" in Example (E19), as Yunyang stated that he was in the preparation for application, but not officially involved in the application system of W University.

(E17) Would you please offer me some information, such as how many doctoral students you plan to enroll, and whether you plan to enroll international students? (2014-08-01 Yunyang Liu)

(E18) ...and, if possible, I intend to apply for the PhD program in your research group. (2014-08-01 Yunyang Liu)

(E19) ...and I am preparing for my application to the 2013 term Fall Ph.D. program. (2014-08-01 Yunyang Liu)

In short, during the first contact, Yunyang stages a debut all about himself to impress the professor. There is no networking capital for him to make use of as the professor was a completely stranger in every sense to him. He appraises himself positively, but with a slice of degrading. He shows interest in the professor, but his interest is not that strong. His alignment with the professor is not an accurate

348

target, neither emphasized since this email with a change of name could be sent to anybody. In addition, the request raised at this stage is about information and offer request is very vague. Nevertheless, Yunyang fortunately received a promising reply from the professor as he reflected in his interview.

(I4) I didn't pay serious attention to the application issue at that time ... I was hardly aware of it. I always thought application is simple, and easy and I made little effort to bond up with the professor. My hardware, I mean my GPA, my academic performance, and my researches are rather good. And I'm confident about myself. After I wrote to him that night, perhaps about three or four hours, he replied me quite fast. He had a good impression about me, and so I had a good impression about him. Although I didn't remember precisely what he said in his email. But he gave me a positive message. He said that I would thrive here in W University. But still the competition is quite fierce and he couldn't give me commitment. But he welcomed me and encouraged me to apply for the program by mentioning his name in my application portfolio. (Interview transcripts, 2014-May Yunyang Liu)

As Yunyang recalled, the professor acknowledged his excellence via a very positive reply, but held up his responsibility for the offer, which foreshadowed his ensuing situation and his discursive strategies to deal with the problem.

5.2.2 The Upsetting Situation: More and Intensifying *Guanxi*-pulling

After the application submission, it is the period for committee review of applicants' materials and decision-making, at least for American universities. Some applicants may receive positive hints about their application status or personal/unofficial offer from their foreign supervisors. The unlucky ones do not but are aware that others do get feedback and would go increasingly upset due to the uncertainty as the offer deadline (usually April 15th) approaches. Yunyang, as he reflected, was one of the unlucky, having no update from Professor Smith as well as no desirable offer from other institutions that he applied for. During this period, Yunyang contacted Professor Smith twice (2014-08-04 Yunyang Liu and 2014-08-05 Yunyang Liu) to convey this concern. However, there was no response to his first try and an indifferent reply with only one sentence of "sometime in April", answering vaguely Yunyang's question of the offer release time, which differs dramatically from the encouraging words he received in the door-knocking phase ("*You can mention in your application that you would like to join [the] my research group*"). The email communication constitutes one aspect of the upsetting situation that Yunyang was facing. He also mentioned his anxiety in the interview:

350

(I5) Actually, I didn't figure out my whole situation because I was overconfident as I mentioned that I felt myself with quite strong background ... Before, I thought application was quite easy. If I emailed you and you didn't reply, that's totally fine for me. Like this professor in W University, I didn't follow him so closely at first. Until March passed, admission comes one by one without funding, so are the MA projects. I was a little, ah, panicked, couldn't sit tight, then I began actively to communicate foreign professors. And I also felt a little frustrated. I had thought, perhaps I couldn't go abroad this year, perhaps I needed to stay home for another year. Later, people told me to change application to European countries. But to tell the truth, I'm not that willing to go there. Since I made the application for American universities, I wanted to nail it down this year. Thus later on, I changed my attitude and tried to do well what I was able to do. (Interview transcripts, 2014-May Yunyang Liu)

When there were neither desirable offers from other applied universities nor promising response from Smith, the interaction came to a confusing halt for Yunyang and he became anxious about his application status. In this email, he basically re-introduced himself to Professor Smith as stranger to stranger in order to create more *guanxi* relationship with the professor and re-present himself as a competent PhD candidate. The speech acts used include new features of old speech acts and new categories of speech acts, listed in Table 5.3.

Table 5.3   Speech acts in the fifth contact

Meso speech acts	Pulling *guanxi*	Promoting self	Negotiating entry
Micro speech act	Deference-oriented: Addressing formally; Making compliment; Exhibiting a formal format	Me-oriented: Introducing academic background; Evaluating self; Listing achievement	Asking for an offer: explicit
	Solidarity-oriented: Magnetizing the professor; Claiming previous association; Keeping frequent contact	Us-oriented: Dialoguing academically	Informing application status

5.2.2.1   New Features in Self-promotion

Forecasting and dialoguing academically are two new categories in this email. The other three old strategies contain some subtle changes of linguistic forms. The strategy of sharing the same interest didn't appear anymore since the first contact already made the claim and the professor had been informed about it.

(a) New Speech Acts: Dialoguing Academically and Claiming My Value to You

(E20) The study on electro-magnetic and photonics requires the comprehension in physics and the skill in programing and simulation; the study on material structure and photolysis requires knowledge in chemistry. (2014-08-05 Yunyang Liu)

The study on electro-magnetic and photonics, and material

structure and photolysis were the professor's research focus. Yuanyang commented on the required knowledge and skills to do this kind of research. It conveyed his better understanding about Professor Smith's work than that of the previous situation.

(E22) These years I've been thinking about what I should do in the future. And I always hoped to do some research that can make good use of all my knowledge. (2014-08-05 Yunyang Liu)

Forecasting prospect is concerned about what Yunyang intended to do for his career. However, he only conceived a rough idea of "do some research that can make good use of all my knowledge" as Example (E22) shows, indicating his imagined identity of being a researcher.

(b) Old Strategies with New Features

First, the strategy of "listing academic achievement" also occurs in the first contact. However, the content of the "achievement" is changed.

(E23) I won the first price of National Chemical Competition when I was in high school. (2014-08-05 Yunyang Liu)

(E24) And as an EE student, my major GPA rank top 10% in my department. (2014-08-05 Yunyang Liu)

The "publication" and "patent" were removed and only the "chemistry award" was left in the email, perhaps because the professor's work was closely related to chemistry. As he was reading Professor Smith's work in depth, Yunyang got a clearer idea about the professor's research. Keeping the only cultural capital of chemistry award in Example (E23) obviously tried to match Yunyang's background with Professor Smith's work. There was a new instance of achievement in the form of "academic performance". In Example (E24) Yunyang stated that he achieved a very top rank of GPA (Grade Point Average) in his department, indicating his excellence. In discussing the genre of personal statement, Swales et al., (2004) mentioned that professionals or professors thought such expression of "I was ranked number one in my program…" very odd. It was not a good way to highlight applicants' uniqueness. However, in China, such kind of ranking has strong symbolic value to students, teachers and parents, and even job employers as it demonstrated excellence and competence. However, the symbolic value might not be recognized by Professor Smith.

Second, the strategy of positive self-evaluation was not a new strategy either, but a nuance was worth mentioning about the manner of self-evaluation. In the first email, there are downgraders about Yunyang's academic ability, for instance, "may" in Example (E7) and "relatively" in Example (E8). However, in this email self-evaluation items are all accompanied with upgraders.

354

(E25) I love doing research, because only doing research can satisfy my curiosity. (2014-08-05 Yunyang Liu)

(E26) I am also very skilled in programming (I am in charge of all the simulation work in my current research group.) (2014-08-05 Yunyang Liu)

(E27) Besides what I mentioned above, I have a lot of practical experiences on doing scientific research. (2014-08-05 Yunyang Liu)

In Example (E25), the affection-laden word of "love" was a highly graded evaluative term to stress Yunyang's strong interest in doing research. The succeeding explanation of "because only doing research can satisfy my curiosity" highlighted the affection. In particular, the contracting term of "only" emphasized the importance of doing research for him. The upscaling term of "very" in Example (E26), and "a lot of practical experiences" in Example (E27) augmented Yunyang's skills and research experience. His cultural capital of research experience and skills was still used as affordances, but with a strong emphasis disclosed in discursive presentation.

5.2.2.2   Intensifying *Guanxi*-pulling

The speech act of magnetizing Professor Smith was used in the first contact but with new characteristics. New categories of micro speech acts in pulling *guanxi* include resorting to previous association, keeping frequent contact and making bribery compliments. The act of

355

keeping frequent contact is exemplified through email turn-taking, as Yunyang initiated four contacts with Professor Smith before his fifth email but with only two replies.

(a) Old Speech Act with New Features: Magnifying Magnetic Attraction

This email was saturated with the professor's strong magnetic attraction realized by both repetition and affectionate vocabulary.

(E28) Your research group is my dream group. (2014-08-05 Yunyang Liu)

(E29) I am really longing for doing research under your instruction. (2014-08-05 Yunyang Liu)

The second paragraph of this email started with Example (E28) and ended with Example (E29). The expressions of "my dream group" and "really longing for" intensified Yunyang's strong inclination towards Professor Smith's group. Compared with the first email, first, there was only one sentence in Example (E15) to mention the professor's attraction to the applicant, while there was almost a whole paragraph in the fifth email, taking up half of the email space, to explain the magnetic attraction. Moreover, the attraction was expanding from the supervisor's recent published papers in the first email to the professor's research group and supervision. Last, such expressions as "dream group" and "really longing for" were invested with more weight of "magnetic force" emitted from the professor.

(b) New Categories of Speech Act

First, "articulating previous association" was used for the first time. Pavlidou (2007) suggested that talking about the relationship itself could affect rapport building. Chinese people typically pull *guanxi* with others through the previous association of "locality (native place), kinship, coworker, classmate, sworn brotherhood, surname and teacher-student" (King, 1991: 70). The previous association for Yunyang to use as affordance was their email communication in Example (E30).

(E30) We've been connected through email before. (2014-08-05 Yunyang Liu)

The word of "connected" sounds more "bonded" than the word of "contact", though both words are usually translated into the same Chinese word *lianxi*.[①]Yunyang had exchanged email with the professor several times and the professor might also know about Yunyang as an applicant for his supervisorship. The explicit articulation of the previous email contact drew the two sides into a kind of factual relation in order to explore existing common ground between them.

---

① In Chinese, it is written as "联系".

Complimenting was another new act. Yunyang mentioned that research in Professor Smith's group made him feel powerful in Example (E31) and energetic in Example (E32). The two episodes expressed a kind of bribery compliment to elevate Professor Smith.

(E31) I always feel my power is not fully utilized not until I know your group... (2014-08-05 Yunyang Liu)

(E32) The research content in your group makes me feel energetic. (2014-08-05 Yunyang Liu)

"Showing loyalty" was conveyed through making promise in Example (E33) below. The usage of negative mood (won't) excluded all the disappointing possibilities. It meant giving the applicant's words to the professor. The utterance declared the applicant's firm loyalty and absolute deference to the professor as a powerful gatekeeper.

(E33) I won't let you down. (2014-08-05 Yunyang Liu)

The acts of intensifying magnetic attraction, showing loyalty and making compliments devote to appreciating the professor as authority and building up their *guanxi*.

5.2.2.3 Asking for Offer: Urging

There are two occurrences of speech act to negotiate the institutional entr, one informing my application status in Example (E34) and the other asking for an offer in Example (E35).

(E34) I've submitted my application of 2014 Ph.D. enrolling, but I did not hear any news from W University. (2014-08-05 Yunyang Liu)

(E35) Now what I need is a chance offered by you. (2014-08-05 Yunyang Liu)

In these examples, Yunyang's institutional role as an applicant was stated through "submitted my application" and "not hear any news". Therefore, he was still in the pending phase, which led to his anxiety when other people had offers. Different from the request for information and implicit request for offer in the first email, the offer request here was raised in a very direct as well as intensifying manner. The time adjunct of "Now" was fronted at the sentence, which created an impression of urgency on the recipient to make a decision.

To this email, the professor replied soon by saying "How likely would you come to W University if we made you an offer?". This response was like an olive branch to Yunyang. Thus Yunyang responded instantly, further clarifying his strong inclination to join the group through the expressions of "I would be very glad to come to your group and If I receive an offer from you, I will accept it at the first time." (2014-08-06 Yunyang Liu). However, still the professor made no commitment, which led to his deadline approaching situation in April.

Under the "no coming offer" situation, Yunyang's competence presentation is full of positive self-evaluation. His comment on the professor's work shows his better understanding about the interlocutor's research. The *guanxi*-pulling speech act increases in types and with strong personal affection. The only networking capital of "previous email association" with professor is improvised. In addition, the offer request is much clearer in the form of direct request. The deployment of all these speech acts is motivated from Yunyang's ongoing anxiety against the situation that no desirable offer comes.

5.2.3 Deadline Approaching: More Accurate Self-promotion

As mentioned, Professor Smith replied by asking how likely Yunyang would choose W University. The indifferent tone in his second email (sometime in April) changed into a possibility of offer. However, at almost the end of the period for admission decision in April, Yunyang still received no good offer and heard no definite answer from Professor Smith. He recounted his situation in the interview.

(I6) "After that [no good offer] I began to take it [the application] seriously... Although I'm not clear about the situation in W University, I thought it is my last straw. So I rewrote an email [the fifth email] and went to my supervisor here, my Chinese supervisor, to ask for his advice. Then he said, he didn't say it toughly, but basically he said my writing couldn't work at all, because I only learnt some key words of the professor's research. He mentioned that there were also many students in other universities writing email to him about intending to do research together with him, so having look at it, he knew the applicants' situation, whether they knew his field for real or not. Therefore, I followed his guidance … Before when I wrote email, I only focused on what research I'm doing, and what I am interested in. My supervisor said it wouldn't work. You should tell the professor what you could bring to him, that is, contribution. So I followed his advice and changed it again and again, about 5 or 6 times, together with my supervisor…. However, in this process, I learned how to write email better. Just like Professor Smith in W University. She asked me whether I accepted an offer else and if he gave me offer how likely would you accept it. I replied her with a short email and said that I would accept it instantly. After a day, I thought my email was not enough, so I sent another email, this one to her. That's the background for this email. " (Interview transcripts 2014-May Yunyang Liu)

At this stage, Yuyang took a more active attitude towards his application and *Taoci* email writing. He even turned to his Chinese supervisor for help about writing tips. They had several rounds of communication about how to write a convincing email to a potential supervisor. The email, as Yunyang mentioned, might be the last straw for him to seize to present himself as a perfect fit into Professor Smith's research group. The speech act categories in Email 7 are listed in Table 5.4.

Table 5.4   Speech acts in the seventh contact

Meso speech act	Pulling *guanxi*	Promoting self	Negotiating entry
Micro speech acts	Deference-oriented: Addressing formally; Using a formal style	Me-oriented: Introducing academic background; Specifying research experience; Looking into the future	Inquiring availability
			Informing application status
	Solidarity-oriented: Showing magnetic attraction; Keeping frequent contact	Us-oriented: Sharing the interest; Knowing the professor's work; Dialoguing academically; Claiming my value to the professor	Asking for illegitimate information

5.2.3.1   More Self-promotion with a Specific Target

Presenting competence became dominant and more personal as the micro speech acts were entirely Smith-oriented. There were three speech acts of the Me-oriented strategies (introducing academic background, specifying research experience, forecasting future), and four subtypes of the Us-oriented strategies (sharing the same interest, knowing the professor's work, dialoguing academically, and claiming personal value). All of these acts had occurred in the previous emails, but with qualitative differences.

(a) Qualitative Change in Me-oriented Speech Acts

First, in the speech act of introducing my academic background,

362

only Yunyang's school name, "A University" was kept to emphasize his solid educational background. Looking into the future was more in detail as Example (E36) shows.

(E36) I wish I could do some interdisciplinary researches that can combine my knowledge on physics, electronics, photonics and chemistry together. Also, personally speaking, I think water photolysis is a great job for human being. Beijing, where I lived now, is one of the most polluted cities in the world. The pollution primarily comes from the steam power plant and car exhaust. If one day solar fuel generation is applicable to our daily life, there would not be that much pollution. I wish I could contribute my power to this great job. (2014-08-07 Yunyang Liu)

In the fifth email, Yunyang only mentioned his imagined identity of "doing research" in the future. By contrast, this email devoted a whole paragraph to his imagined future academic aspiration. At the very beginning, he claimed he wished to make contribution to the academic society by combining his interdisciplinary knowledge. In the rest part of the paragraph, he expressed his opinion of the importance of water photolysis for human being, then introduced a real-life scenario—the polluted city of Beijing and concluded that to help solve the pollution problem by developing more solar fuel was his ambition for the benefit of all human beings.

363

Second, Yunyang's talking about his own research experience was more specific with the usage of multiple "I+Action" structures in reporting the research procedures as Example (E37) shows below. The two process verbs of "investigated" and "studies" together with the "I" subject contributed to the emphasis on his independence to carry out researches.

(E37) **I investigated** the mode-lock fiber ring laser, a source that generates femtosecond pulses, and **I studied a lot** on nonlinear effects, especially on supercontinuum generation. (2014-08-07 Yunyang Liu)

(b) More Us-oriented Speech Acts

The Us-oriented speech acts were richer in category. First, there was a claim of the shared interest at the opening of the email in Example (E38). Knowing better the professor's work was demonstrated in Example (E39). Yunyang also made a brief comment on the professor's work in Example (E40), in which he appraised the professor's work as interdisciplinary and pointed out the research method used in the professor's work.

(E38) I am writing to tell you my interests to your group…(2014-08-07 Yunyang Liu)

(E39) To my knowledge, research on surface plasmons (SPs) is an important topic of your group. (2014-08-07 Yunyang Liu)

364

(E40) Research on SPs is quite interdisciplinary—it requires the knowledge in optics, photonics, material science, etc. ... For another instance, in your Novel Nano EUV Light Sources, you use femtosecond pulses to excite the SPs and generate EUV by nonlinear effects. (2014-08-07 Yunyang Liu)

Claiming personal value to the professor was in much detail together with the introduction of Yunyang's own experience, which was emphasized to fit the professor's lab well. Telling professors what work applicants could accomplish was another way to demonstrate their academic potential. Yunyang took his Chinese advisor's suggestion to underscore his possible contribution to the foreign professor's lab in Examples (E41) and (E42). "SPs" and "the Novel Nano EUV light sources program" were two important research topics in the Smith group.

(E41) I think my research background on optics and photonics can facilitate the **SP**s research a lot. (2014-08-07 Yunyang Liu)

(E42) "Those experience will help a lot in the **Novel Nano EUV light sources program**. (2014-08-07 Yunyang Liu)

5.2.3.2   Less *Guanxi*-pulling Speech Acts

The *guanxi*-pulling speech act occurred less than the previous contact and didn't change much. The only difference worth mentioning was showing the professor's magnetic attraction, which was used with an intensifying tone as Example (E43) presented.

(E43) Your group could be my ideal research group. (2014-08-07 Yunyang Liu)

5.2.3.3 Negotiating Entry More Eagerly

There were three occurrences of speech act to negotiate the institutional entry.

(E44) I'm writing ... to inquire about your plan of PhD enrolling.

(E45) After all, the deadline of PhD application is approaching, so I have to make my decision recently. (2014-08-07 Yunyang Liu)

(E46) Finally, I want to ask about your attitude toward my application to be your PhD student. (2014-08-07 Yunyang Liu)

Example (E44) exemplified a direct request for information. This speech act of information request was used in the first contact before but repeated here. In Example (E45), Yunyang explained that he had to make a decision about his life after graduation, updating his application status. This was also the reason for the face-risking move to bring the illegitimate information request in Example (E46). This request raised an inappropriate question for the professor to answer—the professor's attitude towards Yunyang's application. Since the professor had no absolute power to decide on an enrollment, he couldn't answer or was not willing to answer this question. It was beyond the professor's institutional duty to show personal preference.

Under the situation of deadline approaching, the Me-oriented strategy was used more to foreground the academically capable image. Moreover, the academic proximity that Yunyang tried to approach with the professor was underscored through the Us-oriented strategy to show how fit Yuyang was with the professor's research lab. Comparably, there were less *guanxi*-pulling strategies since Yunyang's strong inclination towards the professor had already been stressed. The speech act of negotiating institutional entry demonstrated a clear request for the offer. The characteristics of these strategies were derived from Yunyang's situation, and were navigated by his active interaction with the situation: taking a more serious attitude and soliciting advice from his Chinese supervisor.

Luckily, Yunyang's re-presentation of self in the seventh email embraced a positive feedback from Professor Smith, as the professor replied by saying "I'd like to let you know on April 10th. Is this ok? Can you wait that long? Where else do you have offers with a full stipend?". It indicated the professor's favorable stance towards Yunyang's application: he was interested in Yunyang and afraid to lose Yunyang, but still couldn't make the final call. It created a new situation for both parties. This reply gave Yunyang a hint of hope, but the pressing deadline was also confronting him. Thus he gave a quick response to illustrate his situation: he had only admission with no funding. Yunyang's application status was clear to Professor Smith, who replied soon with "Please let me discuss with my colleagues", another promising answer. Before long, Yunyang received a notice of admission and funding source from W University and his journey ended with a perfect period.

5.2.4 Summary of Speech Act Variation Across Situations

As the analysis of Yunyang's email package shows, the speech acts and their linguistic features vary across the actual situations that he has gone through. There are some speech acts that are used throughout his emails, such as addressing formally, following a formal format, using response solicitor. Some speech acts appear with new linguistic features such as showing the professor's magnetic attraction, whereas there are also new speech acts appearing in later stages not used in his earlier emails. Table 5.5 summarizes the most prominent changes of each speech act and their correspondent situations.

Table 5.5   Speech acts changing across the three situations

	Phases/situations		
Speech act	Door-knocking phase: Taking application easy, overconfident in application, no specific targeted professor	Pending phase: Anxious with no desirable offer, Indifference shown by Professor Smith, beginning to take application serious	Resolution phase: Increasing anxiety, deadline approaching, getting advice from Chinese advisor, taking application really serious, taking Professor Smith as the last straw
Pulling guanxi	Magnetic attraction: e.g. *I find it appealing to me...*	Intensifying magnetic attraction: e.g. *Your research group is my dream group.* Making bribery compliment: e.g. *make me feel energetic* Showing loyalty: e.g. *I won't let you down.* Articulating previous association: e.g. *We connected before.*	Intensifying magnetic attraction: e.g. *You group could be my idea research group.*
Promoting self	Listing achievement: *prize, patent, paper* Evaluating self: some downgraders	Listing achievement: *prize, schooling performance* Evaluating self: all upgraders Dialoguing academically	Specifying research experience e.g. *I investigated the mode-lock fiber...* Forecasting future: e.g. *I wish I could do some interdisciplinary researchers...* Dialoguing academically Claiming value to professor

369

Continued

Negotiating entry	Inquiring availability	Urging an offer	Asking for illegitimate information
Overall effect	More competence presenting; Less *guanxi*-pulling	Balanced, with affectionate *guanxi*-pulling	More competence presenting targeting the professor; Less *guanxi*-pulling

All the details of the content have been specified in the previous analysis. Each *Taoci* email is written against a specific situational exigency for Yunyang to act, and at the same time creates the situation. To stay in the interactional line of *Taoci* and maintain his competent applicant face, Yunyang shows an acute awareness of taking responsibility for the situations, acting in a thoroughly calculating manner, or "expressing himself in a given way solely in order to give the kind of impression to others that is likely to evoke from them a specific response he is concerned to obtain" (Goffman, 1959: 17), which confirms Darvin and Norton's (2015) emphasis on learners' agency in rational investment in their imagined identity. Although these are institutional restrictions that an applicant could not possibly surpass, Yunyang had an active participation in his discursive performance, both with himself, with the situation, with his Chinese advisor and with the foreign professor. This dynamic usage of discourse strategies reflects the applicant's practical mastery of language and of situations

370

to produce "adequate speech" (Bourdieu, 1977).

5.3 Writing into an Imagined Future

Yunyang's active engagement in doing *Taoci* foreign professors represents his genuine effort of investment in his study-abroad desire and imagined identity. This part is going to deepen the discussion of the second question of "In what sense is *Taoci* an investment into applicants' imagined future?" by referring to the Darvin and Norton (2015) investment model.

5.3.1 Imagined Identity of "World Viewer" and "Successful Returnee"

Yunyang's goal of pursuing an international education was depicted by himself as "open my eyes" to a new world. His personality and experience at domestic university had a great influence on his choice to go abroad. He described himself as follows.

(I7) I am a person who, when I stayed in a place for a long time, I would like a change ... I'm actually not good at knowing about it through the ways of "hearing about" or "reading about", or rather, I don't like this way to know a new place. I would rather try it and know it in detail. When I moved into a new environment, I knew how it looked like, but you know I was also very uneasy in a new place. However once I was in it, at first I was not getting used to it, or

371

作为投资的言语行为
——"套磁"话语实践研究

becoming anxious, afraid that I couldn't hang on, but I would try to conquer my fear, and then get myself accustomed to it step by step. And I would try to take in the essence, the good essence, cultural or ideas like that. After I feel I learned all of them, I would not be happy with the status quo and would try to move to the next place that I like. This kind of thing seems to form a cycle in myself. This is also true to the application issue. I just want to open my eyes to the new place [America] (Interview transcripts 2014-Dec. Yunyang Liu)

As a young and talented student, Yunyang was not content with his status quo. He would rather choose to try new things and new places, and improve himself, which pushed him to step outside of his current comfort zone of staying at A University and to move to a novel environment and feel it physically, with naked eyes.

(I8) I was determined not to stay at A University anymore, though I could be in the graduate program with exemption from the graduate entrance examination... but it is best to walk out of China. Although I had no clear concept about what's like in a foreign country, no concept at all, I knew it was different and to see a different world is good. I don't want to be the frog sitting at the bottom of the well, only knowing the square of sky up its head. (Interview transcripts 2014-Dec. Yunyang Liu)

Primarily, Yunyang's going abroad was motivated by his idea to open his eyes to new spaces, which was inseparable from his personality. Nonetheless, he also had practical reasons for the investment in

372

international education.

(I9) I didn't think much about my future career in the long term. Certainly, if I do well abroad [doing research], I want to be back home as a successful person, like to be "imported" by the "Thousand Young Researcher Plan" of China. I know A University will hire this kind of young and academically strong talent. But there is still a long time and things change, and I'm not sure whether I will stay abroad or come back. I don't want a long-term plan as you cannot see it... I think the academic research in America is better than the domestic, that is one of the driving forces for me to choose the States. (Interview transcripts 2014-May Yunyang Liu)

To Yunyang, the practical attraction of going to America for further education included the academic environment and becoming a successful young researcher to be "imported" one day. However, he would rather downplay it at that moment, but stressed the importance of seeing the world through the international education experience. The imagined identities of "being imported returnee" and of "the world-viewer" in a new space motivated his investment of economic capital, cultural capital and social capital in the application, also his doing *Taoci* and changing speech acts in *Taoci* emails demonstrated above.

5.3.2   Accumulating Capital for Global Offer Hunting

As Bourdieu argued, there was a minimum requirement of capital to make investment (Bourdieu, Wacquant, 1992). For his investment in the overseas PhD program, Yunyang had to possess a certain amount of economic capital to pay for all the preparative tasks, for example the language proficiency test, application fee and English training. Meanwhile, the language proficiency certificate acquired became his cultural capital and even symbolic capital, which illustrated the convertability of different forms of capital (Bourdieu, 1977). Educational background and other academic achievements (e.g. articles, prize, research experience) were embodied and objectified form of cultural capital accumulated through time. The *Taoci* interaction represented a move to bring these existing capitals as affordance (Darvin, Norton, 2015) to compete for the global offer that he longed for. Capitals were invested to different degrees against different situations as the previous discussion goes.

5.3.2.1　Cultural Capital of English

Yunyang had invested a great deal of capital in his study-abroad project starting from English learning, which cost time, physical efforts, emotion, and economical capital. He started to take English learning seriously when he had a rough idea about going abroad and he needed to get a language proficiency certificate for the application.

(I10) I started to prepare for the English proficiency test like TOEFL and GRE in

2012, and my English was improved much during the time. I was thinking more about study-aboard at the end of 2012, because at that time I was considering my future, my graduation seriously. Before that, I was "slippery", fooling around, and no aspiration. (Interview transcripts 2014-May Yunyang Liu)

In order to pass or get a satisfying score in those tests, Yunyang had economic capital, i.e. money invested as he took classes in private English training agencies to achieve higher levels of English proficiency. Although Yunyang didn't mention that these classes cost money, the names of New Oriental and Cloud English of private training center were self-obvious.

(I11) …other people also gave me suggestion, so I took a TOEFL class in New Oriental … For GRE, I signed in a Cloud English training center. My roommate went there. At first, I didn't give it a damn. I thought it might be a cheating agency. However, my roommate went there when the training center was just established and he felt very effective learning there. The Cloud English focuses on vocabulary. It would tell you all the academic words in GRE by teaching the Indo-European roots, just like the Chinese skillful bone disassembler. I went there and had a try of it. It's not cheating at all. (Interview transcripts 2014-May Yunyang Liu)

Not only had he put money in acquiring the cultural capital of English, but also he spared great efforts into the learning activity. He used the word "hard" for his feelings (literally it means "painful" in

Chinese) several times in Example (I11) below. The word of "devil training" was used to describe the preparation for GRE in Example (I12). However, his persistence (9 a.m. to 11 p.m. everyday in two months) and repeated practices (e.g. listening to it again and again) bear out fruit: he got 98 out of 120 in TOEFL and $151+170$ in GRE, which were usable for his application.

(I12) At first, the listening part, I couldn't understand it at all. After listening to a paragraph, I caught nothing, everything is blurring … **Everyday**, I listened to a joke and read out the material while listening to looking at it and then I could recite it. I practiced this for 31 episodes of listening materials and felt almost in command of the listening part. In TOEFL testing, I got a full score in listening. I got 98 in the TOEFL test in March, 2013, and it's usable for the application … **The whole month** of June after I took TOEFL, I went there [Cloud English], and studied **hard**. That kind of **devil training**, each day we learned from 9 a.m. to 11 p.m. Everyone went there and people were all hardworking. There were a lot of students from S University. I achieved $151+170$ in GRE, which is also usable for application. If I didn't get the training there, but did it myself, it might have been a **painstaking headache**. I thought reciting words is **really hard**, you have to **work hard and work hard**. (Interview transcripts 2014-May Yunyang Liu)

(I13) But at that center, when you see people weaker than you work so hard, you will be touched. The two months' staying there for the GRE training is just like **devil training**, but I stuck to it and I felt satisfied with myself... (Interview transcripts 2014-May Yunyang Liu)

What he reaped through the English training process was further invested into other English practices, for example, making presentation in English. The practical use of English was both a reward of his previous investment and re-investment into his further success in using English for communicative purpose, like the *Taoci* emails he contacted foreign professors, to enhance his language capital.

(I14) At the end of 2013, I had a chance to present report in English. In our department, we have presentation of excellent graduates' project each year. Just like international conferences, there is poster as well as oral report and I had an oral presentation in English. To prepare for that oral presentation, I practiced a lot of times and I felt it very interesting. There are a lot of students and professors in our department, and we even had two foreign professors attending. My presentation is about 8 minutes. This was the first time that I used English in talking, to practice English. You know, English on stage and backstage is quite different. When you present in front of people in English, it's very different. (Interview transcripts 2014-May Yunyang Liu)

Yunyang felt empowered when he used English to do the oral report as Example (I13) shows. "Competence in the restricted sense of linguistics becomes the condition and sign of competence in the sense of the right to speech, the right to power through speech." (Bourdieu, 1977: 649) When he used English to communicate with Professor Smith and got positive feedback, he also felt the return of

377

the labor. English, as both his investment subject and his possessed cultural capital, infiltrated and backed up his whole process of the practice of *Taoci*.

5.3.2.2 Academic Capital

Academic competence or potential was the most important factor in PhD program application. Academic capital refers to different forms of cultural capital that characterize a person as academically capable and promising researcher. The academic capital involved in Yunyang's application included his school performance (GPA), educational background, publications, prize, patent, command of knowledge, skills, etc. Some of them were embodied such as the programming skill that he had acquired, others had materialized form, like published papers, patent certificate, prize medal, and all of them could be turned into symbolic capital of his competitive candidature. The different forms of capital were accumulated over time as Yunyang reflected.

(I15) I joined the research lab earlier, in my third year. For undergraduate [who wants to go abroad], researches are big deal. I stayed in the lab, even at night, to do lab work. Although nobody forced me to stay there, but everyone stayed there, even at weekend. (Interview transcripts 2014-Dec. Yunyang Liu)

(I16) My Chinese supervisor can be counted as a very good researcher. He is our big boss. He has a lot of contacts with international sources. Our lab could be thought at an international level. Not only our research topic, but also what we published. (Interview transcripts 2014-Dec. Yunyang Liu)

Yunyang had input time and energy in his research as he mentioned that he went to the lab almost every day. In particular his Chinese supervisor was a top-class academia, which influenced the students' vision. Being trained in such environment, Yunyang produced several English articles and took charge of a patent, which indicated that he was involved in his own disciplinary community. The details of his academic capital were presented in the previous discussion of speech acts and were changed across his own evaluation of situations.

5.3.2.3　Social Networking Resource

Doing *Taoci* emails is a kind of symbolic means to serve as networking resource. For Yunyang, there was little existing social capital that he could take advantage of. *Guanxi* capital is confined to a certain field. In Yunyang's *Taoci* emails to another foreign professor, he purposefully mentioned his Chinese supervisor as he reflected below.

(I17) If between you and the professor there is a third person that both of you know, the application could be much easier. This professor and my own Chinese professor, they know each other quite well. So I said *** is my supervisor directly at the beginning … However, later I got the funded offer from Professors Smith.

379

(Interview transcripts 2014-Dec. Yunyang Liu)

The "middleman" networking resource can only be afforded as capital to use among relevant people. However, in the case of Professor Smith, there was no middleman between them. Yunyang had to depend all on himself to create the relation from scratch by resorting to other speech acts of pulling *guanxi*.

Yunyang spoke high about the role of *Taoci* investment in his own application, in which he emphasized that *Taoci* communication would make two persons know each other better.

(I18) Without these email exchanges, I might not have that offer. I think *Taoci* is necessary for anyone … For ordinary applications, *Taoci* is to let foreign professors know about you, know whether you're countable, like personal statement. However, I think *Taoci* is more important than personal statement, because personal statement is more a matter of form … Foreign professors would also like to know the applicant person-in-person, like the email communication and phone interview, to know who you really are and whether you can do work for me. (Interview transcripts 2014-May Yunyang Liu)

Taoci in Yunyang's understanding had developed a new connotation of "interaction makes communication better", shedding its original derogatoriness of the dialectal sense. And "…this practical sense enables learners to (a) master the rules, norms, genres, and multimodal features specific to different communicative contexts; (b) seamlessly shift codes, practices, and strategies while moving across spaces..." (Darvin, Norton, 2015: 48) as Yunyang did in his *Taoci* journey.

5.3.3　The Dynamic Investment in Yunyang's *Taoci*

Through the lens of investment theory (Norton Peirce, 1995, 2000; Darvin, Norton, 2015), we can see more clearly Yunyang's *Taoci* practice for his imagined study-abroad program. First, Yunyang's imagination of "seeing the world" and "being a successful returnee" was integral to his own identity and the driving force to spur him to learn English hard, stay in the lab late, and communicate actively through *Taoci* email with foreign professors, since it is in the realm of the imagination, or imagined identities (Norton, 2013; Kanno, Norton, 2003; Pavlenko, Norton, 2007) that people are able to express this desire. Imagination allows learners to re-envision how things are as how they want them to be (Darvin, Norton, 2015). Receiving an offer from W University and having Professor Smith as his supervisor signaled the change of institutional membership and a progress Yunyang's imagined identity of the world viewer, to become an excellent academia and contribute to his imagined interdisciplinary arena.

Second, capital is power and can be used as affordance to invest only in correspondent fields (Darvin, Norton, 2015). Yunyang's cultural capital of education, skill, knowledge, paper, patent, etc., were recognized symbolically powerful because it was put in the international higher education field to compete for a PhD program. These capitals might not be that powerful if he wanted for example to look for a job in a trading company. Moreover, because "occupying new spaces involves not only acquiring new material and symbolic resources" (Darvin, Norton, 2015: 45), *Taoci* investment helped Yuyang have access to new and more capitals, not only his English language capital, but also the educational resources that would tie him with new institutional networking, a platform to reach his disciplinary community and other education resources that were not available domestically. Through the examination of Yunyang's positive participation into the pending situations, we can observe his agency to navigate his options and negotiate his identity and relation with the foreign professor.

Third, along with his *Taoci* practice, new dispositions might be added to his habitus. For example, he recognized the importance of fighting for himself or thrusting himself even if he was in front of the higher-status authority, which is more often than not related to the Western self-promotion style as he reflected below.

(I19) Doing *Taoci* is also a way of learning. I did *Taoci*, not because of I grasped it, but I learned from it or learned within it … My strongest feeling is that you must fight for your goal to the end, though this might not be related to English study. As I told you before, I was slippery, not serious about everything. The application issue spurred me and changed my attitude. Without the application issue, I might still have indulged myself in playing DOTA game. (Interview transcripts 2014-May Yunyang Liu)

5.4   Summary

By focusing on the individual *Taoci* investment trajectory, we have tried to answer the sub-question of "How were the speech acts employed across situations in the application process?" as well as to deepen the discussion on the second question of "In what sense was speech act, as cultural and historical encounter between linguistic habitus and linguistic market, investment into applicants' imagined identity and imagined future?". It is demonstrated how the speech acts in the three meso speech acts of pulling *guanxi*, promoting self and negotiating entry evolved with Yunyang's situation in the application process. Meanwhile different types of academic capital, which are invested as affordances into the *Taoci* communication were presented differently as the interaction moved on. As one of international education offer hunters, Yunyang's case served to present an individual investment trajectory of *Taoci* practice for overseas education offer. His successful application at the same time constitutes a part of the flow of different capitals across boundaries, especially the mobility of academic talent in the globalized education field.

Chapter 6

The Dynamic
Investment Model

This chapter is going to make a synthetic discussion of the findings in the previous two chapters, and to propose the Dynamic Investment Model based on the empirical study of *Taoci* praxis.

6.1   General Discussion on Major Findings

Chapter 3 has given an intensive description of all speech acts in our *Taoci* email data and interpreted how investment has been made with configurations of different capitals. Chapter 4, by focusing on a particular applicant's *Taoci* journey, has revealed the variation of speech acts across situations and personal investment trajectory. Chapter 3 serves to paint an overall picture of *Taoci* as investment among Chinese applicants while Chapter 4 zooms in an individual *Taoci* process.

Based on the email analysis, the hierarchy of speech acts has been teased out. The emerging genre of *Taoci* emails among Chinese applicants is considered as a macro speech act at a generic level, directed at a goal of bringing about positive changes for their application through an ensemble of lower-level speech acts. The meso speech act consists of pulling *guanxi*, promoting self and negotiating entry, which are higher-level strategies driven by the practical goal of *Taoci*. Under each meso speech act, a specific repertoire of micro speech act has been

386

generalized to mediate linguistic forms and actions. The meso and micro level has been the focus of analysis. The meso speech act of pulling *guanxi* consists of deference-oriented strategy and solidarity-oriented strategy. The meso speech act of promoting self is categorized into Me-oriented strategy and Us-oriented strategy. The meso speech act of negotiating institutional entry is constituted of five micro speech acts.

There are five general types of working mechanism of these speech acts, illustrated in sub-figure (a), (b), (c), (d) and (e) of Fig. 6.1 below. The capital letter "A" represents Chinese applicant while "P" is foreign professor. In sub-figure (e), "DI" means domestic institution while "FI" is foreign institution. The arrows in each sub-figure indicate the moving direction of the two parties in each speech act. Details of each sub-figure are explained below.

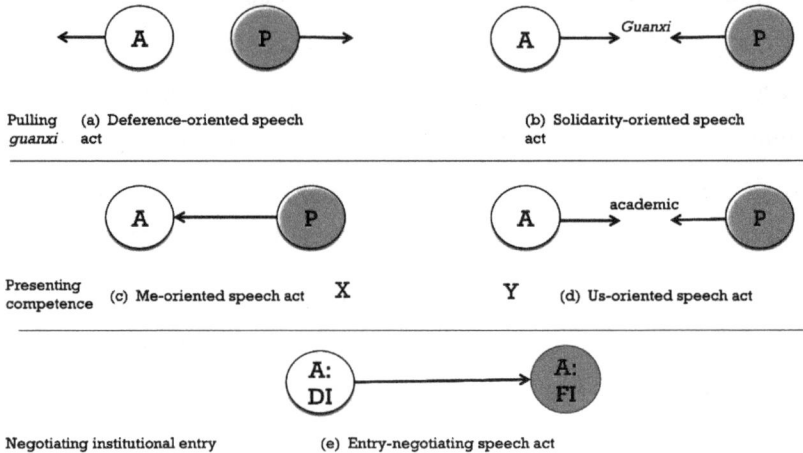

Fig. 6.1　The working mechanism of speech acts in *Taoci*

Sub-figure of (a) shows the force flow in deference-oriented speech acts. The outward arrow directions indicate that applicants and professors are driven apart, creating a big difference between them either horizontally or vertically and profiling professors' higher or respectful status as capital possessor and allocator. Sub-figure (b) is about the solidarity-oriented speech acts, which draws applicants and professors together, emphasizing their common ground or sameness for *guanxi*-building. The solidarity strategy emphasizes togetherness or involvement while the deference strategy underscores differentiation

388

or difference, but both pulling towards applicants and pushing away from applicants work for building or consolidating the relationship with professors. In this sense, the solidarity-oriented category is a complement to the deference-oriented one.

In the meso speech act of self-promoting, sub-figure (c) explains the force of Me-oriented speech acts, to impress and attract foreign professors' attention or favor through highlighting their individual competence or potential. The arrow, which points from professor to applicant, means that the former is supposed to be attracted by the latter's academic capitals. Sub-figure (d) resembles (b), but with a different content of sameness, i.e. academic similarity. The Us-oriented speech acts focus on the shared common ground in terms of academic issue, but also oriented to attracting professors through the demonstration of applicants' academic capital. Both strategies are deployed to impress and convince professors through explicit or implicit self-promotion in order to increase their stakes in the offer-hunt wrestling.

In the speech act of negotiating entry, sub-figure (e) illustrates the ultimate goal of *Taoci* investment, i.e. moving applicants from a domestic institution to a foreign institution, usually a better one. The micro speech acts of negotiating institutional entry are all request, direct or indirect request, request for information or offer, and illegitimate or legitimate request. Both the meso speech acts of pulling *guanxi* and presenting competence are oriented towards the speech act of negotiating institutional entry. All of these speech acts and their specific linguistic features can vary across situations that an individual applicant comes upon, which has been illustrated by Yunyang's case.

Targeted foreign professors are regarded to own the capitals that Chinese applicants longed for and competed for. For example, economic capital of research funding that professors could allocate to support applicants, cultural capital or more specifically their academic capital of research achievement, even their social capital of being involved in the applicants' desirable disciplinary circle. All of these capitals that professors possess are, in the case of *Taoci*, turned into symbolic capital—gate-keeper power, authority, prestige, recognized by these applicants, which explains why they spare no efforts in pulling *guanxi*, either pulling themselves toward or pushing themselves away from professors.

On the other side, Chinese applicants are equipped with different types and amounts of capital when they start their *Taoci* investment. First and foremost, they could resort to their academic capital: the embodied form of acquired skills, the objectified form of research articles, books, and awards, and the institutionalized form of language certificate, diploma and degree. Second, using English itself demonstrates their linguistic capital and switching to other codes boasts multilingual edges. Third, the social capital of middleman and previous acquaintance are available *guanxi* resource to mediate applicants with unfamiliar foreign professors. Therefore, facilitated with the minimum amount of capital (Bourdieu, Wacquant, 1992), Chinese applicants can manipulate their cultural capital of knowledge, skills, publications and talent through such speech acts as making positive evaluations about themselves and dialoguing academically. They turn to such speech acts as introducing the intermediary and articulating previous association for *guanxi*-building. Therein these capitals have been used strategically as affordances for their investment in future study-abroad programs and their imagined identities of being scholar, scientist, researcher, etc.

In the *Taoci* investment, there are speech acts which value the hierarchical student-teacher relationship, represented by formal addressing, honor statement; there are speech acts, which attach great importance to the indigenous concept of *guanxi*, such as introducing the middleman. "…knowing how to make a good *guanxi* is a prerequisite for the achievement of harmony and competence in Chinese communication."

(Chen, 2010: 206) The usage of these speech acts is connected with the cultural habitus of traditional Confucianism of maintaining *li* as well as cherishing harmonious interpersonal relationship as an essential social resource. On the other hand, the necessity to advertise themselves in order to compete with international applicants for better educational opportunity drives Chinese applicants to behave discursively towards the self-promotion style, which is not inherently rooted in traditional Chinese value (Gao et al., 2007), but the typical, familiar, and natural way to act with strangers among Americans (Tice, Butler, Murayen et al., 1995) and particularly strongly characterizes the individualistic countries for agentic traits (Kurman, 2001). Moreover, the micro speech acts of negotiating institutional entry further demonstrates how initiatively applicants were behaving to hunt a global offer, as they raised different kinds of request and even illegitimate ones to claim for their own power to speak, contrary to the indirectness and lack of self-appraisal often stereotypically characterizing Asian or Chinese (Kaplan, 1966; Bhatia, 1993). The change of discursive strategy reflects what Darvin and Norton argued, "…their styles and registers are measured against a value system that reflects the biases and assumptions of the larger sociocultural context." (Darvin, Norton, 2015: 45)

In the continuous process of massive as well as repeated discourse practice of *Taoci* among Chinese applicants, it is perceived that the belief of reserved or plain self-presentation with Chinese traditional value is tilting towards the value of self-promotion characterizing individualism in "western" countries (Elliot, Chirkov, Kim et al., 2001; Hosftede, 1980; Xin, Tsui, 1996), reflected through the predominant proportion of promoting personal competence (52%). Thus, if we draw a continuum between the traditional Chinese habitus of being sensitive to *guanxi* and the western cultural habitus of stressing individual competence in high-stake self-presentation, different speech acts can be placed at different positions on the continuum as Fig. 6.2 illustrates.

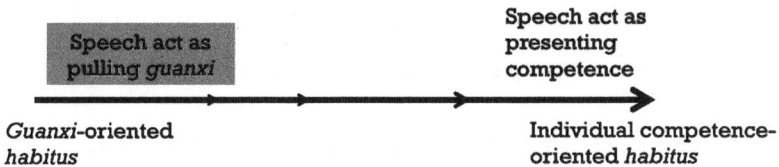

Fig. 6.2　Self-presentation habitus with speech acts: durability and changeability

As Fig. 6.2 shows, the speech act of pulling *guanxi* represents more of the Chinese habitus of maintaining *li* in particular between hierarchical interlocutors and taking great care of harmonious interpersonal relationship for networking resources. The speech act of presenting competence reflects more of the belief in individual competence in self-presentation and directness to go straight to the point. On the one hand, we can also feel the durability of habitus dispositions of Chinese applicants, clinging to pulling *guanxi* and alluding to the subconscious level of investment, while one the other hand, we can observe the dynamism or variability of habitus changing to cater for the exigency of self-advertising on the competitive international higher education market. Because of the duality of habitus, *Taoci* practice exists as natural and reasonable activity, as what Bourdieu argued, "… the field structures the habitus … Habitus contributes to constituting the field as a meaningful world." (Bourdieu, Wacquant, 1992: 127) Traditional Chinese values linger on while "Western" values seep in.

6.2 The Dynamic Investment Model

Based on the investigation of Chinese English learners' *Taoci* practice, we try to propose the Dynamic Investment Model (Fig. 6.3) to enrich the existing investment model of Darvin and Norton (2015) and to better explain sociolinguistic phenomena with tilted concern about the micro level of language. The Darvin and Norton (2015) investment model has three interconnecting constructs: identity, capital and ideology, with investment navigating the three. In this new model, habitus is introduced to replace the more static concept of ideology.

Speech act is taken as investment to involve the microstructure of language. Moreover, the dynamism is reflected through potential change of the three constructs of identity, capital and habitus due to investment.

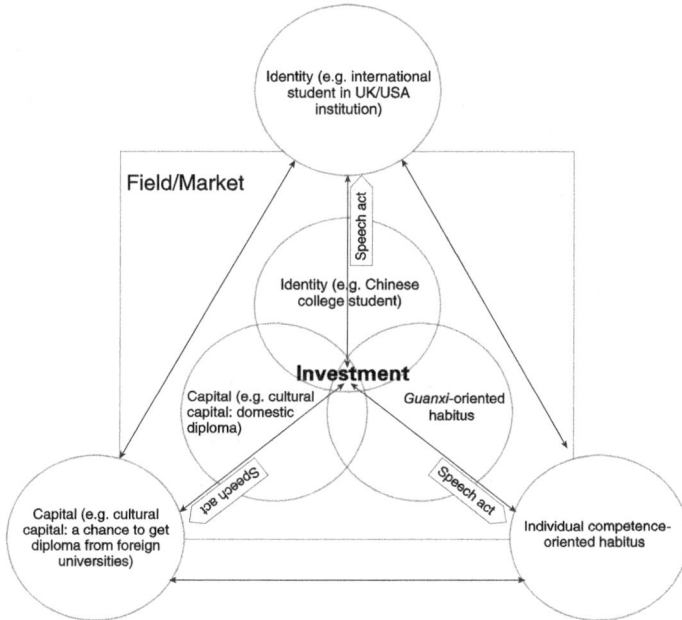

Fig. 6.3   The Dynamic Investment Model

In Fig. 6.3, investment is still placed at the very center of the interaction between identity, capital and habitus of the three interconnecting circles inside, and takes place in a certain field/market, shown by the rectangle.

395

The bidirectional arrows connecting investment in the center and the outward three circles of identity, capital and habitus mean that speech acts are the bridge of current identity and imagined identity and are used to mobilize existing capital as affordance to invest in desirable future and identity, and the interaction between old dispositions of habitus and newly emerging and structured ones. Thus, the outward three constructs of identity, capital and habitus can be changed or added with new features to different degrees due to speech act investment, indicating the dynamism of investment. These changes are relevant to each other shown by the bidirectional lines connecting them and new investment practice can be remolded or "embezzled" based on these new features of identity, capital and habitus in other fields. However, the newly added features only grow out of and cannot be completely cut from the old constructs, alluding to the continuum of the existing structure, indicated by the three outward circles embedded partially in the field where investment happens.

Since the constructs of identity and capital in the Darvin and Norton (2015) investment model are kept intact in this model and have been introduced in the literature review part, details of them will not be repeated, but will be integrated into the focal discussion on speech act, habitus and the dynamism.

6.2.1   Speech Act: Doing Investment with Words

The introduction of speech act into the investment model draws our attention to the fact that speech is action, action brings change and creates identity. Speech act hereby could mean all the three levels of macro, meso and micro as discussed before. Darvin and Norton argued that their model of investment aimed to "go beyond the microstructures of power in specific communicative events and to investigate the systemic patterns of control that communicative events are indexical of" (*ibid*: 42). The present model goes the other way around: to dive into the microstructures of message construction, and to straighten out the discrete events with communicative practices and the value-laden linguistic forms with their socio-historical lineage.

Speech act is intention-oriented just as investment is desire-oriented, executed by speakers with a goal, a purpose or an intention in mind, at the macro, meso or micro level, though sometimes speakers might not be aware of the pragmatic function of their speech. "… persons want their goals, possessions, and achievements to be thought desirable not just by anyone, but by some particular others especially relevant to the particular goals, etc." (Brown, Levinson, 1987: 63) For instance, the greeting speech act of "How're you doing today?" is taken as a default and spontaneous opening when people see each other day in and day out in America, and its purpose has been "misrecognized as arbitrary" (Bourdieu, 1991: 170) and thus taken for granted. Nonetheless, its function is embedded into the form with or without the speaker's conscious intention, and this purposeful act steers peoples' way of behaving them discursively. Investment is driven by investors' ambivalent desire, and "...it is through desire that learners are compelled to act and exercise their agency ... learners invest because there is something that they want for themselves" (Darvin, Norton, 2015: 46). The same holds true to the use of speech acts. In order to achieve what they want, different speech acts are employed by Chinese applicants to invest in their successful application, and the intention or goal of each speech act represents the purpose of *Taoci* investment practice at a micro level.

Each speech act is made under a specific context just as investment takes place within a certain market or field. "Any speech act or any discourse is a conjuncture, the product of the encounter between, on the one side, a linguistic habitus ... and, on the other hand, a linguistic market." (Bourdieu, Wacquant, 1992: 193) The market produces and censors the value or price of linguistic products. The socially constituted dispositions of linguistic habitus preset a certain way of speaking. Thus, preferred ways or conventional ways of speaking vary across cultures or societies. However, linguistic habitus interacts constantly with its linguistic market, which is influenced by other markets. When enough sedimentation is accumulated after repeated and massive linguistic practices, like the genre of *Taoci* email, market will be reregulated and habitus will change accordingly, and so is the "price" of a speech act to its own field.

"A speaker's linguistic strategies ... are oriented ... by the chances of being listened to, believed, obeyed, even at the cost of misunderstanding; ... by the chances of profit for that particular speaker, occupying a particular position in the structure of the distribution of capital." (Bourdieu, 1977: 654) Therefore, when linguistic habitus and linguistic market are incompatible or incongruent with each other, people "may not know how to act and may literally be lost for words" (Thompson, 1991: 17). However, rational people have their agency to either adjust their own behaviors to the market, just as Chinese applicants have followed the western style of promotional self-presentation in their *Taoci* email, or "he is likely to find that there are already several well-established fronts among which he must choose" (Goffman, 1959: 27), which corresponds to the usage of *guanxi*-oriented strategies to stick to the traditional Chinese value of *li* between the teacher and the student. The co-existence of *guanxi*-oriented and self-promotion-oriented speech acts represents the discursive hybridity in the new genre of *Taoci*.

Speech act can be invested to change identity in so far as linguistic behavior is taken as "a series of acts of identity in which people reveal both their personal identity and their search for social roles" (Le Page, Tabouret-Keller, 1985: 14). Speakers' choice of linguistic forms is to negotiate their identity in interaction under the steering propensity of habitus. With every speech act, individuals perform an act of identity, revealing their gender, ethnicity, occupation, social rank, etc., which is further invested in their imagined identity. A range of diverse identities are thus switched on and off in strategic ways so that they may fit in or be distinguished, and more importantly to negotiate and frame their desirable benefits with the investment of capitals. "Speech acts contribute to reproducing society (social identities, social relationships, systems of knowledge and belief) as it is, yet also contributes to transforming society." (Fairclough, 1992: 65) *Taoci* speech act amounts to the action that applicants take to invest in their study-abroad program. The form of a specific speech act is affected not only by the applicants' linguistic competence in the narrow sense but also governed by their possession of capital, predisposed language habitus, and the market on which their capitals come into contest.

6.2.2   Habitus: Perpetuating Yet Changing

Habitus is introduced to replace the original construct of ideology in Darvin and Norton (2015) for the following reasons. First, ideology is more related with social political aspects as their case analysis shows whereas habitus can deal with the sociocultural aspect of investment of particular importance to the present study of *Taoci*. Second, ideology in Darvin and Norton (2015) is described as a systemic pattern of control, which appears quite static and cannot adequately reckon with the undercurrent and vicissitude of culture sedimentation in the fast-changing fields in the globalized world. Nonetheless, it doesn't mean that ideology is totally out of the scene in the present investment model.

As structured structures play the role of structuring structures, habitus mediates the dialectical relationship between structure and agency, objectivism and subjectivism, and manifests itself through each individual in the society. In Darvin and Norton (2015: 45) habitus is regarded as "an internalized system shaped by ideology" and "shaped by structures that govern and are perpetuated by ideology". However, Bourdieu's habitus is "**durable, but not eternal**" (Bourdieu,Wacquant, 1992: 133, bold added by the present author), which indicates on the one hand its inertiality as *opus operandi* and on the other hand its potential for change as *modus operandi*. "Habitus ... can adapt to

401

new circumstances and generate novel response." (Block, 2013: 135) The adaptation and response to a new environment or a new field, is possible to engender new dispositions. The addition of habitus into this model is to infill both a historical and individual perspective towards investment by stressing a more elastic view towards habitus so as to explain the changes occurring to individuals as well as a cultural group, or small culture (Holliday, 1999).

To both a whole class and an individual, habitus is historical in that it is "the product of a chronologically ordered series of structuring determinations" (Bourdieu, 1995: 86). The class habitus of bourgeois is formed along with the appearance of capitalism and still lingers on. The inculcation of a propensity to act of a person is acquired starting from his or her early childhood and may last throughout adulthood. "[I]ndividual's internalized dispositions … are formulated out of engagement in situated social practices as well as actions linked more directly with larger social structures." (Block, 2013: 135) Habitus is also individual because the subjectiveness of habitus is externalized through the daily routines of perception, action, and investment of individuals. Habitus gives individual a sense of practice (or game), against its historical and collective tradition, which enables us to discern a historical continuity of culture and identity as well as a reference to the future/imagined identity.

Field shapes the structure of habitus, which in turn becomes the basis of perception and appreciation of the ensuing experience of social individuals (Bourdieu, 1995). In this way, habitus can guide peoples' action and ways of practice to achieve their objectives by investing appropriate volumes and types of capitals in a specific social field. The practice of investment reproduces habitus itself as well as the structure of the field. Meanwhile, the appearance of new habitus and shedding of old dispositions usually happen in a slow and subtle way.

In the context of globalization, the flow of goods, money, resources, and talents are accelerated worldwide while the digital era transforms the speed, mode and range of such flows. These facts invariably define and redefine the existing fields, like the international higher education field in this research, which correspondently breeds new habitus among its field participants, for instance, through the repeated and large-scale discourse practice of writing personal statement or writing self-presentation email to foreign professors among Chinese applicants.

Speech act or discourse practice plays the forming and reforming role at a micro level in cultivating new dispositions of habitus as well as new fields. This dialectical formulation between habitus and field, mediating through speech act, prevents us from drifting with and being immersed in the tide of postmodern deconstructionism, and grounds us to the solid structure of field, but also not neglecting the perspective of identity as multiple and social structure as porous. Therefore, the introduction of habitus in this model could better explain the changes brought by investment occurring to individuals as well as groups.

Chinese applicants' *Taoci* speech act of pulling *guanxi* reflects more the *guanxi*-oriented habitus in traditional Chinese cultural value of Confucianism. The hierarchical relationship between student and teacher is stressed by students' self-abasing and raising the teacher's higher status. The maintenance of *li* has probably been inculcated through family and school education of using formal titled addressing to teachers and behaving modestly in front of the higher-status, which constitutes the subconscious part of habitus that refuses to back out easily. "[I]t is therefore through the dispositions of the habitus that the conjunctural configuration of the linguistic production relation modifies practice." (Bourdieu, 1977: 655) On the other hand, in the competitive application for PhD programs in developed countries, Chinese applicants' speech act of presenting competence and negotiating institutional entry with foreign authorities displays the feature of the individual-competence-oriented habitus which characterized the "Western" culture advocating individualism of self-promotion even in front of higher-status authorities. The fast development of different fields as well as the wide spread of dominant ideology of powerful English-speaking countries exerts influence on and modify Chinese young generation's practice to handle their "upward communication" (Ho, 2010).

6.2.3　Dynamism of Investment

Investment is driven by investors' anticipation of profit and their ambivalent desire of imagined identity and imagined community, which "allows learners to re-envision how things are as how they want them to be" (Darvin, Norton, 2015: 46). Investors, positioned by the structural relation of a given field, are bearers of capital, and can employ their capitals as affordances to make a change of their identity, and reproduce or subvert the current capital distribution in terms of volume, category and form. Therefore, through the practice of investment, investors come closer to their imagined identity and have access to different capitals and even acquire new dispositions of habitus, which is the dynamism of investment.

In the field of international higher education market, talents and resources flow world-wide, but concentrates in developed countries of English-speaking nations, which have been attracting applicants all over the world. However, usually only the most excellent will get that pass. The cross-border influx to a more developed country itself contains symbolic value. Chinese applicants' *Taoci* is one of their eager investment projects for their imagined study-abroad programs. In their initiative engagement in *Taoci* email exchanges, they appropriated and employed a spectrum of capitals hunting for their foreign education offer investment: cultural capital of digital literacy, language skills, knowledge of politeness, academic ability, social capital of intermediary person as valuable liaison as well as economic capital[1] to pay for their English training and test. The forms and amount of the capitals were under transformation after the application, at least for those successful applications. Becoming an international student affiliated to a western university is a symbolic capital as overseas credential may mean a profitable job, an international position, or a better start-off. For example, Chinese universities would love to pay more money for recruiting PhD returnees as faculty than domestic graduates.

---

[1] Economic capital such as funding source or program grant is especially crucial in those visiting scholar programs in my data from applicants for visiting positions in foreign universities. The applicants mentioned explicitly their available government funding.

In this process, applicant's identity also changes. At least they have a new institutional identity, migrating from a domestic institution to a foreign university, more often than not a better one. The opportunity of going abroad is a new capital afforded to applicants and can be mobilized to acquire more capitals and to attain their imagined future. For instance, they will be involved in new disciplinary circles, starting their professional career, and making friends of culturally diversified backgrounds. In this process, the cross-border enrollment reproduces the structure of the international higher education field.

The meaning of *Taoci* in Beijing dialect is partially preserved and partially subverted to different extents. It has been enregistered (Agha, 1999; Dong, 2012) from a local term to the nation-wide discourse practice among study-abroad applicants in China, which changed the *sens pratique* of dialectal *Taoci* that responds to the complexities of the digital era. What is more important, the young generation's habitus has been revealed to undergo changes as well. The speech act of pulling *guanxi* is more oriented towards the traditional Chinese value of cherishing networking while the speech acts of presenting academic competence and negotiating institutional entry are justified as legitimate means to fight for their educational resources, resembling the individualism of promoting personal interest. The newly charged meaning contrasts with traditional Chinese politeness of *li* and maintaining harmonious relation with others in that the focus is no longer the relational hierarchy, but self, the emphasis on individual. That is a diversion from the dominant respect for power hierarchy and *guanxi* construction, to the focus on self-presentation of individual strengths. This difference might indicate an important change in the Chinese habitus of *Taoci* born and metamorphosed in the study-abroad heat propelled by globalization and digitalization over the past two decades. Drawing on a Chinese idiom, we may say the individualism-based self-promotion is "new wine in an old bottle". From a social constructivist perspective, the despotic "bottle" of language can be quietly transformed to accommodate new "wine" in subtle connection with the old, ushering new dispositions of habitus. The imagined identity of better education and better jobs modifies Chinese applicants' linguistic practice to accommodate to the convention of the "Western" in a broad sense.

Only a fast-developing market would accelerate the merging of cultural values. As new field is forming, new habitus will come into being as well. "...the field structures the habitus ... Habitus contributes to constituting the field as a meaningful world." (Bourdieu, Wacquant, 1992: 127) It is not impossible that the mixture of *guanxi*-pulling, presenting competence and negotiating entry would one day become

408

a norm followed by foreign applicants from other countries seeking PhD programs in China as China is rising as a powerful country in the world and gradually becoming a hot study-abroad destination for foreigners. The structure of global higher education market will be in upheaval and perhaps the *guanxi*-oriented habitus will be formed among foreign applicants for Chinese educational programs and they will turn to match their cultural norm and value of self-presentation to the traditional Chinese ways.

To summarize, in our proposed Dynamic Investment Model, speech act is introduced to the Dynamic Investment Model to offer a socio-pragmatic perspective to the investment model by focusing more on language forms and uses. Habitus, as a replacement of ideology in the Darvin and Norton (2015) investment model, gives more leverage to the dynamism of investment and the delicate change occurring to individuals as well a group in terms of identity, capital and habitus. Braiding insight from Bourdieu's habitus into the existing investment model could enhance its theoretical and explanatory rigor. However, it should also be alerted that the newly generated features of identity, capital and habitus are not accomplished at one action of investment. The change is constant and continuous. When they move to new communities, applicants still carry with themselves their existing identity, capital and dispositions of habitus.

Chapter 7

Conclusion

This research has investigated Chinese applicants' *Taoci* discourse practice in their hunting for international education offer. Their *Taoci* email texts and interviews were collected as data for analysis. Brown and Levinson's (1987) politeness theory was adopted as the analytical framework for speech act analysis in *Taoci* emails. Darvin and Norton's (2015) investment model was deployed as the theoretical lens to examine *Taoci* as investment in applicants' imagined identity and future.

For the first big question of "What is *Taoci* as 'doing things with words' in study-abroad application in China?", a hierarchical approach to speech acts in terms of macro, meso and micro has been teased out to give an overall picture of the nature and function of *Taoci* in Chinese applicants' email texts. *Taoci* as a type of self-promotional genre was treated as the macro speech act of general function of bringing changes into current situation. Three meso speech acts of pulling *guanxi*, promoting self and negotiating entry were generalized, and their respective micro speech acts with rich linguistic realizations were categorized and analyzed in Chapter 4 to answer the first sub-question of "What speech acts were used in *Taoci* email texts?". An in-depth analysis of the research participant Yunyang Liu's email package and interviews was conducted in Chapter 5 to unfold the flexible mixture of different speech acts to cater for situational contingency based on the applicant's active interaction with his own situation. The case analysis, as a vertical dimension, made a complement to the horizontal description of the overall picture of *Taoci* and addressed the second sub-question of "How were the speech acts employed across situations in the application process?".

As to the second big question, "In what sense was speech act, as cultural and historical encounter between linguistic habitus and linguistic market, investment into applicants' imagined identity and imagined future", the analysis of email texts and interviews has manifested that Chinese applicant, when they started *Taoci* with foreign professors, were already equipped with different types and volumes of economic, cultural, social capitals, which were used as affordances (Darvin, Norton, 2015) through various speech acts to invest in their imagined identities illustrated both in Chapter 4 and Chapter 5. This responded to the first sub-question of "What and how capitals were served as affordances for applicants' application for overseas education?". What is more, by tapping into the features of their *Taoci* speech acts as the encounter of linguistic habitus and language market, it further revealed the fact that the more *guanxi*-oriented habitus was mixed with and moving towards the individual-competence-oriented habitus in the applicants' upward self-presentation, which addressed the second

413

sub-question of "Through the investment of different speech acts in what way did the Chinese young people's habitus undergo changes perceived through their *Taoci* practice?". The large-scale and repeated *Taoci* practice among Chinese study-abroad applicants, along with the maintenance and transformation of cultural habitus, is perhaps a necessary characteristic of changing fields or markets.

By applying the Darvin and Norton (2015) investment model to exploring the less-known topic of *Taoci*, this research has filled in the niche of the underexplored area of Chinese English learners' email writing practice in real life. Moreover, based on the observation of *Taoci* as investment involving the flow of cultural, economic and social capital for their imagined education projects, we proposed the Dynamic Investment Model to enhance the theoretical and explanatory rigor of existing investment model in terms of the following two aspects: (1) By paying more attention to discourse at a micro level of language, the new model adds a socio-pragmatic perspective to connect speech act and investment; (2) The new model gives more dynamism to habitus evidenced by *Taoci* speech act and can better explain the individual change of identity and capital through the practice of investment driven by their imagined identities.

414

7.1   Implications

The findings of the study on Chinese applicants' *Taoci* practice shed insights into theoretical implications on speech act as the link between words and the world. Bourdieu's (1991, 1995) argument of speech act or any discourse segment as the interaction between linguistic habitus and linguistic market drives us to take into consideration the underlying mechanism of social and cultural factors to analyze discursive actions. In other words, "A genuine science of discourse must seek truth within discourse but also outside it" (Bourdieu, 1977: 650). This point of view is also significant for analysis of the other aspects of micro level language practice.

On the other hand, the involvement of microscopic analysis of language into the existing investment theory helps us better understand people's investment practice of doing their imagined identity with their words. Combining the macro structure of society with the hierarchical analysis of speech act in *Taoci* emails, this research has demonstrated how *Taoci* serves as students' investment in their imagined future of going abroad and imagined identity of being a researcher, a scholar, an international sojourner, etc., which at the same time deepens our understanding of the performativity of speech act itself. Moreover,

415

the emerging factuality, boosted by prevalence of computer-mediated communication across cultures, nations, and areas, that the original dialectal sense of *Taoci* has been enregistered as a nation-wide norm among study-abroad applicants to communicate with potential foreign supervisors, also gives us the lens to observe the discursive hybridity in *Taoci* emails and to be keen to the delicacy of cultural confluence between different cultures.

7.2 Limitations

This study is not impeccable. There are two general limitations. First, the data coverage and consistency are not adequate enough. The data were collected from applicants in four universities located in the city of Beijing, and the majority of research informants were from one of the four universities. Although the collected amount of data was rather substantial, the population coverage might challenge the generalizations drawn from the collected data. Furthermore, a small number of research participants joined the interview part and only four of them completed in-depth interviews, which poses the problem of data consistency. However, the researcher had tried hard to elicit as rich data as possible from the respondents and used supplementary evidence such as field notes, online discourse to support the arguments made.

In addition, there was a lack of interview data from the receivers of such *Taoci* emails, i.e. foreign professors, which could not be possibly to get access to in this research. The professors' understanding and feedback about the emails they received could have provided more insiders' perspective towards the analysis. However, I did consult two American professors for their reaction and appraisal of the email data in order to strengthen my interpretation.

Second, with regards to the email textual analysis, because I learned English as a second language, there might be a lack of native speaker's linguistic and cultural instinct and I might unconsciously examine the data from a Chinese perspective from time to time. My subjectivity was thus inevitably imposed on the analysis and interpretation. However, as a native Chinese speaker with one-year's educational experience in America and going through similar *Taoci* experience with foreign professors, I did offer an insider's perspective towards the data. To secure the validity of the analysis, I also tried to adopt a systemic linguistic analysis for each speech act category and consulted my Chinese supervisor and American professors' to corroborate the analysis. What is more, I did inter-coding with a fellow researcher to ensure the reliability of the analysis.

7.3 Suggestions for Future Research

Future work can be launched in different directions. The first one is about Chinese people's email practice. The less mined field of email writing, either in English or in Chinese, is still worth excavating. A promising area might be English email writing literacy among Chinese English learners to enhance both their language ability and intercultural awareness. There has been, up to now, no longitudinal research on Chinese English learners' English email practice and it could be a valuable research topic in many facets. Apart from English emails, research on emails written in Chinese is also in a great lack and awaits academic exploration. More researches on intercultural student-teacher email interaction are also needed to accommodate new challenges in the international education environment. Contrastive researches can be conducted to compare *Taoci* emails with those written by applicants' of other cultural backgrounds. In terms of research method, corpus could be introduced to collect and analyze more email texts so as to expand the data pool and generalize more representative findings.

The other line would be about L2 investment in the digital world. With the convenience of and easy access to the Internet resources, which has changed both the social and language landscape, students

418

are endowed with more affordances of capitals in terms of both type and volume. For instance, the wide spread of MOOC (Massive Open Online Courses) provides a golden opportunity for them to develop their literacy and intellect, and to communicate with talents from all over the world. People who have access to such resources are multiplicatively empowered while those who cannot are relatively handicapped, which poses more severe yet invisible challenges for current L2 investment theory and needs to be addressed instantly. Moreover, Chinese English learners' investment practice calls for more vibrant empirical researches. Their acquired language capital, is more often than not driven by an instrumental incentive, sediments and becomes a part of their habitus, and prepares them for future identity, which will generate an invaluable insight into the interaction between habitus, capital and identity in the Chinese context.

Appendixes

Appendix A English Translation of Participant Recruitment Email

Dear ***,

I am Xiao Lin, a PhD student in School of Foreign Languages, Peking University. We are conducting an investigation on Chinese students' English emails written to foreign professors for application (*Taoci* emails in brief). We are collecting such email samples and hope you can give a hand. It's guaranteed that your personal information and other privacy will be secured. If you would like to help us and join us, would you please give me a reply so that I can tell you more about the details of the project? You can either reach me through the bulletin board short message or my email (********@pku.edu.cn), or my phone (********).

Thanks very much and really looking forward to your reply.

Best regards,

***

Appendix B   English Translation of the Interview Design

Theme 1 About *Taoci*

(e.g. What's your understanding about the word of *Taoci*, its original meaning as well as the meaning in the study-abroad application field?)

Theme 2 About doing *Taoci* with foreign professors

(e.g. Can you talk about your experience of doing *Taoci* with the foreign supervisor (s) during your application process? Before you wrote the *Taoci* email, did you make any preparations for it? How do you appraise your doing *Taoci* with your supervisor?)

Theme 3 About learning English

(e.g. Can you talk about your experience of learning English in the past years? How do you think about English in your life?)

Theme 4 About going abroad

(e.g. Can you share your overseas application experience? Why did you choose to go abroad?)

Appendix C   Samples of Email Data in the Year of 2013, 2014 and 2015

Sample 1   2013-01 Qiang Miao

Dear Prof. ***,

Hello! My name is Qiang Miao. Currently I am a student working for the degree of Master of Philosophy (MPhil) in the department of *** of A University. I have applied to the Ph. D. program of your department and indicated that I wish to join your group. So I would like to briefly introduce myself.

Before studying in A University, I received the degree of Bachelor of Science in EE department of H University, China, where I learnt most basic courses of mathematics, signal processing and communications. Now I am with the *** Lab of *** department in A University. The research here is design and fabrication of high performance photonic circuits for telecommunications, data centers and high performance computing. My research topics is applications of silicon photonics devices for advanced optical communication systems. At this stage, I have one first-authored international conference publication and several co-authored conference and journal publications.

During MPhil studies, I attended Advance Wireless Communications course of Prof. Tang and went to several classes of Network Coding Theory of Professor Yun. These two courses guide me to the fields of wireless communications and networking, and information theory. Upon graduating from A University, I have been thinking about working for a Ph. D. degree in these areas. Especially, the research in your group, such as wireless networking of energy harvesting systems, information-theoretic secrecy in wireless systems, and resource allocations, are all interesting topics worth exploring. I am interested in these topics and willing to devote to research, especially those related to applied mathematics.

I hope your group can be my research home and thank you for your consideration. Thank you!

P. S. Attached is my CV!

Warm regards,

Qiang Miao

Sample 2   2014-01-01 Nan Zhou

Dear Prof. ***

I am a graduate student with a degree in electrical engineering in Peking University ***, who would like to apply for your school.

My research concentration was put on the study of millimeter wave devices, such as tunable RF MEMS filters and radiation pattern reconfigurable microstrip antennas. I utilized multimodal techniques to analyze the signals in CPW and slot line. Also, conformal mapping was used to calculate the characteristic impedance of some non-standard transmission lines. Our group also introduced RF MEMS switches into a single antenna element to alter the physical dimensions of antenna, hence changing the radiation pattern.

On your website, I notice that your research interests include MEMS, electromagnetic analysis and design of optical structures, which I am very interested in. Therefore, I am here to ask if there is a Ph.D.

position open for 2014 fall admission.

Best,

Nan Zhou

Sample 3   2015-01 Zhi Gao

Dear Prof. ***,

My name is Zhi Gao, from *** University. Wang Lin may have mentioned me to you.

I am very sorry to contact you so late after Ding Peng's email, because this week I went to *** City for a workshop on causality, and I left the material about visiting student program in Beijing.

I am glad to introduce the visiting student program to you. The original material is in Chinese, for convenience, I list the main points in the "intro" attachment. If there are some points that are not stated clearly, please tell me and let me introduce them in detail. If it's convenient to you, you can also ask ***, who is now a visiting student in Professor Hudson Will's group, and he has almost the same background as I.

I also make a brief introduction of my recent work and my research interest in CV and CL. If you are interested, please find attachments for them.

Invitation from *** is the beginning point of my applying. If you are interested in the program, I can introduce more details about the program and requirements on invitation.

Thank you very much for your attention. I wish to have your response soon.

Sincerely,

Zhi Gao

References

AGAR M, 1985. Institutional discourse[J]. Text, 5(3): 147-168.

AGHA A, 2003. The social life of cultural value[J]. Language & communication, 23(3-4): 231-273.

AKKAYA A, 2007. Student-teacher email interaction: pragmatic markers of gender, nationality and status of the students [D]. Carbondale: Southern Illinois University.

ALTBACH P A, 2013. Frontier issues of international higher education[M]. Shanghai: Shanghai Jiaotong University Press.

ARKOUDIS S, DAVISON C, 2008. Chinese students perspectives on their social, cognitive, and linguistic investment in English medium interaction[J]. Journal of Asian Pacific communication, 18(1):3-8.

AUSTIN J L, 1962. How to do things with words[M]. New York: Oxford University Press.

BARDOVI-HARLIG K, HARTFORD B S, 1990. Congruence in native and nonnative conversations: status balance in the academic advising session[J]. Language learning, 40(4): 467-501.

BARGIELA-CHIAPPINI F, 2003. Face and politeness: new (insights) for old (concepts) [J]. Journal of pragmatics, 35(10-11): 1453-1469.

BARON N S, 1998. Letters by phone or speech by other means: the linguistics of e-mail[J]. Language and communication, 18:133-170.

BAUMAN R, BRIGGS C, 1990. Poetics and performance as critical perspectives on language and social life[J]. Annual review of anthropology, 19: 59-88.

BELL A, GIBSON A, 2011. Staging language: an introduction to the sociolinguistics of performance[J]. Journal of sociolinguistics, 15(5): 555-572.

BENWELL B, STOKOE E. 2006. Discourse and identity[M]. Edinburgh: Edinburgh University Press.

BHATIA V K, 1989. Nativization of job applications in South Asia[R]. Islamabad: International Conference on English South Asia.

BHATIA V K,1993. Analyzing genre: language use in professional settings[M]. London: Longman.

BI J, 1996. On the cultural characteristics of "politeness" [J].World Chinese teaching, 35(1): 51-59.

BIESENBACH-LUCAS S, 2005. Communication topics and strategies in e-mail consultation: comparison between American and international university students[J]. Language learning and technology, 9: 24-46.

BIESENBACH-LUCAS S, 2007. Students writing emails to faculty: an examination of e-politeness among native and non-native speakers of English[J]. Language learning & technology, 11(2): 59-81.

BIESENBACH-LUCAS S, WEASENFORTH D, 2001. E-mail and word processing in the ESL classroom: how the medium affects the message[J]. Language, learning & technology, 5: 133-165.

BLOCH J, 2002. Student/teacher interaction via email: the social context of internet discourse[J]. Journal of second language writing, 11: 117-134.

BLOCK D, 2013. The structure and agency dilemma in identity and intercultural communication research[J]. Language and intercultural communication, 13(2): 126-147.

BLOMMAERT J, 2010. The sociolinguistics of globalization[M]. Cambridge: Cambridge University Press.

BLUM S D, 1997. Naming practices and the power of words in China [J]. Language in society, 26(1): 357-379.

BLUM-KULKA S, JULIANE H, KASPER G, 1989. Cross-cultural pragmatics: requests and apologies[M]. Norwood, NJ: Ablex.

BLUM-KULKA S, HOUSE J, 1989. Cross-cultural and situational variation in requesting behavior [M]//BLUM-KULKA S, KASPER G. Cross-cultural pragmatics: request and apologies. Norwood, NJ: Ablex.

BLUM-KULKA S, OLSHTAIN E, 1984. Requests and apologies: a cross-cultural study of speech act realization patterns (CCSARP) [J]. Applied linguistics, 5(3): 196-213.

BOND M H, 1991. Beyond the Chinese face: insights from psychology[M]. Hong Kong: Oxford University Press.

BOURDIEU P, 1977. The economics of linguistic exchanges[J]. Social sciences information, 16(6) : 645-668.

BOURDIEU P, 1984. Distinction[M]. Oxford: Polity.

BOURDIEU P, 1986. The forms of capital[M]//RICHARDSON J G.

Handbook of theory and research for the sociology of education. New York: Greenwood Press.

BOURDIEU P, 1990a. The logic of practice[M]. Stanford, CA: Stanford University Press.

BOURDIEU P, 1990b. In other words: essays towards a reflexive sociology[M]. Oxford, UK: Polity Press.

BOURDIEU P, 1991. Language and symbolic power[M]. Cambridge, MA: Polity Press.

BOURDIEU P, 1994. Academic discourse: linguistic misunderstanding and professorial power[M]. Cambridge, MA: Polity Press.

BOURDIEU P, 1995. Outline of a theory of practice[M]. New York: Cambridge University Press.

BOURDIEU P, PASSERON J, 1977. Reproduction in education, society, and culture[M]. London/Beverly Hills, CA: Sage Publications.

BOURDIEU P, WACQUANT J D, 1992. An invitation to reflexive sociology[M]. Chicago: The University of Chicago Press.

BROWN G, YULE G, 1983. Discourse analysis[M]. Cambridge: Cambridge University Press.

BROWN P, GILMAN A, 1968. The pronouns of power and solidarity[M]//FISHMAN J A. Readings in the sociology of language. Cambridge, MA: MIT Press.

BROWN P, LEVINSON S C, 1987. Politeness: some universals in language usage[M]. Cambridge: Cambridge University Press.

BROWN R, 2004. Self-composed: rhetoric in psychology personal statements[J].Written communication, 21(3): 242-260.

BUTLER J, 1990. Gender trouble: feminism and the subversion of identity[M]. London: Routledge.

BUTLER J, 1999. Performativity's social magic[M]//SCHUSTERMAN R. Bourdieu: a critical reader. Oxford: Blackwell.

CARGILL M, 2000. Intercultural postgraduate supervision meetings: an exploratory discourse study[J]. Prospect, 15(2): 28-38.

CHANG H, HOLT G R, 1991. More than relationship: Chinese interaction and the principle of guan-hsi[J]. Communication quarterly, 39: 251-271.

CHANG H, 2010. Clever, creative, modest: the Chinese language practice[M]. Shanghai: Shanghai Foreign Language Education Press.

CHANG M, et al., 2015. Do Chinese students waffle in their apologies?:

an exploration into EFL learners' emails[M]//CHEN Y D, RAU V, RAU G. Email discourse among Chinese using English as a lingua franca. Singapore: Springer Publisher.

CHANG Y, et al., 1998. Requests on e-mail: a cross-cultural comparison[J]. RELC journal, 29: 121-151.

CHARMAZ K, 2014. Constructing grounded theory: a practical guide through qualitative[M]. 2nd ed. London: Sage Publications.

CHEN C E, 2006. The development of e-mail literacy: from writing to peers to writing to authority figures[J]. Language learning & technology, 10(2): 35-55.

CHEN G, 1985. Beijing colloquial terms dictionary[M]. Beijing: The Commercial Press.

CHEN N, 2014. Analyzing factors influencing Chinese students' cross-boarder higher education mobility[M]. Beijing: China Renmin University Press.

CHEN X, 2015. Emailing requests to international researchers: the construction of identity by Chinese EFL graduate students[M]// CHEN Y, RAU D V, RAU G. Email discourse among Chinese using English as a lingua franca. Singapore: Springer Publisher.

CHEN X, CHEN C C, 2004. On the intricacies of the Chinese *guanxi*: a process model of *guanxi* development[J]. Asia Pacific journal of management, 21(3): 305-324.

CHEN G, 2010. Study on Chinese communication behaviors[M]. Hong Kong: China Review Academic Publishers.

CHEN Y, 2015. Developing Chinese EFL learners' email literacy through requests to faculty[J]. Journal of pragmatics, 75: 131-149.

CHEUNG F M, 2004. Use of western and indigenously developed personality tests in Asia[J]. Applied psychology, 53: 173-191.

CHIANG S, 2009. Personal power and positional power in a powerful 'I': a discourse analysis of doctoral dissertation supervision[J]. Discourse & communication, 3(3): 255-271.

CHOW I H, NG I, 2004. The characteristics of Chinese personal ties (*guanxi*): evidence from Hong Kong[J]. Organization studies, 25(7): 1075-1093.

CLARK H H, 2009. Context and common ground[M]//MEY J L. Concise encyclopedia of pragmatics. Oxford: Elsevier.

CONNOR U, DAVIS K, RYCKER T D, 1995. Correctness and clarity in applying for overseas jobs: a cross-cultural analysis of U.S. and

Flemish applications[J]. Text, 15(4): 457-476.

CONNOR U, MAURANEN A, 1999. Linguistic analysis of grant proposals: European union research grants[J]. English for specific purposes, 18(1): 47-62.

CRYSTAL D, 2001. Language and the internet[M]. Cambridge: Cambridge University Press.

CUMMINS J, 2006. Identity texts: the imaginative construction of self through multiliteracies pedagogy[M]//GARCIA O, SKUTNABB-KANGAS T, TORRES-GUMAN M. Imagining multilingual schools: languages in education and glocalization. Clevedon: Multilingual Matters.

DANIELEWICZ-BETZ A, 2013. (Mis) use of e-mail in student-faculty interaction: implications for university instruction in Germany, Saudi Arabia and Japan[J]. Jaltcall journal, 9 (1): 23-57.

DARVIN R, NORTIN B, 2015. Identity and a model of investment in applied linguistics[J]. Annual review of applied linguistics, 35: 36-56.

DING H, 2007. Genre analysis of personal statements: analysis of moves in application essays to medical and dental schools[J]. English for specific purposes, 26(3): 368-392.

DONG J, 2010. The enregisterment of Putonghua in practice[J]. Language & communication, 30(4): 265-275.

DONG P R, 2012. Identity and style in intercultural institutional interaction: a multi-modal analysis of supervision sessions between British academics and Chinese students[M]. Beijing: Higher Education Press.

DREW P, HERITAGE J, 1992. Talk at work: interaction in institutional settings[M]. Cambridge: Cambridge University Press.

ECONOMIDOU-KOGETSIDIS M, 2011. "Please answer me as soon as possible": pragmatic failure in non-native speakers' e-mail requests to faculty[J]. Journal of pragmatics, 43: 3193-3215.

ELLIOT A, CHIRKOV V I, KIM Y, et al., 2001. A cross-cultural analysis of avoidance (relative to approach) personal goals[J]. Psychological science, 12: 505-510.

ERVIN-TRIPP S, 1976. Is Sybil there? The structure of some American English directives[J]. Language in society, 5(1): 25-66.

FAIRCLOUG N, 1992. Discourse and social change[M]. Cambridge: Polity Press.

FAIRCLOUGH N, 2006. Language and globalization[M]. London:

Routledge.

FAERCH C, KASPER G, 1989. Internal and external modification in interlanguage request realization[M]// BLUM-KULKA S J, HOUSE, KASPER G. Cross-cultural pragmatics: requests and apologies. Norwood, NJ: Ablex.

FEI X T, 1948. Earthy China[M]. Shanghai: Observatory Publishing Company.

FEI X T, 1992. From the soil: the foundations of Chinese society[M]. Berkeley: University of California Press.

GAO A, FU M, 2001. Beijing dialect dictionary[M]. Beijing: Peking University Press.

GAO Y, 2009. Sociocultural contexts and English in China: retaining and reforming the cultural habitus[M]//LO BIANCO J, ORTON J, GAO Y H. China and English: globalization and the dilemmas of identity. Bristol: Multilingual Matters.

GAO Y, CHENG Y, ZHAO Y, et al., 2005. Self identity changes and English learning among Chinese undergraduates[J]. World Englishes, 24: 39-51.

GAO Y, et al., 2007. The social psychology of English learning by

Chinese college students: motivation and learners' self-identities[M]. 3rd ed. Beijing: Foreign Language Teaching and Research Press.

GAO Y, JIA Z, ZHOU Y, 2015. EFL learning and identity development: a longitudinal study in 5 universities in China[J]. Journal of language, identity & education, 14(3): 137-158.

GAO Y, ZHAO Y, CHENG Y, et al., 2007. Relationships between English learning motivation types and self-identity changes among Chinese students[J]. TESOL quarterly, 41: 133-155.

GEE J P, 1999. An Introduction to discourse analysis: theory and method[M]. London: Routledge.

GLESNE C,1999. Becoming qualitative researchers: an introduction[M]. 2nd ed. New York: Addison Wesley Longman.

GOFFMAN E, 1959. The presentation of self in everyday life[M]. London: Penguin Group.

GOFFMAN E, 1967. Interaction ritual[M]. New York: Anchor Books.

GOFFMAN E, 1974. Frame analysis[M] . New York: Harper and Row.

GRENFELL M, KELLY M, 1999. Pierre Bourdieu: language, culture and education: theory into practice[M]. Bern, Switzerland: Peter Lang AG.

GRICE H P, 1975. Logic and conversation[M]//COLE P, MORGAN J L. Syntax and semantics 3: speech acts. New York: Academic Press.

GU M, 2008. Identity construction and investment transformation college students from non-urban areas in China[J]. Journal of Asian Pacific communication, 18(1): 49-70.

GU Y, 1990. Politeness phenomena in modern Chinese[J]. Journal of pragmatics, 14: 237-257.

GU Y, 1992. Politeness, pragmatics and culture[J]. Foreign language teaching and research, 4: 10-17.

HALL E T, 1976. Beyond culture[M]. New York: Doubleday.

HALLIDAY M A K,1994. An introduction to functional grammar[M]. London: Edward Arnold.

HARTFORD B S, BARDOVI-HARLIG K, 1996. "At your earliest convenience": a study of written student requests to faculty[M]// BOUTON L F. Pragmatics and language learning monograph series. Urbana, IL: University of Illinois at Urbana-Champaign.

HE Z, CHEN X, 2004. Contemporary pragmatics[M]. Beijing: Foreign Language Teaching and Research Press.

HEINE S J, 2003. Making sense of East-Asian self-enhancement[J].

Journal of cross-cultural psychology, 34(5): 596-602.

HERRING S C, 2001. Computer-mediated discourse[M]//TANNEN D, SCHIFFRIN D, HAMILTON H. Handbook of discourse analysis. Oxford, UK: Blackwell.

HERRING S C, 2002. Computer-mediated communication on the internet[J]. Annual review of information science and technology, 36: 109-168.

HO V, 2010. Constructing identities through request e-mail discourse[J]. Journal of pragmatics, 42(8): 2253-2261.

HOFSTEDE G, 1980. Culture's consequences: international differences in work-related values[M]. Beverly Hills, CA: Sage Publications.

HOLLIDAY A R,1999. Small cultures[J]. Applied linguistics, 20: 237-264.

HOLMES J, 1986. Compliments and compliment responses in New Zealand English[J]. Anthropological linguistics, 28(4): 485-508.

HOLMES J, 1988. Paying compliments: a sex-preferential politeness strategy[J]. Journal of pragmatics, 12: 445-465.

HOLMES J, 1990. Apologies in New Zealand English[J]. Language in society, 19: 155-199.

HORN L R, 1984. Towards a new taxonomy for pragmatic inference: Q-based and R-based implicature[M]//SCHIFFRIN D. Meaning, form, and use in context: linguistic applications. Washington D.C.: Georgetown University Press.

HOUSE H, 2012. Identity and face in institutional English as lingua franca discourse[J]. Utrecht studies in language and communication, 24: 187-204.

HUANG M C, 1993. Request across cultures: a contrastive study of request speech acts in English and in Chinese [D]. Urbana-Champaign: University of Illinois.

HWANG K K, 1988. Human emotion and face: the Chinese power game[M]//HWANG K K. The Chinese power game. Taipei: Juliou Books Company.

HYLAND K, 2002. Activity and evaluation: reporting practices in academic writing[M]//FLOWERDEW J. Academic discourse. London: Pearson Education.

HYLAND K, 2009. Academic discourse: English in a global context[M]. London: Continuum.

HYLAND K, 2012. Disciplinary identities: individuality and community in academic discourse[M]. Cambridge: Cambridge University Press.

HYMES D H, 1972a. On communicative competence[M]//Pride J B, HOLMES J. Sociolinguistics: selected readings. Harmondsworth: Penguin.

HYMES D H, 1972b. Models of the interaction of language and social life[M]//GUMPERZ J, HYMES D. Directions in sociolinguistics: the ethnography of communication. New York: Holt, Rinehart and Winston.

JAMES C, SCHOLFIELD P, YPSILADIS G, 1994. Cross-cultural correspondence: letters of application[R]. Dublin: Centre for Language and Communication Studies, Trinity College.

JIANG W, 2000. Pragmatics: theories & applications[M]. Beijing: Peking University Press.

JONESTONE B, 2008. Discourse analysis[M]. 2nd ed. Oxford: Blackwell Publishing Ltd.

KACHRU B B, 1982. The other tongue: English across cultures[M]. Urbana: University of Illinois Press.

KANNO Y, NORTON B, 2003. Imagined communities and educational possibilities: introduction[J]. Journal of language, identity, and education, 2(4): 241-249.

Kaplan R, 1966. Cultural thought patterns in inter-cultural education[J]. Language learning, 16(1): 1-20.

KASPER G, ROSE K R, 2002. Pragmatic development in a second language[M]. Oxford: Blackwell Publishing Limited.

KECSKES I, 2014. Intercultural pragmatics[M]. New York: Oxford University Press.

KECSKES I, ZHANG, F. 2009. Activating, seeking and creating common ground: a socio-cognitive approach[M]. Pragmatics and cognition, 17(2): 331-355.

KHAN A, TIN T B, 2012. Generic patterns in application letters: the context of Pakistan[J]. RELC journal, 43(3): 393-410.

KING A Y C, 1985. The individual and group in Confucianism[M]// MUNRO D J. Individualism and holism: studies in Confucian and Taoist values. Ann Arbor: University of Michigan.

KING A Y C, 1991. Kuan-hsi and network building: a sociological interpretation[J]. Daedalus, 120 (2): 63-84.

KINNEL M, 1990. Introduction[M]//KINNEL M. The learning experiences of overseas students. Buckingham & Bristol: The Society

445

for Research into Higher Education & Open University Press.

KIRKPATRICK A, 1991. Information sequencing in Mandarin in letters of request[J]. Anthropological linguistics, 33: 183-203.

KURMAN J, 2001. Self-enhancement: is it restricted to individualistic cultures? [J] Personality and social psychology bulletin, 27:1705-1716.

KURMAN J, 2003. Why is self-enhancement low in certain collectivist cultures? An investigation of two competing explanations[J]. Journal of cross-cultural psychology, 34: 496-510.

LAM W S E, 2006. Re-envisioning language, literacy and the immigrant subject in new mediascapes[J]. Pedagogies: an international journal, 1(3): 171-195.

LEE C F K, 2004. Written requests in emails sent by adult Chinese learners of English[J]. Language, culture and curriculum, 17(1): 58-72.

LEECH G N, 1983. Principles of pragmatics[M]. New York: Longman.

LEGGE J, 2014. The Chinese classics: Confucian analects, the great learning, the doctrine of the mean[M]. Shanghai: SDX Joint Publishing Company.

LE PAGE R B, TABOURET-KELLER A, 1985. Acts of identity[M]. Cambridge: Cambridge University Press.

LEVINSON S C, 1987. Pragmatics[M]. Cambridge: Cambridge University Press.

LI Z, GAO Y, LI F, 2007. Academic identity construction through appraisal resources and modesty strategy in Chinese applicants' personal statement[M]//GAO Y, et al. The social psychology of English learning by Chinese college students: motivation and learners' self-identities. Beijing: Foreign Language Teaching and Research Press.

LO BIANCO J, ORTON J, GAO Y, 2009. China and English: globalization and the dilemmas of identity[M]. Bristol: Multilingual Matters.

LUO M, 2010. A pragmatic analysis of cross-cultural requests: a case study of Chinese college students' English e-mail communication with a U.S. professor[J]. Journal of Zhejiang normal university, 1: 115-120.

MALINOWSKI B, 1947. The problem of meaning in primitive languages[M]//OGDEN C K, RICHARDS I A. The meaning of meaning: a study of the influence of language upon thought and of the science of symbolism. New York: Harcourt Brace.

MAO L R, 1994. Beyond politeness theory: 'face' revisited and renewed[J]. Journal of pragmatics, 21: 451-486.

MARGINSON S, WENDE M V D, 2009. The new global landscape of nations and nstitutions[M]//Center for educational research and innovation. Higher education to 2030, vol. 2, globalisation. OECD: OECD Publishing.

MARTIN J R, WHITE P R R, 2008. The language of evaluation: appraisal in English[M]. Beijing: Foreign Language Teaching and Research Press.

MATSUMOTO Y, 1988. Reexamination of the university of face: politeness phenomena in Japanese[M]. Journal of pragmatics, 12: 403-426.

MCCARTHY M, 2000. Mutually captive audiences: small talk and the genre of close- contact service encounters[M]//COUPLAND J. Small talk. Harlow: Pearson Education.

MCKAY S, WONG S C, 1996. Multiple discourses, multiple identities: investment and agency in second language learning among Chinese adolescent immigrant students[J]. Harvard educational review, 66(3):

577-608.

MEY J, 1993. Pragmatics: an introduction[M]. Oxford: Blackwell.

MIAO Y K, 2012. Doctoral advising: a grounded theory exploration of female Mainland Chinese international students [D]. Rochester: University of Rochester, New York.

MOTALLEBZADEH K, MOHSENZADEH H, SOBHANI A, 2014. Investigating Iranian University students' emails for pragmatic features[J]. Procedia-social and behavioral sciences, 98: 1263-1272.

NASH T, 1983. An instance of American and Chinese politeness strategy[J]. RELC journal, 14: 87-98.

NORTON B, 1995. Social identity, investment, and language learning [J]. TESOL quarterly, 29: 9-31.

NORTON B, 2000. Identity and language learning: gender, ethnicity and educational change[J]. Essex: Pearson.

NORTON B, 2013. Identity and language learning: extending the conversation[M]. 2nd ed. Bristol: Multilingual Matters.

NORTON B, GAO Y, 2008. Identity, investment, and Chinese learners of English[J]. Journal of Asian Pacific communication, 18(1): 109-120.

NORTON B, TOOHEY K, 2011. Identity, language learning, and social change[J]. Language teaching, 44 (4): 412-446.

PAN B, CAI J, 2005. A contrastive study on Chinese and American college students' email text[J]. Journal of Xi'an foreign languages university.

PAULHUS D L, WESTLAKE G B, CALVEZ S S, et al., 2013. Self-presentation style in job interviews: the role of personality and culture[J]. Journal of applied social psychology, 43: 2042-2059.

PAVLENKO A, NORTON B, 2007. Identity, language learning and imagined communities[J]. International handbook of education: English language teaching, 2: 669-680.

PAVLIDOU T, 2007. Telephone conversations in Greek and German: attending to the relationship aspect of communication[M]//SPENCER-OATEY H. Culturally speaking: managing rapport through talk across cultures. Shanghai: Shanghai Foreign Language Education Press.

PENNYCOOK A, 2007. Global Englishes and transcultural flows[M]. London: Routledge.

PITTAWAY D S, 2004. Investment and second language acquisition[J]. Critical inquiry in language studies: an international journal, 1(4):

203-218.

QI X, 2013. *Guanxi*, social capital theory and beyond: toward a globalized social science[J]. The British journal of sociology, 64(2): 308-324.

REN W, 2015. Strategies used in Chinese university students' ELF emails to remedy or prevent problems in understanding[M]//CHEN Y, RAU D V, RAU G. Email discourse among Chinese using English as a lingua franca. Singapore: Springer Publisher.

RUI X, GAO Y, 2008. Review on the concept of L2 investment[J]. Modern foreign languages, 31(1): 90-98.

SAPIR E, 1921/2002. Language: an introduction to the study of speech[J]. Beijing: Foreign Language Teaching and Research Press.

SARANGI S, ROBERTS C, 1999. The Dynamics of interactional and institutional orders[M]//SARANGI S, ROBERTS C. Talk, work and institutional order: discourse in medical mediation and management setting. Berlin and New York: Walter De Gruyter.

SAUSSURE F, 1960. Course in general linguistics[M]. London: Peter Owen.

SCHIFFRIN D, 1994. Approaches to discourse[M]. Oxford and

Cambridge: Blackwell.

SCHIFFRIN D, 2006. From Linguistic reference to social identity[M]// DE FINA A, SCHIFFRIN D, BAMBERG M. Discourse and identity. Cambridge: Cambridge University Press.

SCOLLON R, SCOLLON S, 1991. Topic confusion in English-Asian discourse[J]. World Englishes, 9: 113-123.

SCOLLON R, SCOLLON S, 2001. Intercultural communication: a discourse approach[M]. Oxford: Blackwell.

SEARLE J R, 1969. Speech acts: an essay in the philosophy of language[M]. Cambridge: Cambridge University Press.

SEARLE J R, 1975. A taxonomy of illocutionary acts[M]// GUNDERSON K. Language, mind and knowledge. Minnesota: University of Minnesota Press.

SEARLE J R, 1979. Expression and meaning[M]. Cambridge: Cambridge University Press.

SMITH D E, 1987. The everyday world as problematic: a feminist sociology[M]. Boston: Northeastern University Press.

SPENCER-OATEY H, 2002. Managing rapport in talk: using rapport sensitive incidents to explore the motivational concerns underlying

452

the management of relations[J]. Journal of pragmatics, 34: 529-545.

SPENCER-OATEY H, 2007a. Theories of identity and the analysis of face[J]. Journal of pragmatics, 39: 639-656.

SPENCER-OATEY H, 2007b. Cultural speaking: managing rapport through talk across cultures[M]. Shanghai: Shanghai Foreign Language Education Press.

SPERBER D, WILSON D. 1986. Relevance: communication and cognition[M]. Oxford: Blackwell.

SWALES J, 1990. Genre analysis: English in academic and research settings[M].Cambridge: Cambridge University Press.

SWALES J, 1996. Occluded genres in the academy: the case of the submission letter[M]//VENTOLA E, MAURANEN A. Academic writing: intercultural and textual issues. Amsterdam: John Benjamins Publishing Co.

SWALES J M, FEAK C B, 1994. Academic Writing for Graduate Students: Essential Tasks and Skills[M]. Ann Arbor, MI: The University of Michigan Press.

SWALES J, FEAK C, BARTON E, et al., 2004. Personal statements: a conversation with John Swales and Chris Feak[J]. Issues in writing,

15(1): 5-30.

THOMPSON J B, 1991. Editor's introduction[M]//BOURDIEU P. Language and symbolic power. Cambridge, Massachusetts: Cambridge University Press.

TICE D M, BUTLER J L, MURAVEN M B, et al., 1995. When modesty prevails: differential favorability of self-presentation to friends and strangers[J]. Journal of personality and social psychology, 69(6): 1120-1138.

TYLER A, 1995. The co-construction of cross-cultural miscommunication: conflicts in perception, negotiation, and enactment of participant role and status[J]. Studies in second language acquisition, 17: 129-152.

UPTON T, CONNOR U, 2001. Using computerized corpus analysis to investigate the textlinguistic discourse moves of a genre[J]. English for specific purposes, 20: 313-329.

VAN DIJK T A, 1977. Text and context: explorations in the semantics and pragmatics of discourse[M]. London and New York: Longman.

VAN DIJK T A, 1980. Macrostructures: an interdisciplinary study of global structures in discourse, interaction, and cognition[M].

Hillsdale: Lawrence Erlbaum Associations, Inc., Publishers.

VAN DIJK T A, 1997. Discourse as interaction in society[J]. Discourse as social interaction, 2: 1-37.

VASILOPOULOS G, 2015. Language learner investment and identity negotiation in the Korean EFL context[J]. Journal of language, identity & education, 14(2): 61-79.

WANG W, GAO X, 2008. English language education in China: a review of selected research[J]. Journal of multilingual and multicultural development, 29(5): 380-399.

WARDHAUGH R, 2000. An introduction to sociolinguistics[M]. 3rd ed. Beijing: Foreign Language Teaching and Research Press.

WATTS R J, IDE S, EHLICH K, 2005. Politeness in language: studies in its history, theory, and practice[M]. 2nd ed. Berlin and New York: Mouton de Gruyter.

WONG S M L, 2000. Cross cultural communication[M]. Frankfurt am Main: Peter Lang.

XIANG B, 2006. Global "body shopping": an Indian labor system in the information technology industry[M]. New Jersey: Princeton University Press.

XIANG H, 2004. A contrastive study into apology strategies: native British, Chinese graduate students and Chinese EFL learners [D]. Melton Keynes: Open University.

XIAO L, 2014. Rapport management in Chinese *"Taoci"* email[J]. Linguistic research, 15: 165-174.

XIAO L, GAO Y, 2015. Intercultural *Taoci* email: new wine in an old bottle [M]//CHEN Y, RAU D V, RAU G. Email discourse among Chinese using English as a lingua franca. Singapore: Springer Publisher.

XIN K R, 2004. Asian American managers: an impression gap? An investigation of impression management and supervisor-subordinate relationships[J]. The journal of applied behavioral science, 40: 60-181.

XING J, 2014. An empirical study of applying e-mail exchange to college English learners' writing[J]. Journal of language teaching and research, 5(4): 856-864.

YANG M, 1994. Gifts, favours and banquets[M]. Ithaca: Cornell University Press.

YANGW, 2012. Small talk: a strategic interaction in Chinese

interpersonal business negotiations[J]. Discourse & communication, 6(1): 101-124.

YUM J O, 1988. The impact of Confucianism on interpersonal relationships and communication patterns in East Asia[J]. Communication monographs, 55: 374-388.

ZHANG Y, 1995. Strategies in Chinese requesting[M]//KASPER G. Pragmatics of Chinese as native and target language. Honolulu: University of Hawaii Press.

ZHAO D, 1996. Foreign study as a safety-valve: the experience of China's university students going abroad in the eighties[J]. Higher education, 31(2): 145-163.

ZHOU J, 2006. Higher education in China[M]. Singapore: Thomson Learning.

ZHU W, 2012. Polite requestive strategies in emails: an investigation of pragmatic competence of Chinese EFL learners[J]. RELC journal, 43(2): 217-238.

ZIMMERMAN D H, 1998. Identity, context and interaction[M]// ANTAKI C, WIDDICOMBE S. Identities in talk. Thousand Oaks, CA: Sage Publications Ltd.